GUY CARLETON

A BIOGRAPHY

GUY CARLETON

A BIOGRAPHY

PAUL R. REYNOLDS

GAGE PUBLISHING LIMITED
Toronto Ontario Canada

Cover and design by Susan Weiss

Cover photo courtesy of the Countess of Malmesbury

Canadian Cataloguing in Publication Data

Reynolds, Paul R., 1904-
  Guy Carleton

Bibliography: p. 201-205
Includes index.
ISBN 0-7715-9300-7

1. Dorchester, Guy Carleton, 1st Baron, 1724-1808.
2. Canada–History–1763-1791.   3. Governors– Canada–Biography.*

FC411.D67R49   971.02'092'4   C80-094261-2
F1032.D67R49

1 2 3 4 5 HR 84 83 82 81 80

Printed and bound in Canada

For
Robbin Reynolds
and the
Robbin Reynolds Agency

TABLE OF CONTENTS

ACKNOWLEDGMENTS

I am grateful to my wife for her patience and her shrewd suggestions, and to my daughters, especially my eldest daughter, Robbin Reynolds of the Robbin Reynolds Agency, without whose help this book would never have been published. I am indebted to Mr. James K. Smith for his revision of my manuscript, although I take full responsibility for everything in this volume, and to my editor, Ms. Colleen Dimson of Gage Publishing Limited. I am grateful to the librarians of the five libraries I have used, especially to Mrs. Grace Hubler of the Bridgeport Public Library, who in her enthusiasm helped me above and beyond the call of duty, and to her boss, Mr. Douglas G. Reid, who gave me an entré to the archives of Quebec, without which I could not have undertaken this biography.

Paul R. Reynolds
March, 1980

INTRODUCTION

The first European to see Quebec, "the place where the river narrows," was Jacques Cartier, in 1535. His countryman, Samuel de Champlain, founded the first European settlement there in 1608. By 1759, the city and the lands along the St. Lawrence River supported a thriving French colony of some sixty-five to seventy thousand people. That year, the British organized a great fleet and an army of nine thousand men under General James Wolfe, to wrest the St. Lawrence colony from the French. Wolfe attacked here and attacked there, but was thwarted for months by the impregnable walls of Quebec. Finally, on the Plains of Abraham, he triumphed over French commander-in-chief Montcalm. The city surrendered, and the next year Canada became a British possession.

Wolfe's capture of Quebec was one of the world's decisive battles. Had he given up the siege—as he very nearly did—had he sailed home in September as Admiral Saunders had advised, Canada would have remained French territory, and the subsequent history of North America would have been greatly different. The American Revolution would not have occurred—or at least not when it did. With France a constant menace, with the French in Canada a perpetual threat to the English on the Atlantic coast, the Thirteen Colonies would have needed British troops and British sea power for their defence. They would have had little stomach for revolt. And Wolfe's quartermaster-general, Lieutenant-Colonel Guy Carleton, might never have earned a place in history.

I first visited the city of Quebec in 1945. Walking across the Plains of Abraham, I wondered why Canada had remained British. I imagined someone at the beginning of the American Revo-

lution speculating about the future of the North American continent. Such a person would have mused that perhaps the
Thirteen Colonies would rebel successfully, perhaps not; but
French, Roman Catholic Quebec—which Britain had taken by
conquest a mere fifteen years earlier—was almost certain to
revolt. Moreover, if, for some incomprehensible reason, French
Canadians remained neutral at the beginning of the war, surely
they would revolt if France entered on the side of the rebels? I
kept asking myself: why did Quebec not join the Thirteen Colonies during the American Revolution?

Another question intrigued me. How was it that the Province
of Quebec has been able to retain its language and culture? The
French founded New Orleans—admittedly much smaller in area
and population—but it rapidly became an English-speaking city
and adopted American culture. The same is true of the Dutch in
New York City, of the Germans or "Pennsylvania Dutch" in
Pennsylvania. How, then, did the Québécois manage to
maintain their identity? Nearly every summer that I returned to
Quebec, these same questions haunted me.

There are many answers to these questions, many threads in
history. However, one man, Guy Carleton, dominated the first
thirty years of Quebec's existence under British rule. A Protestant, born in Northern Ireland, he was governor of the Province
of Quebec from 1766 to 1778 and from 1786 to 1796.

As a statesman, Carleton conceived and formulated the Quebec Act, which guaranteed the inhabitants of Quebec their language, their civil law, their religion, and, in the case of Roman
Catholics, the right to hold public office. Carleton spent four
years in England securing all these rights. Yet, at that time, the
British hated the French, who had been their enemy for centuries. Nine out of ten Britons were blatantly anti-Catholic; no
Catholic in the British Isles was permitted to hold public
office—or even to vote. It was almost a miracle that this pro-
French, pro-Catholic legislation, drawn up as Carleton had recommended, should have been passed by Parliament and signed
by King George III. Furthermore, legislation becomes effective
only if successfully implemented. The implementation of the
Quebec Act was, to a considerable extent, in the hands of Carleton. And he was involved, although to a lesser extent, in the cre-

ation of another Act, one that divided the old Province of Quebec into two parts. The French part preserved its language and culture, whereas the rest of Canada adopted the English language and culture. So it is today.

As a soldier, Carleton's contribution to history was significant. When American forces invaded Quebec in 1775, Carleton's miniature army was forced to surrender and he had to abandon Montreal. However, with a makeshift fighting force, he defended the citadel of Quebec and defeated its besiegers. Had Carleton failed, and a lesser man might have failed, Quebec might have become the fourteenth member of the emerging United States of America. As it was, the gateway to Canada was saved, and the following year he drove the invaders out of the entire Province of Quebec.

For a year and a half Carleton was in New York City as the commander-in-chief of all the British forces in North America. Cornwallis had surrendered, and shortly after Carleton's arrival, England acknowledged the independence of the Thirteen Colonies. Carleton's assignment involved the prevention of skirmishes between British Loyalists and American colonists, the withdrawal of a large British army spread along the Atlantic seaboard, and above all the transportation of some thirty thousand Loyalists to new areas, especially to Nova Scotia. These emigrant Loyalists, constantly persecuted in the Colonies, required clothes, provisions, farm tools, and above all land on which they could locate. All of this Carleton provided.

When Carleton died in his eighty-fourth year, his wife obeyed her husband's injunction to burn his collection of private papers upon his death. Thus, we know almost nothing about the first half of his life, and only hints and suggestions as to his life during the days of his prominence. His public life is well documented, but the motives behind his actions are often obscure.

In many ways Carleton was an enigma. Although trained to lead men in battle, he tried to avoid killing American rebels, whom he considered to be deluded Englishmen. To the consternation of the British government, he kept releasing and returning American prisoners of war. He cultivated the friendship of Indians, but refused to use them as military allies, in disobedience to instructions from London. Carleton was an austere man with a manner that was cold and aloof. He was a dictator, at times a ruthless one, and yet he was often praised for his kindness and humaneness.

Ethan Allen, Major André, Benedict Arnold, John Burgoyne, Edmund Burke, Aaron Burr, Lord Chatham (William Pitt the Elder), Sir Henry Clinton, Thomas Gage, King George II, King George III, Alexander Hamilton, William Howe, Lord North, George Washington, King William IV, and James Wolfe move through the pages of this book. Most of these men praised or even adored Carleton, a couple of them feared him; all of them, with the exception of George II, respected him.

Carleton seems to have had a magnificent constitution. He recovered from four wounds received in four different battles. He made the dangerous Atlantic crossing fourteen times. On his last voyage, shortly after his seventy-second birthday, he was shipwrecked but he came through unscathed. At the age of forty-seven, he married a girl of eighteen, Lady Maria Effingham, whom he scarcely knew. Maria became devoted to him, shared his long life, and bore him eleven children.

His biographers, A. G. Bradley in 1907, William Wood in 1916, and Pierre Benoit in 1961, were ignorant of much material concerning Carleton that modern research has unearthed. The first two of these biographies are so extravagant in their praise as to make Carleton almost superhuman, while during the last fifty years, his critics have been virulent. Carleton has been criticized as a general for being too cautious—a criticism that has some validity—but among British officers of high rank during the American Revolution, only Carleton's reputation was enhanced. They denounce Carleton as a statesman for his occasional pettiness, for his misleading or even deceitful reports to the British government, for his antagonism toward Lord George Germain and, above all, for his lack of interest in and his opposition to representative government in Quebec. That Britain in the eighteenth century was hardly a democratic nation, and that there was little enthusiasm for democracy in Quebec seems to have been overlooked. But even Carleton's severest critic, the brilliant Canadian historian Alfred Leroy Burt, cannot refrain from referring to Carleton's prophetic vision of a Canadian federation and to his incorruptibility in a corrupt age.

Only a handful of men in the eighteenth century can have any claim to have changed history. Surely Sir Guy Carleton must be numbered among those few.

CHAPTER 1

Early Years and the Capture of Quebec

Guy Carleton was born at Strabane in the County of Tyrone, Northern Ireland, on September 3rd, 1724.[1] He was the third son in a family of four boys and two girls. His father's family, staunch Anglicans and established in Northern Ireland for several generations, had originally emigrated from Cumberland County, England.[2] His mother, Katherine, was the daughter of Henry Ball of Donegal County, Northern Ireland.

Christopher Carleton owned a little land in the village of Strabane, some thirteen miles southwest of the port of Londonderry. Here Guy Carleton spent his childhood, not in luxury but hardly in poverty. When he was fourteen, his father died. Soon afterward, his mother married the Reverend Thomas Skelton, an Anglican clergyman who had a small parish in or near Newry, County Down, Northern Ireland. Guy's education has been attributed to his stepfather.[3]

In 1742, the eighteen-year-old Carleton was commissioned an ensign in the 25th Regiment of Foot. To obtain an officer's commission, it was usually necessary to pay several hundred pounds to someone who was resigning the commission, or to the officer or politician who recruited or controlled the regiment. William Conolly, a wealthy Irish landowner and an old friend of Christopher Carleton, seems to have purchased the commission for his friend's son.[4]

Promotion came slowly to an army officer lacking money and connections. After three years, Carleton had been promoted to lieutenant; but after ten years he was only a captain. Luckily, he

1

had a close friendship with another army man, James Wolfe,[5] his junior by two and a half years, but an officer with many connections and already, in 1752, a lieutenant-colonel. In December 1752, Wolfe did Carleton a favor. The second Duke of Richmond had purchased for his eldest son a captaincy in Wolfe's regiment, the 20th Foot. The father asked Wolfe to recommend a military tutor for the youth. Wolfe proposed his "friend Carleton."[6] In the spring, the eighteen-year-old future Duke of Richmond and the twenty-eight-year-old Captain Guy Carleton spent six weeks visiting and studying the fortified towns of the Low Countries. Carleton had made a connection of value.

In 1756 the Seven Years' War broke out, and Britain was once again at odds with France. William Pitt the Elder, the prime minister of Great Britain, had worked out his war strategy. While his European allies fought the French on the continent, he was determined to conquer New France so that all of North America would belong to Britain.

The gateway to New France was the St. Lawrence River. It flows past the city of Quebec and finally empties into the enormous Gulf of St. Lawrence. Two fortresses protected the approach to New France by sea. Louisbourg on Cape Breton Island commanded the southern, easiest entrance to the Gulf, and the citadel of Quebec stood inland where the river narrows. From British-held Nova Scotia, Louisbourg was the closest, and hence the first, fortress to assault and capture.

Pitt put Major-General Jeffrey Amherst in command of the expedition to attack Louisbourg, and appointed James Wolfe one of Amherst's brigadiers. Wolfe wanted Carleton, now a lieutenant-colonel, to be his aide. With Amherst's permission, Carleton's name was forwarded to King George II for approval. The King promptly drew his pen through the request. Carleton had more than once spoken disparagingly of the German troops—especially the Hessians—whom the British hired as mercenaries. George II was also King of Hanover, and had no use for anyone who slighted his German subjects. Ascertaining how he discovered what Carleton said is a matter of guesswork. Carleton had served under the Duke of Cumberland, one of the King's sons. Perhaps Carleton's impolitic remarks had been brought to the Duke's attention and Cumberland had reported them to his father. At any rate, Wolfe wrote his mother: "The King has refused Carleton leave to go [to Louisbourg] to my very great grief and disappointment, and with circumstances unpleasant to him."[7] He also complained about the circumstance in a letter to Lord Sackville:

> I find that a Lieutenant of the First Regiment is put over Carleton's head. Can Sir John Ligonier [commander-in-chief of the British forces] allow His Majesty to remain unacquainted with the merits of that officer, and can he permit such a mark of his displeasure without endeavoring to soften or clear the matter up? A man of honor has the right to expect the support of his Colonel and of the Commander of the troops, and he can't serve without it. If I were in Carleton's place I would not stay an hour in the army after being aimed at and distinguished in so remarkable manner.[8]

Carleton did not resign from the army. The British captured Louisbourg, where Brigadier James Wolfe was the outstanding hero. But his failure to have Carleton along with him on the expedition still rankled. In another letter to Lord Sackville, he remarked: "If His Majesty had thought proper to let Carleton come with us [to Louisbourg] as engineer, it would have cut the matter much shorter."[9] And in yet another letter he wrote: "He [Amherst] will tell your Lordship his opinion of Carleton, by which you will probably be better convinced of our loss."[10]

In December 1758, Wolfe, now a major-general, was given command of the expedition to capture the citadel of Quebec. Wolfe was determined to have Carleton accompany him as quartermaster-general. His name, along with those of other officers Wolfe wanted, was submitted to the King for approval. The King accepted all the submissions except one. Again, he ran his pen through Carleton's name. Prime Minister Pitt intervened, claiming that without Carleton the entire expedition under Wolfe was in jeopardy. The King remained adamant. A third effort was made. Pitt wrote to General Sir John Ligonier (now Lord Ligonier), whom the King respected on military matters. Pitt asked Ligonier to obtain an audience with the King and "tell His Majesty that in order to render any General [i.e. Wolfe] completely responsible for his conduct, he should be made as far as possible inexcusable if he should fail, and that consequently whatever an officer entrusted with a service of confidence requests, should be complied with."[11] Ligonier understood Pitt's clumsy English and persuaded the short-tempered monarch to sign Carleton's commission.

By mid-February 1759, a large fleet, including one hundred transports carrying nine thousand soldiers, had been assembled near Portsmouth on the south coast of England. On the morning of February 17th, the admiral of the fleet, Sir James Saunders, the general of the army, James Wolfe, and the quartermaster-general, Lieutenant-Colonel Guy Carleton, were rowed out to the flagship *Neptune*. They had scarcely been on board an hour when vessel after vessel began to spread its sails, and the fleet began its long journey across the Atlantic. One port of call was Halifax, Nova Scotia. After refitting and reprovisioning there, the fleet would carry on north to Quebec.

At Halifax, Carleton left the *Neptune* to assume command of six hundred grenadiers. These troops were to accompany an advance squadron of ten warships under Rear-Admiral Durell. It was hoped that he would capture any French cargo vessels supplying Quebec. As matters turned out, Rear-Admiral Durell was too late. He missed a convoy of French supply ships.

Carleton had providentially brought ample fishing line and hooks, and he and his troops spent a lot of their time fishing. Eventually, the boredom of patrolling the St. Lawrence River came to an end. When Durell's ships came in sight of the Ile-aux-Coudres, some fifty miles below Quebec, he sent a frigate ahead with a French flag at its mast. A dozen or so French-Canadian pilots, assuming that this frigate was the precursor of a French fleet, scrambled into their canoes and paddled out to get the job of guiding the ships to Quebec. Durell's frigate took the pilots on board; the French flag was lowered and up ran the Royal Ensign. At musket point, a captive pilot was then assigned to each Royal Navy vessel with orders to guide it safely past the many sandbanks and shoals that made navigation extremely hazardous. Each pilot was assured that if he failed he would be hung from the yardarm.[12] The threat was most effective: not one ship went aground.

The British fleet reached Quebec at the end of June. For weeks thereafter, Wolfe failed to force French commander-in-chief

Montcalm to engage in battle. Indeed, an attempt to break through French defence lines east of the city ended in a bloody repulse. By continuous, indiscriminate bombardments, the British destroyed two-thirds of the fortress city but were no nearer capturing it in September than they had been all summer.

Carleton was in charge of the main encampment on the Ile d'Orléans, which is in the middle of the St. Lawrence just below Quebec.[13] As quartermaster-general, he was responsible for the wellbeing of Wolfe's army: food, drink, clothing, accommodation (tents), arms and ammunition, and hospital facilities. He also seems to have acted as engineer, supervising the placement of the cannon that blasted Quebec.

Wolfe also assigned Carleton a minor independent mission. The British had an encampment across the river from Quebec not far from where the town of Lévis stands today. A couple of French deserters had been brought to the Lévis camp. They alleged that at Pointe-aux-Trembles, eighteen miles upriver from Quebec, there was a depot with supplies, small arms, ammunition, and papers describing French battle plans. Carleton was ordered to capture the depot and its contents.

On the evening of July 20th, Carleton, in command of some six hundred soldiers, rowed and paddled up the St. Lawrence.[14] Not a lantern could be lit; the stars were their guide. Unalerted, the French on the north bank of the river did not fire. At dawn, the raiders landed at Pointe-aux-Trembles, where a motley collection of Indians was driven off. From his headquarters in the vestibule of a parish church, Carleton supervised a thorough search, but neither supplies nor papers were found.

Close to the shore was a group of shacks and tents housing a hundred or so old men, some women, and their children. These French Canadians, their houses destroyed in the bombardment, had been evacuated from Quebec. They were in a bad state. Almost out of food, without carriages or wagons to transport them back to Quebec, they were pestered by Indians eager for tobacco, rum, trinkets, none of which these refugees possessed. The women constantly feared rape; the men expected to be scalped. To their great relief—and to the exasperation of his soldiers and sailors—Carleton offered to take them back with him. At twilight, he crowded them into his boats. As they pulled away from the shore, Carleton watched the Indians pillage and burn the miserable quarters where the refugees had been living.

The little flotilla reached the safety of the Lévis camp the next morning. Carleton could have been reprimanded for overloading his boats with non-combatants, and French-speaking ones at that. Instead, Wolfe was pleased with his humane action. The following evening, Wolfe and Carleton entertained some of the ladies at dinner. The next day, Wolfe arranged with Montcalm a six-hour truce, during which all the men, women and children were released a mile or so from the city.

Carleton played an active part in the Battle of the Plains of Abraham. Wolfe had spotted a virtually undefended cove, Anse au Foulon (now called Wolfe's Cove), on the north shore of the St. Lawrence and a little to the west of the city, which still defied the besiegers. Noting a steep path that led to level ground at the top of formidable cliffs, Wolfe hoped he had found a way for his army to infiltrate enemy defences, line up for battle, and challenge Montcalm to risk everything in a face-to-face encounter.

In the early hours of September 13th, Wolfe set out in the lead boat. (This was the circumstance in which he is said to have recited out loud Gray's "Elegy in a Country Churchyard," with its prescient line: "The paths of glory lead but to the grave." Legend has it that Wolfe stated that he would rather have written the poem than take Quebec.[15])Wolfe landed at the cove and led his infantry up the cliffs. By nine a.m., they were drawn up in two long, redcoated lines on the Plains of Abraham, facing the walls of Quebec. Caught by surprise, Montcalm lined up his troops against the British. During the preliminary skirmishing, Carleton, positioned in the front line at the head of his grenadiers, was wounded in the head. At first a fracture was feared, but the wound was not serious.[16]

About ten a.m., the French received the order to advance. The regimental colors were unfurled, the drums rolled out the charge, and the white-uniformed men gave a deep-throated cheer and advanced at a run toward the two silent, motionless lines of British redcoats awaiting them. In twenty minutes, it all was over. At close range, British musketry drill paid off and tore tremendous gaps in Montcalm's regiments. The French reeled and retreated. The casualties on both sides were great; and both Montcalm and Wolfe died of their wounds.

Wolfe had written his will on board the *Neptune* while sailing from Halifax to Quebec. He bequeathed to Carleton £1,000, a sum approximately twice as large as Carleton's annual salary as lieutenant-colonel.[17] Carleton was also left all of Wolfe's books and papers, both at Quebec and in London. One of the books contained Gray's "Elegy."[18]

Most of the British army remained in Quebec. The captured city had to be defended, and once the approaching winter was over, the rest of New France remained to be conquered. However, when the fleet sailed for England in October, Carleton was aboard one of the ships. Why didn't Carleton stay in Quebec with the army? He may have felt that his head wound was too severe for him to continue as quartermaster-general; or perhaps he felt that his duty was to return to his own regiment.

CHAPTER 2

Carleton's Arrival in Quebec

Once New France had been conquered, William Pitt decided to capture Belle-Ile-en-Mer, an island in the northern part of the Bay of Biscay, ten miles off the coast of France. Pitt hoped to transform it into a great naval base, a sort of northern Gibraltar. On March 29th, 1761, a British fleet of thirty-three vessels carrying ten thousand soldiers left Plymouth, England, en route to the Bay of Biscay. One of the regiments was the 72nd Foot, to which Lieutenant-Colonel Carleton was attached. King George II had died the previous year, and his successor, George III, had no objection to Carleton's assignment.

On April 7th, Belle-Ile-en-Mer came into view. The coast was rocky, with bluffs and enormous caves. The terrain was flat, almost treeless, and the highest elevation a mere hundred and thirty feet. The fleet sailed down the southwestern coast, found no harbors, and came to anchor at the southeastern tip, just offshore from Port Andro, a little hamlet of perhaps two dozen fishermen's huts. Some five hundred soldiers under Carleton landed without opposition, but as they advanced they encountered a small contingent of French troops. Carleton, leading the attack, was wounded seriously enough to prevent his taking any further part in the fighting. The French retreated the seven miles to the chief town and harbor of the island, Le Palais.

After four weeks of fighting, the British captured Le Palais and the rest of Belle-Ile at a cost of over fifteen hundred casualties. However, Pitt's dream of an island naval base was not to be realized. The harbor of Le Palais was only thirteen feet deep, far too small for more than two or three sailing ships to manoeuvre and anchor, and also vulnerable to storms from the east. The other so-called harbors on the island were mere inlets, even less suitable as naval bases.[1]

A year later Carleton saw action again. On March 5th, an expedition set forth from Spithead to attack Havana, the capital of the Spanish island colony of Cuba. Carleton, raised to the rank of colonel, was the quartermaster-general. The army was ferried ashore not far from Havana. The capital was defended by a great citadel, the Moro Castle, which the British took by storm. This meant the end of any successful defence of Havana or the rest of the island. On July 22nd, Carleton, leading an attack against a Spanish outpost, was wounded for the third time, again not seriously. Fortune also smiled on him in the matter of what was termed "prize money." By agreeing not to sack Havana, the British received a ransom from the Spanish of approximately £736,000. This sum was allotted, in varying amounts, to every sailor and soldier who took part in the attack on the Moro Castle. As a colonel, Carleton's share was £1,600.

British control of Havana was shortlived. By the Treaty of Paris, which ended the Seven Years' War, Cuba was restored to Spain in exchange for Florida.[2] By the same treaty, Louis XV of France surrendered to Britain almost the entire territory of New France, from Ile Royale (Cape Breton Island) in the Gulf of St. Lawrence to the western plains and the Gulf of Mexico. (The exceptions were that part of Louisiana lying west of the Mississippi and the tiny islands of St. Pierre and Miquelon off the south shore of the British colony of Newfoundland. Intended as "a shelter for French fishermen," these islands still belong to France today.) An enormous stretch of territory from Labrador to Florida now became part of a single British North American empire.

In June 1766, Brigadier-General Carleton accepted the position of acting governor of Quebec. With no experience in public affairs, Carleton must have been surprised to be offered this position. All his adult life had been spent in the army, where his record was good but hardly outstanding. How did the opportunity arise and why was Carleton chosen?

9

After Wolfe's victory, Brigadier-General James Murray had been appointed military governor and then, in 1764, civil governor. Murray ended up being at odds with the commander of the British troops in Canada, Major-General Ralph Burton, and particularly with the English-speaking merchants of Quebec and Montreal. These merchants had forwarded bitter complaints about Murray to the secretary of state, the Duke of Grafton, and Murray had been asked to return to England to answer their charges. Theoretically, if Murray answered the accusations satisfactorily and was cleared of the charges, he would remain governor. However, it is a fact of practical politics that when an official has been unsuccessful, he is apt to be replaced. Moreover, Major-General Burton, Chief Justice William Gregory, and Attorney-General George Suckling—"two ignorant needy lawyers," in Murray's words—had also been recalled. The British cabinet had made up its mind to replace the Murray regime.

In 1766, the third Duke of Richmond replaced Grafton as secretary of state for the North American colonies. If Murray was going to be replaced, Richmond would recommend his successor. Fourteen years earlier, Carleton had been a military tutor to the Duke. In 1758, the Duke had been made colonel of the 72nd Foot, whereupon two or three months later Carleton had been made lieutenant-colonel of the same regiment. Perhaps the Duke arranged for Carleton to join the regiment, perhaps the matter was coincidental. At any rate, the two members of the same regiment renewed their friendship. It was the consensus of opinion that the governor of Quebec should be an army officer, one who spoke the language of the inhabitants, and one who had at least some knowledge of the colony. The Duke's friend, Brigadier-General Carleton, fulfilled these requirements.

Carleton, forty-two years old, stood six feet tall and walked with an erect military posture.[3] His portraits show a resemblance to George Washington. Both men had a bald, sloping forehead, a bold nose, an unsmiling, set mouth, a double chin, and grizzled sidelocks brushed forward over the ears. However, Carleton's grey eyebrows were bushier, his eyes more sunken, his cheeks more filled out, and his mouth perhaps smaller than Washington's. Carleton was a handsome, aristocratic-looking man, with a stern, serious, aloof manner. It is hard to imagine him laughing. Indeed, Wolfe referred to the "grave Carleton,"[4] and the Duke of Richmond described Carleton as "distant and reserved in manner."[5] General Haldimand, a later governor of Quebec, said of Carleton that one "should not be repelled by his cold manners, that he was a perfect gentleman and one of the best officers in the service."[6]

Carleton was given the powers of governor, but for a time he was to have only the title and salary of lieutenant-governor. The new lieutenant-governor was also appointed commander-in-chief of all British troops stationed in Canada. (Toward the end of the French regime, the names "Canada" and "New France" were both being used to designate all the lands discovered, explored, and settled or claimed by the French in North America. It was in 1763 that a royal proclamation gave the St. Lawrence colony the official name of the Province of Quebec.) Carleton was given effective legal support with a new chief justice, the youthful William Hey, and a new attorney-general, the scholarly Francis Maseres. Both were able lawyers and could converse in French as easily as in English. Carleton may have suggested these two men to Richmond; certainly Carleton was consulted and approved of the appointments.

There was another important position in the Canadian administration: executive secretary to the governor. Because this position was considered personal, Carleton could fill it without consulting London. Governor Murray's executive secretary, Hector Theophilus Cramahé, had been ordered to London to report on conditions in Quebec. Carleton met Cramahé, a Swiss by birth but a British Army officer by occupation, and liked him. When Carleton asked Cramahé to stay on in his old post as executive secretary he was taking a chance. Cramahé, a close friend of Murray's might prove to be secretly working for Murray's return to Quebec. However, Carleton trusted Cramahé to serve him faithfully, and his judgement proved correct.

Hey, Maseres, and Cramahé planned to leave London in August and sail directly to Quebec. Carleton had a different plan. Before he took office, he wanted to learn as much as possible about Quebec. A new governor ran the risk of being shown only what his officials wanted him to see, and of being told only what they wanted him to hear. Thus, in the middle of July,

Carleton sailed from Falmouth on a packet, the *Halifax*, and landed in New York City on August 21st. Stationed in this city was General Thomas Gage, commander-in-chief of all His Majesty's troops in North America. Gage had been military governor of Montreal from 1760 to 1763 and Carleton no doubt gained useful insights into the colony from his conferences with Gage.

Three days later, Carleton sailed up the Hudson River to Albany. From there he continued almost in a straight line along Lakes George and Champlain and down the Richelieu River, reaching the fort at Chambly. From Chambly he crossed the St. Lawrence to Montreal Island. The second largest town in Quebec, Montreal was already an important supply centre of the western fur trade. Located between the great "River of Canada" and the tree-covered Mont Royal that dominated the surrounding countryside, it was protected by a narrow, eighteen-foot-high stone wall, complete with loopholes and bastions, and now in a state of ill repair. Within this ancient palisade were a few private mansions—the Château de Vaudreuil, the Château de Ramezay—and the convents and seminaries, churches and chapels that bespoke the town's religious origin. Some of the old tin-roofed, roughstone houses were being replaced by handsome structures of carefully dressed limestone from local quarries, but generally Montreal's streets were narrow, unpaved and badly lit. Townspeople and *habitants* haggled daily in the principal marketplace, and the *voyageurs* of the fur trade could be heard carousing in the dingy taverns of the rue de la Capitale.

From Montreal, Carleton journeyed by carriage along the rutted King's Highway to the community of Trois-Rivières, where reputedly the finest birch-bark canoes in the colony were produced, and then on to Cap Rouge at the outskirts of Quebec City. Here, on September 22nd, he was welcomed by his council and by Hey, Maseres, and Cramahé, all of whom had arrived two weeks earlier.[8]

Quebec City was built on two levels. High on a plateau was the Upper Town. Here stood government offices, the governor's residence, convents, churches, hospitals, the bishop's palace and the Jesuit college, and the homes of the wealthy few. City walls with gates that were closed at night protected the north and west sides of the Upper Town. Its south and east sides ended at cliffs, almost perpendicular and dropping two hundred feet to the Lower Town, which was built on a strip of land shaped like a half-moon with a width of from five hundred to one thousand feet, bounded on one side by the St. Lawrence River and on the other by the cliffs. This was a well-populated area with many houses, stores and businesses, steep, winding, narrow streets, and busy docks. To reach the Upper Town, one had to climb many stone steps or take a steep, circular road up to the Prescott Gate of the Upper Town.

Carleton was driven to the governor's mansion, the enormous Château St. Louis. This building, long and rectangular in the Norman architectural tradition, had two storeys, plus a cellar and an attic. The front of the building was wood, the roof copper-slated, the rear walls entirely of stone. The structure faced a driveway and garden and boasted seven chimneys. Its entrance was a handsome porte-cochère, supported by two columns. On the ground floor were a council chamber and a lofty banquet hall, which could seat sixty people. A passageway from this hall led to a balcony at the rear, buttressed by a sixteen-foot stone wall.[9] From this balcony Carleton had an aerial view of the Lower Town. Raising his eyes, he could gaze across the St. Lawrence River to the little community of Lévis, where with Wolfe he had helped install cannon to shell the city, and from which he had set forth on his expedition to Pointe-aux-Trembles. Turning to the left, he could see the gentle Ile d'Orléans, where he had first landed with Wolfe.

The colony of Quebec was markedly unlike the thirteen British colonies to the south. Each of these had been settled by Englishmen, mainly Protestant, and had grown by peaceful expansion. King George III's "new subjects" belonged to a completely different culture. The language of Quebec was French (a French enriched by local terms, Indian words, and idiosyncratic idioms); scarcely one person out of fifty could speak English. They were a devoutly Catholic people—more Catholic than Catholic France itself.

Before the conquest, the seventy-five thousand French-speaking people of Canada[10] had considered themselves to be in a land governed by France but not part of France. Nearly all were native born; practically no immigration had taken place for

13

many decades. Moreover, few of Quebec's inhabitants had ever visited France. In their isolation, they had developed their own indigenous customs and laws, of which they were fiercely proud and protective. They had endured French rule with its corruption, but few felt a deep allegiance to France. They felt neither loyalty nor bitterness toward their new British rulers. All they wanted was to continue to live the way their fathers had, and they were unlikely to revolt unless their way of life was disrupted.

The French Canadians lived predominantly on small farms. The city of Quebec had a population of perhaps eight thousand, Montreal almost five thousand, and the third largest community, Trois-Rivières, had barely fifty households. The other sixty-two thousand inhabitants lived along or close to the two-hundred-and-fifty-mile shoreline of the St. Lawrence River between Montreal and Kamouraska.

The typical farmer, or *habitant*, although illiterate,[11] was highly intelligent. Living in a harsh but healthy climate of long winters and hot summers, he had remarkable vigor and stamina. In addition to farming, he was a hunter, fisherman, wood-cutter, canoeist in summer, and skater in winter. He was also a great "do-it-yourself" man. He fashioned his own tools, furniture and kept his house and outbuildings in good repair. The average *habitant* had one or two horses or a couple of oxen. He owned a cow or two, some calves, a few sheep and some pigs.[12] He produced enough to feed his family, his animals, and to give him a small surplus that fetched enough cash to buy tobacco, gunpowder, and other household needs he could not supply himself. The *habitant* was neither ambitious nor materialistic. He did not want a large farm, which only meant more work, and had little yearning for luxuries. He was happy if he could live each year as he had lived the last.

The *habitant* loved dancing, storytelling, gossiping, and joking. He was usually an inveterate smoker, and at the many parties during the winter he would consume a considerable amount of brandy. A passionately independent character, he particularly loved litigation. (One lawsuit involved the ownership of a featherbed!) The *habitant* was willing to show his landlord respect, but not the mute submission of the French peasant.

Indeed, French Canadians had successfully protested the imposition of the numerous taxes for which peasants were liable in France. *Habitants'* wives took great pride in their homes, their housekeeping and their cooking. They spun and wove the wool from their own sheep and made most of the family's clothes. At harvest time, they worked in the fields alongside their men. Quebec women were prolific child bearers, and although the mortality rate among babies was high, the population doubled roughly every twenty-five years. In the opinion of one aristocratic French visitor, the *habitant* and his family had a "very comfortable" existence and lived like minor aristocracy in France.

Habitants farmed their land under a quasifeudal system. The valley of the St. Lawrence had been partitioned into *seigneuries*, or estates. French-Canadian society had a class of leaders made up of about four hundred prominent families. Of these, about a quarter were landowners (*seigneurs*), another quarter independently wealthy gentlemen, and the remainder merchants, lawyers and doctors. Governor Murray had confirmed the seignorial system. The rent the *habitant* paid was small, and it was often paid in kind with bags of grain, poultry or livestock. The *habitant* also paid the *seigneur* for the privilege of using his mill.

Most of the *seigneurs* were only slightly better off than their tenants. The *habitant's* house had one chimney; a *seigneur's* manor house had two, possible three. Both were simple wooden structures, built with the traditional steep roof of Normandy, which was ideal for shedding the heavy snowfalls of Quebec. Compared with the estates of English and French nobility, the *seigneur's* mode of living was unpretentious. There were social distinctions between *seigneur* and *habitant*, but the relationship was not that of lord and vassal. The *habitant* bowed to no one, and the *seigneur* mingled with all.

There were one hundred and thirty-four parishes of the Catholic Church in the Province, with some one hundred and fifty resident priests.[13] In most of the parishes, the church was the social and information centre. The feast of the patron saint of the parish was an annual holiday and high mass was celebrated. On some Sundays after mass, worshippers would remain to hear the priest give a neighborhood report. Perhaps he talked about

15

the problems of an individual parishioner, who might be sick and in need of help to harvest his crops. Any breach of custom on the part of a *habitant* or *seigneur* would be brought up for discussion. And it was after the church service on Sunday that the priest or the captain of the militia read out the latest laws and orders. These meetings after church were the nearest equivalent in Quebec of the town meeting so common in the New England colonies.

Other groups who inhabited Quebec included shopkeepers, fishermen, lumbermen (who shipped masts and spars to Britain, but whose wood was produced mostly for home consumption), and notaries, who were kept busy drawing up the papers for the litigious *habitants*. The British employed some two hundred officials and clerks, mostly Frenchmen who had served the old regime. There were also sixteen hundred British soldiers, one thousand stationed in Quebec City and six hundred in Montreal.

An important factor in the economy of Quebec was the fur trade. Badly disrupted by years of war, it was now beginning to resume its former profitable role, under the direction of British entrepreneurs. The Canadian fur trade owed its existence to a European mania for beaver hats that persisted throughout the seventeenth and eighteenth centuries and on into the first half of the nineteenth. Society, whether royal or aristocratic, clerical or lay, rarely appeared in public without a beaver hat—plumed, bejewelled, braided or embroidered; high, flat or tricorne, according to the fashion of the moment. About the time that the beaver was dying out in Europe, countless numbers of the animal were being discovered in the northern half of the New World. In this cold climate, the animal grew heavy, lustrous pelts.

The quiet life of the villages and farms of the St. Lawrence had no appeal for the bolder sons of New France. Instead, scores of adventurous traders had travelled westward from Montreal, taking canoeloads of European trinkets and tools, combs and clothing—and, above all, brandy—to barter for furs in Indian villages. They slipped away from their river-lot homes for the far more profitable and exciting life of a *coureur de bois* ("runner of the woods") who traded for furs, with or without a *congé* or official licence. In time, they traded with Indian tribes living farther and farther from Montreal and, in so doing, had advanced the territorial claims of France into the heart of the continent. The English in the seaboard colonies were hemmed in by the barrier of the Allegheny Mountains, whereas the St. Lawrence enabled the *coureurs de bois* to reach the Great Lakes. From these, they paddled and portaged into the drainage basin of the Mississippi or ventured northwestward into the watershed of the Saskatchewan River.

Sometime around 1700, the *voyageur*, or French-Canadian canoeman, came on the scene. The fur trade operating out of Montreal had become big business. Only tough tireless *voyageurs* had the strength and stamina to take hundreds of tons of goods thousands of miles into the continental interior. They were the indispensable workhorses of the trade who skilfully navigated their fragile, heavily laden birch-bark canoes safely through the seething white waters of a *sault* or, more laboriously and almost as dangerously, "lined" or hauled their craft all the way past it. The strength to carry two ninety-pound *pièces*, or packs, over a stony portage trail at a steady dogtrot, was another requirement of this rigorous career.

The men who managed the posts in the "Indian country" were sometimes French-speaking and sometimes English-speaking. However, after the Conquest, the merchants who financed and carried on the fur trade—as well as the entire import-export business of Quebec—were nearly all English-speaking. They were about a hundred in number, colonials from the south, or immigrant Scots who had scented an opportunity to make money. Many of them had been contractors or purveyors with Wolfe's army or with British reinforcements that arrived after the surrender of New France. Because they spoke English and had British connections, these men had replaced most of the French businessmen. A compact, exclusive group, these newcomers constituted the *nouveaux riches* of Quebec. To these entrepreneurs, Canada was a place to exercise a power they could never have had in the Old Country and to turn a quick buck. Although they had their business rivalries, they

17

were almost unanimous in their opposition to Murray, and they expected Carleton to conform to their wishes by being less conciliatory toward the French population.

Some antagonism had grown up among the three groups of the population: the French Canadians, the army, and the English-speaking merchants. The Québécois disliked and distrusted the merchants because they were rich, influential and arrogant. Conversely, as a general rule, the merchants were contemptuous of the Québécois and thought of them as a conquered people. The merchants and the army, too, were at odds. Not without reason, the merchants thought the officers snobbish. The average army officer was high-born, had an ingrained prejudice against anyone "in trade," and scorned the merchant class. (This contempt was not extended to the merchants' wives and daughters, who were invited to garrison balls—without their husbands and fathers.) At the same time, the officers envied the merchant his ability to amass wealth. Although there was no threat of aggression on the part of any of these three groups, their tensions aggravated the problems that faced the colony and its new governor.

Within and surrounding Quebec was yet another population: the Indians of the eastern forests. In a heavily wooded, four-hundred-mile-wide swath between Quebec City and the Great Lakes, there were perhaps as many as ten thousand Indians, divided into roughly one hundred tribes. Each tribe was further divided into innumerable clans. Men did the hunting and fishing for the clan; women performed all other labor. The Indian's intimate knowledge of the forest and his peerless skill as a hunter were a source of great pride to him.

The Indian's great gifts to the European were the birch-bark canoe and the snowshoe. Without them, the fur trade could never have flourished. For his part, the European revolutionized life in the eastern forests. For centuries, the Indian had fashioned his own stone or bone implements, clothed himself in skins and furs, and made his own bow and arrows. Now he was captivated by a labor-saving technology: steel hatchets and knives; iron pots and kettles; clothes and blankets; and above all the superior weaponry of musket, ball and powder. As a result, the Indian's self-sufficiency was destroyed, and he became a trapper of fur-bearing animals, especially the beaver, in order to exchange their pelts for the white man's luxuries. The Indians and the Europeans were mutually dependent: the *habitants* produced little surplus food, there was no manufacturing, and thus many items—salt, sugar, wines and liquor—had to be imported. The sale of furs to Europe paid for a large percentage of the imports.

Despite normally friendly relations with the forest Indians, despite their essential function in the economy of Canada, many a British official feared them. After all, it was only three years since Pontiac's Rebellion had brought bloodshed and death to the western frontiers of the Thirteen Colonies. Sensing that British settlers would inevitably spread west and take over Indian hunting grounds, Pontiac, of the Ottawa tribe, had tried to organize a military alliance of the Great Lakes tribes to drive all Europeans off the continent. He succeeded only in rousing the Wyandot, Potawatomi, and Chippewa, but they were numerous enough to besiege Fort Detroit for several months, capture several other British frontier posts, and raid groups of settlers who had crossed the Alleghenies to farm in the Ohio Valley. At least two thousand settlers, five hundred soldiers, and an equal number of Indians lost their lives before troops and militia put down the rebellion.

Carleton must have talked with Thomas Gage about the "Indian problem," and doubtless he learned of Lord Amherst's failure to solve it by military garrisons. One of the serious challenges facing Carleton was to reassure the Indians that they would not lose their ancestral lands, and thus avoid the bloodshed of a native uprising.

CHAPTER 3

Carleton's First Council

Carleton arrived at the Château St. Louis on September 23rd, 1766. The next day, standing before Chief Justice Hey, he took the oath of office as lieutenant-governor. He then listened to three separate addresses of welcome: one from the magistrates; one from English-speaking merchants; and one from Murray's councillors.[1] To these Carleton replied with the usual polite generalities, although his words contained an implication that he intended to run the province without interference from anyone. In reporting to London about his reception, Carleton observed dryly that he suspected the reason for three addresses was because these groups, mutually jealous, were unable to co-operate.

How the Province of Quebec was to be governed was defined in the Royal Proclamation of October 7th, 1763, and in instructions to Murray that had been signed by the King on December 7th, 1763. Carleton, theoretically acting for Murray, was bound by these instructions. They indicated that the normal apparatus of British colonial government would be instituted: a governor, a council, and an assembly, plus a system of law courts headed by a chief justice. However, the instructions assumed that the immediate creation of an assembly might not be practical and permitted government by governor and council. Thus Quebec was ruled by a council of eleven men approved by London and by a governor, who was the chairman of the council. Ten of the eleven were members of Murray's former council. The eleventh was Hey, whose position as chief justice automatically made him a councillor. The governor could veto any action the council wanted to take and there was no provision for the council to be able to override such a veto by a majority. However, London's instructions explicitly required the council's consent to just about every decision the governor would ordinarily make. In other words, the council was both a legislative and an executive body, and this could result in an impasse and leave the governor's power much restricted.

Today, we accept the fact that the power to govern is often vested in one individual, a president or prime minister. Although the chief executive can delegate this power, he can also withdraw it at any time. Two hundred years ago in Britain, there was little understanding of the desirability of placing executive power in the hands of one person. The British government itself operated in haphazard fashion. Undefined executive power rested in the hands of the monarch, the prime minister, members of the cabinet, and in various committees, and years would pass before executive power was placed firmly in the hands of the prime minister.

Carleton had two firm supporters in the council, Hey and Cramahé. The opinions of the other members he had yet to determine, but they had been councillors for three years and doubtless felt they knew how the Province should be run. One of them, Lieutenant-Colonel Paulus Irving, had been acting governor during the summer, before Carleton had arrived. However, Carleton may well have suspected that the councillors expected him to do what they wanted. He must have wondered how he was going to persuade—or force—a majority of them to accept his leadership. As commander-in-chief, he automatically had the authority to run the army, but as governor, how was he going to obtain the authority to run the government? If Carleton did not obtain the power to govern, would he not follow Murray into oblivion?

Carleton had been appointed to govern a people who followed a different religion, lived by a different culture, and spoke a foreign language. They had been recently conquered and might prove restive. The English-speaking merchants were thoroughly frustrated by the lack of a representative assembly in which they would have some say in running the Province.

Carleton's task was not going to be easy. Would it even be possible if he could not control the council?

For two weeks Carleton did not call any council meetings. Then, early in October the leadership came to a head. There were four Indian trading posts northeast of Quebec City known as the King's Posts. They were owned by the Crown and leased to merchants for a yearly rent. Four years earlier, in consideration of an annual fee of £400, Murray had leased these posts to two merchants, Thomas Dunn and John Gray. In the early summer of 1766, another merchant, George Allsopp, had erected rough buildings to set up a fifth trading post in this area. Dunn and Gray vigorously protested Allsopp's intrusion into their trade monopoly. On August 8th, the council, with Irving presiding, had sided with Dunn and Gray and ordered Allsopp to tear down his buildings. Now Allsopp appealed to Carleton to rescind the council's order. Carleton was sympathetic. Although the greatest part of the trade took place west of Montreal, nonetheless another post downriver might help to increase the flow of pelts to Britain. However, a council that had ordered the destruction of Allsopp's post was hardly likely to reverse itself and cancel the order two months later.

Carleton must have known that a decision in the Allsopp matter, while of little importance in itself, was vitally significant in its implications, so he devised an expedient. He did not call a meeting of the full council. On October 9th, he met with four councillors, Hey, Cramahé, Irving, and Samuel Holland. Carleton could count on a majority including himself, Hey, and Cramahé. These five members, assembling in the Château, unanimously passed a resolution to suspend the order of the full council of August 8th and to let Allsopp's trading post stand. They also appointed themselves a committee to report on the matter.[2] Then the minutes of the meeting were entered in the council book as if they were the minutes of the full council, and these minutes were signed by the new lieutenant-governor.

At this time, neither Irving nor Holland objected to a meeting limited to five council members. However, some of the councillors who had not been invited to the meeting—namely, James Cuthbert, Walter Murray (a relative of the former governor), Dr. Adam Mabane and François Mounier—were alarmed. They complained to Irving that they were being ignored. A couple of days later, Irving had a talk with Carleton, as the two men walked back and forth in the garden of the Château at sunset. Carleton tried to be conciliatory. When Irving said the men who had been excluded felt justified in preparing a written remonstrance and insisting on their right to attend, Carleton seemed to agree. The conversation ended with Carleton asking Irving to come to dinner at the Château two nights later and suggesting that he bring along the aggrieved councillors.[3]

The next day, Carleton received a polite but pointed remonstrance signed by the excluded councillors and by Irving. Carleton exhibited no ire, said he would respond in writing, and did not cancel the dinner date. The dinner, however, was a stormy one because Carleton lost his temper.[4] He cast aside the persona of the conciliatory politician and was blunt and forthright. Irving, he said, had not understood him. It was not an accident that they had been left out of the meeting. That was intentional.[5] In his anger, he either said or implied that he was going to remove some of the present members of council.

Carleton called no further meetings of the full council, or of any of its members, during the next six weeks. Then another problem arose. Two years earlier Thomas Walker, an Englishman who had lived in Boston and was now a Montreal merchant and a justice of the peace, had been assaulted in his home by several men with blackened faces. Walker had been brutally beaten and one of his ears had been cut off. He had exhibited considerable animosity towards the army, and soldiers or officers undoubtedly were his attackers. For various reasons, the crime had remained unsolved and the criminals unpunished. Now, an ex-soldier, albeit a man with a record as a deserter and a criminal, was accusing three army officers and three prominent Montreal citizens of having attacked Walker. All six were arrested and brought to Quebec to appear before Chief Justice Hey.

The arrests aroused excitement and fury in Montreal and Quebec City. Many believed the accused innocent and considered the arrest the result of a Thomas Walker plot. (When the case came to trial a few weeks later, all six were exonerated, the jury reaching a decision within five minutes.) Hey would not allow bail on the ground that Walker said his life would be in danger if the accused were at large. This refusal of bail, a dubious decision to say the least, enraged the people. A petition was drawn up on behalf of the accused and signed by a large number of eminent Quebec citizens. It was presented to Lieutenant-Governor Carleton, who replied that he would try to alleviate the conditions of imprisonment of the six and press for a speedy trial.

The aggrieved councilmen who had attended the dinner at the Château were among the many citizens who had signed the petition. Carleton, sensing an opportunity to deal with them, consulted Maseres as to the legal options available. Maseres found an old statute of King Charles II to the effect that a petition signed by more than twenty people could be considered seditious. Carleton did not punish all the members of council who had signed the petition. He simply dismissed two of the most prominent signatories, Councillors Irving and Mabane.

The conditions prescribed in the King's instructions for the removal of a councillor were as follows: a specific charge or charges against a member had to be heard and examined in council, and a majority vote decided whether the councillor should be dismissed. Copies of the proceedings had to be forwarded to the Board of Trade. (At this time the Board of Trade and the secretary of state were jointly in charge of Britain's colonies.) If a governor found reason "not fit to be communicated to the council," he could dismiss on his own authority, provided he sent a full report to the Board of Trade.[6] Carleton dismissed Irving and Mabane upon his own authority.

On Monday, December 1st, Carleton called a meeting of the remaining councillors. He opened the meeting with the simple statement that he had dismissed the two and that his reasons would be sent to London. Not a voice was raised in opposition. Carleton had obtained a co-operative if not a subservient council, and he was now the decision maker.*

* There is an interesting sequel to the dismissal of the two most prominent councillors. Irving returned to London. Dr. Adam Mabane, however, remained in Quebec. As the months and years rolled by, he and Carleton became friends. The two men retained no bitterness toward each other and found out that they thought alike on many issues and problems. As a result, in 1774, Carleton asked London to reinstate Mabane as a councillor, which was duly done.[7]

Carleton's reports to the Board of Trade and to Lord Shelburne, who had replaced the Duke of Richmond as secretary of
state in charge of Canada, were far from candid. In writing to
the Board of Trade about the order to demolish Allsopp's new
Indian trading post, Carleton remarked that this order had been
"flagrantly unjust" and that he himself had suspended it. He
admitted that he had received a remonstrance from certain
councillors who had not been at the meeting. He claimed that
these men were unavailable to attend the meeting. By innuen-
do, he cast aspersions upon their characters. Carleton then went
on to say that he was not calling a further meeting of the council
for a while "to give them time to cool and reflect."[8] To Lord
Shelburne, Carleton wrote that for citizens to sign and present
to him a petition on behalf of the six accused of assaulting
Walker was "the first attempt to disturb the peace and interrupt
the free course of justice since my arrival in the Province."[9]
Actually the presentation of the petition was orderly, and Carleton's accusation had little relation to the truth.

Carleton has been bitterly criticized by historians for his high-
handed actions and distortions of the truth. He, of course, could
rationalize what he had done and say to himself that the instructions written to Murray three years ago were for the purpose of
setting up Murray's government and no longer applied. Did
London want the new lieutenant-governor to be hamstrung by
Governor Murray's council after Murray had been recalled and
when London was looking for a thorough house-cleaning and a
new, effective regime?

To the citizens of the city of Quebec, the motives behind
Carleton's actions were easily understood. They knew that
Carleton had not called a full meeting of the council over the Allsopp affair because he did not have a majority to legitimize his
leadership. Later, he summarily dismissed two councillors to
cow the others and thus obtain a majority following. Carleton's
actions were an obvious power play.

His distorted report to London is more difficult to justify. It
can be argued that there was no point in his asking Lord Shelburne or the Board of Trade for permission to dismiss one or
more councillors because their reply would not reach ice-bound
Quebec until the following May. Also, Murray was still the real

governor. Shelburne and the Board of Trade would have hesitated to authorize the lieutenant-governor to discharge members of Murray's council. Once Carleton had been evasive—perhaps it should be said, once he had lied—about his handling of the Allsopp affair, it was difficult for him to be candid about his dismissal of Irving and Mabane.

Carleton obviously wanted to avoid interference from London. In this, he was successful. The following May he received a letter from Lord Shelburne saying that His Majesty was pleased at the way Carleton had been conducting the government of Quebec and taking care of problems as they arose. The dismissal of the two councillors was not commented upon, but the implication was clear: London had no objection. Carleton had this letter to wave in the face of any councillor who might be tempted to become recalcitrant.[10]

CHAPTER 4

The Problems Facing the New Lieutenant-Governor

Once Carleton had obtained control of the council, he became, in effect, the government of the Province of Quebec. Unlike our present-day multilayered governments, each with its own complex bureaucracy, the government of Quebec was solely in the hands of Carleton and the subservient councillors. The lieutenant-governor was accountable to no elected assembly or legislature. As chief executive of the colony, Carleton dealt with Indians, with the Thirteen Colonies and with Great Britain, in addition to being the equivalent of the mayor of the city of Quebec, of Montreal, and of the tiny community of Trois-Rivières.

Carleton talked to people of all types, and the major complaint he heard during his first few weeks in office concerned the fees that citizens had to pay to government officials, only a few of whom were paid salaries, and meagre ones at that. If a citizen had a case in court, he had to tip the clerk of the court or his case would not be heard. A mill or tavern owner paid for the application for a licence, for the licence to be processed, and for its endorsement. A *habitant* taking farm produce to the market in Quebec or Montreal had to pay a harbor official for the right to tie up his boat to a wharf and another tip to allow his produce to be displayed. On the whole, fees were small but they were so numerous as to become burdensome and to open the way to corruption of officials. The Quebec *Gazette* listed some three hundred and fifty types of fees in 1765.[1]

On November 7th, 1766, the *Gazette* announced that Lieutenant-Governor Carleton was relinquishing all his own fees. His services would be free, with the exception of those for licensing taverns and public houses. These, Carleton said, would be collected and turned over to the receiver-general to become part of the public revenue.[2]

Carleton in his report to London made the following comment: "There is a certain appearance of dirt, a sort of meanness in exacting fees on every occasion. I think it is necessary for the King's service that his representative at least should be thought unsullied."[3] To Lord Shelburne, he wrote:

> It seems to me no less essential that none of the principal officers of government and justice, neither Governor, Judge, Secretary, Provost Martial, or Clerk of the Council should receive fee, reward, or present from the people on pain of the King's displeasure, tho' an equivalent should be allowed them by way of salary, and that the inferior officers be restrained to the fees authorised under the French Government.[4]

In relinquishing his own fees, Carleton was giving up of between £500 and £600 a year.[5] Even if Carleton had been a rich man, his decision would have been commendable. However, Carleton had little money behind him. His income was £600 to £700 a year as a brigadier-general, plus a £600 salary as lieutenant-governor.[6] Nonetheless, £1,200 to £1,300 was barely sufficient to maintain the upkeep of the Château St. Louis and take care of his other living expenses.

Governor Murray, who was living in London, was furious that Carleton had renounced his personal fees. In a London newspaper, *Lloyde's Evening Post*, Murray published a letter that tried to justify his fees while chastising Carleton. Murray stated that the fees that he personally collected did not exceed £65 during his three years as governor.[7] Actually he had collected almost ten times that amount.

For the next thirty years Carleton continued to denounce the fee system to little avail. It was ingrained not only among the officialdom in the Province of Quebec but also in Britain. The British government did not want to reduce fees because it would then have to increase the existing salaries of officials, at home and abroad. The most Carleton could do was to check the worst features of the fee system. In May 1767, he issued the following order:

> All the officers of the civil government, magistrates, clerks, Deputy-Marshal, must deliver exact lists of all fees they have been accustomed to take or claim by value of right within the space of three months of this notice, lists to be sent to James Polk, Clerk of the Council, and likewise to set forth in the said lists the ground on which they take or claim such fees.[8]

Carleton tried to stipulate the amount of each fee and he threatened officials with expulsion if they were caught overcharging. When Thomas Ainslie, the collector of customs at the port of Quebec, increased the fees that incoming and outgoing ships' captains had to pay, Carleton went into a rage and forced him to return to the old schedule. Without success, Carleton tried to reduce the size of dockage fees charged at the ports of Halifax and New York.[9]

One of Carleton's first actions upon his arrival at Quebec had been to pardon all army deserters who surrendered and returned to duty before January 1st, 1767. The proclamation of the proffered pardon was published in the Quebec *Gazette*, a bilingual weekly paper, with a circulation in the neighborhood of three hundred copies. In order to inform the seventy thousand or so near-illiterate *Canadiens*, Carleton had his proclamation printed in French as a handbill. He then requested Bishop Briand, the bishop of Quebec, to forward this handbill to each of his one hundred and fifty Catholic priests, directing that they read the proclamation to their parishioners.[10]

Carleton's humaneness was exemplified in other actions. On October 7th, 1767, a Simon La Point of Montreal was convicted of robbing a man named Sourbroun of £25. There seemed to be no irregularity in the trial, no reasonable doubt as to the man's guilt, and no extenuating circumstances. The judge sentenced La Point to be hung on October 22nd. This was the first time since the institution of civil government in the Province that one of his Majesty's "new subjects" had been sentenced to death. Carleton lacked the power to reduce the sentence, but he could pardon La Point, which he did, with the proviso that the thief leave the Province within thirty days and never return.[11] Carleton's leniency tended to restrain the courts from imposing excessive sentences.

One perennial problem in the Province was the control and prevention of fires. The year before Carleton arrived, a fire in Montreal had damaged over one hundred houses, rendering homeless seven to eight hundred people. In the city of Quebec, there were between five and six hundred houses huddled closely together. The walls of the houses were built of stone (no new house could be built with wooden walls in the cities of Quebec and Montreal), but it was not practicable to construct the roof of stone, so these were usually wooden, sometimes with thatching on top. Most chimneys were connected to one or more stoves, in which fires burned twenty-four hours a day during the severe Quebec winter. If a chimney caught fire, the roof would easily ignite, and the flames—especially if the day was windy—would race swiftly from one roof to the next. In 1768, an ordinance was published over Carleton's signature stipulating that every householder must have two buckets, a hatchet, a ladder, and two fire poles. There was a five-shilling fine if one of these articles was found missing.[12] The fire poles were each ten feet long, five or six inches thick, and had crossbars at one end. Thus, four men, two to a pole, could wrench loose a burning roof and topple it off the walls. Once the roof was on the ground, it was relatively easy to extinguish the flames. By law, every householder had to have his chimney swept every four seeks at the cost of sixpence. The penalty for any delay in doing this was five shillings. In addition, if a house caught fire from the chimney or from a stove, a forty-shilling fine was levied.

Carleton took measures to resolve many other domestic problems. Against bakers who were accused of cheating their customers by reducing the size of a loaf, Carleton and the council passed an ordinance stipulating that a sixpenny loaf of white bread was to weigh three pounds, twelve ounces, and a sixpenny brown loaf four pounds, twelve ounces.[13] To reduce drunkenness, an ordinance was passed prohibiting tavern keepers from giving credit in excess of half a Spanish dollar (the equivalent of about four shillings). If the tavern owner disobeyed the ordinance, he was not fined, but he was not allowed to collect for the excess drinks. The drinker or drinkers got their beer or liquor free.[14]

Due to the tricky currents of the St. Lawrence and its strong tides, competent pilots were needed. Yet unqualified men were acting as pilots, and pilotage charges were not uniform. To avoid these charges, when a ship was being guided upriver, instead of paying for a pilot, the next ship would copy the movements of the ship ahead. This bred bitterness between ships' captains and between captains and pilots. Carleton drew up an ordinance creating the new position of commissioner of pilots, who was required to investigate the qualifications of applicants for a pilot's licence, to check on the efficiency and competence of pilots, and to regulate their activities. The most dangerous part of the channel below Quebec was the passage across the river at the northeastern end of the Ile d'Orléans called the Traverse. Here were numerous reefs, sandbars, and little islands that were submerged at high tide. The commissioner was made responsible for ensuring that guide buoys were laid in the Traverse in the late spring after the ice had broken up and taken out again in the late fall before freeze-up. Pilot's fees were made uniform and determined by the number of feet of a ship's water line: the longer the water line, the higher the fee. A ship's captain could refuse a pilot, but he was required nevertheless to pay half the pilot's fee.[15]

A particularly prickly problem that Carleton faced was acquiring revenue to pay the expenses of government. The chief source of income was the duties that London had placed on the importation of liquor and wines. These were as follows: rum, one pound a hogshead; brandy, sixpence a gallon; wine, ten shillings a hogshead; ordinary wine bottled, one halfpence a bottle; sweet wine bottled, one and one halfpence a bottle.[16] For six years, the income from these had been insufficient to meet expenses, and the British treasury had had to pay the deficit. Officials in London were beginning to object. In June 1766, a Thomas Mills had arrived from Britain with the title of receiver-general. He had been sent to Quebec to audit accounts, to try to reduce expenses, to increase revenue, and to balance the provincial budget. Murray had already sailed for England, Carleton had not arrived, and Acting Governor Irving dissuaded Mills from taking any action until the advent of the new lieutenant-governor.

Duties on liquor were difficult to collect because a ship's captain often insisted upon unloading as soon as his ship docked, so that he could start the return trip as soon as possible. Since there were no warehouses where the spirits and wine could be stored, the customs collector could not prevent the owners from picking up their consignments on the dock. If the customs collector could not obtain immediate cash, he had to accept a note or I.O.U. Thus Mills found a large collection of unpaid notes. As most of the importers came from the Thirteen Colonies to the south and were influenced by the current agitation there against "taxation with no representation," they complained that these duties were unfair. Why should they, and they alone, provide the government of Quebec with much of its income? They refused to honor their notes. Carleton insisted on legal action, and Attorney-General Maseres brought suit in November 1766. Because the amount involved was over £500, the case came before the King's Bench presided over by Chief Justic Hey.

During the trial, the genuineness of the notes was not denied, and there was no logical defence against the fact that they had to be paid. Judge Hey therefore instructed the jury to bring in a judgement in favor of the plaintiff, the government. However, the jury solemnly brought in a judgement in favor of the defendants, the merchants.

The explanation of the jury's action was quite clear to every citizen of Quebec. Hey's court was conducted in English. French citizens were eligible for jury service, but because ninety-nine per cent of them could not understand English, they were, in practice, never called. Only one hundred, possibly one hundred and fifty, men were available for jury duty in the city of Quebec. They were either merchants, or worked for merchants, or were members of families who were friends of the merchants. This close-knit group of English-speaking businessmen was determined not to pay these duties.

Carleton had come to Canada with the conviction that he must co-operate with the powerful English-speaking commercial community, who had engineered Murray's recall when he had displeased them. Very soon, however, Carleton began to change his attitude. As early as 1766, he was beginning to feel that he must restrain and control the merchants and work on behalf of the King's "new subjects," who made up ninety-eight per cent of the province's inhabitants. The outcome of this trial was one of the factors that changed Carleton's mind. On December 24th, 1767, he wrote to Lord Shelburne: "The Canadians in general, particularly the gentlemen [the *seigneurs*], greatly disapprove of the verdict given last year against the crown on the trial of the duties . . . "[17]

In the winter of 1767, forty *seigneurs* from the Montreal area signed a petition to George III. They thanked the King for the repeal of the Stamp Act, requested that Governor Murray return to Quebec and resume his duties, and pleaded for the right of Catholics to hold public office.[18] Carleton had not as yet spent any time in Montreal; he had been too busy at Quebec. Because of the distance between the two cities, few if any of these *seigneurs* had ever met Carleton. On the other hand, they knew and trusted Murray. The *seigneurs* near Quebec City did not sign the petition. Many of these had met Carleton, liked him, and doubtless realized that he was on their side. Carleton was not disturbed by the petition; however, it did bother Carleton's supporters and they started to circulate a counter-petition asking the King to make Carleton the full-fledged governor of Quebec. Carleton vigorously objected to this petition and successfully quashed it.

In April 1767, His Majesty's Privy Council repudiated the complaints that had been made against Governor James Murray. No witnesses had appeared, and no evidence had been brought forward to sustain any of the charges. Murray was totally exonerated. However, he resigned the governorship and never returned to Quebec.[19]

On Tuesday, November 1st, 1768, on the parade ground of the Upper Town in front of a large concourse of people, His Majesty's letters patent naming Guy Carleton governor of the Province of Quebec were read. The oath of office was administered by Chief Justice Hey, and an honor guard fired a salute.[20]

CHAPTER 5

The Need for a Constitution for Quebec

The Catholic Church posed yet another problem for Carleton. In 1760, the Bishop of Quebec had died, and for six years the Province had had no spiritual leader. Thus no priests could be ordained to replace those who had retired or died. In 1766, Jean Olivier Briand, a devout, able and popular Quebec priest, was consecrated bishop in a private chapel in France. He returned to Quebec some months before Carleton arrived. However, there was no coadjutor; if Bishop Briand should die, the same problem would arise. Briand started inquiries among Quebec priests as to who might be a good man for the position. These inquiries reached Carleton's ears and he requested a conference with Briand. When the two met, Carleton told Briand bluntly that no coadjutor could be appointed without the governor's approval. Briand, a pragmatic man, decided to acquiesce.

Carleton wanted the Church to be administered not in the interests of France, or of Rome, or even of London, but in the interests of the French Catholics in the Province. He insisted that he have a veto over any suggestion for a coadjutor because he suspected that an able priest, Abbé de la Joncaire, would be appointed. Although born in Canada, Joncaire had lived in France for twenty-seven years, and Carleton feared that Joncaire would look to France for decisions and orders. The matter dragged on without being resolved. Finally, in the spring of 1770, Carleton suggested Louis-Philippe Mariéchau Desglis, a curé on the Ile d'Orléans, as coadjutor and Briand agreed. However, it was two years later before all the necessary papers were signed and Desglis was consecrated.

When the Earl of Dartmouth, who in 1772 succeeded Hillsborough as secretary of state for the colonies, heard of this consecration, he was enraged at Carleton's presumption and sent Cramahé, who was acting governor in Carleton's absence, letters of bitter reproach. In the end, Dartmouth was powerless: the deed had been done. At a later date, Carleton explained his rationale by writing to London to request that "the head of the ecclesiastical arrangements be left as much to himself as possible, and begs he may be left at liberty to use his own discretion in this very difficult business."[1]

Carleton was, of course, a Protestant, a member of the Church of England, and he and his co-religionists had a very minor problem. The Protestants, being few in number, had no church building of their own. (The present Anglican cathedral in Quebec was not completed until 1804.) The Recollets, a Roman Catholic missionary order, had a chapel scarcely six hundred feet from the Château St. Louis, in which they permitted the Protestants to conduct a service each Sunday. The service was held thirty minutes after the completion of mass, but because the duration of the mass varied, there was some confusion as to the time the Protestant service began. In May 1767, Carleton announced in the Quebec *Gazette* that he was ordering drummer boys from the garrison to beat their drums for three minutes at the conclusion of the mass. Exactly half an hour after the sound of the drums, the Protestant service would commence.

One of Carleton's biggest headaches was the courts and the legal system operating in the Province. In 1764, Governor Murray had set up a judiciary in four tiers. Justices of the peace, or magistrates, comprised the lowest tier. The next was the Court of Common Pleas, above which, presided over by Chief Justice Hey, was the King's Bench or Supreme Court. The fourth tier, a court of appeal to the council, was almost never used.

The magistrates had jurisdiction over minor criminal cases and some civil suits. Only cases involving more than £30 could receive their initial hearing in a higher court, and there were few such cases. The average *habitant* had no dealings with the higher courts. To him, law and justice were dispensed by the magistrates and their bailiffs, who were on the whole a sorry lot. Because no Roman Catholic could hold public office and because there were so few Protestant lawyers in the province, Murray had been forced to appoint as magistrates English-speaking merchants, some British and some American, who were ignorant of the law. To help the magistrates understand the cases, it was necessary to appoint French-speaking bailiffs. These, many of whom were former French soldiers—in some cases, former deserters—were remunerated by fees. It was in their interests to encourage lawsuits among the *habitants*, in order to collect exorbitant fees, which were often shared with the magistrate. Debtors were imprisoned, sometimes for a debt as small as two pounds. The magistrates' and bailiffs' handling of civil suits was all too often a mockery of justice. Carleton raged that "not a Protestant butcher or publican became bankrupt who did not apply to be made a justice." And he complained to the Earl of Hillsborough that "three or four hundred families have been turned out of their houses, land sold for not one eighth of its value, debtors ruined, and debts still uncharged, fees absorbing everything."[2]

At first Carleton tried halfway measures. He found grounds to discharge two magistrates who were the worst offenders. He wrote the others, asking them to change their regulations and received querulous replies. He tried without success to regulate fees. Carleton was a cautious man but finally he became impatient with the whole situation. In August 1769, he appointed Hey to chair a committee to investigate the administration of justice by the magistrates. The committee reported that the magistrates had more power and fewer qualifications than did justices of the peace in Britain. The committee found that magistrates, especially in Montreal, used their authority illegally and harshly. Acting on this report, Carleton had a statute prepared to transfer all civil cases from the justices of the peace to the Court of Common Pleas. The existing criminal jurisdiction was left with the magistrates as before.[3]

The new statute stipulated what fees the Court could charge: a writ of summons cost sixpence when written by the plaintiff; a shilling if written by the clerk of the court. A successful plaintiff was prohibited from executing judgement against real property unless that judgement was in excess of £12. Read in council on January 10th, 1770, this ruling was revised and passed on February 1st. Carleton immediately freed sixteen debtors, whose combined debts did not exceed £40. Robert Mackay, the keeper of His Majesty's jail in Montreal, was accustomed to charge a fee to a family member or friend who wanted to visit a prisoner, or to anyone who wanted to pay for extra food for a prisoner. Carleton's reform so reduced the local prison population that Mackay could no longer live on his fees and had to petition for a salary.

Not unexpectedly, the magistrates, whose comfortable incomes had been suddenly reduced, were furious at Carleton's action, but they managed to subsist under the new system. The English-speaking merchants were also upset and not a little bitter. Usually they were creditors; very rarely were they debtors. Fearing that their trade would be ruined because it would be difficult for them to collect payment for debts, they organized meetings of protest. But Carleton stood firm: when a delegation of merchants came to see him at the Château, he rebuked them in no uncertain terms. The agitation of the merchants eventually died down, partly because they were powerless and partly because trade was not seriously hurt. However, Carleton had sided wholeheartedly with the French-speaking population, and the animosity of the merchants remained alive and watchful.

Carleton informed Hillsborough of what he had done. (Carleton was in the habit of doing what he thought was best and accounting in detail for what he did. Neither Hillsborough nor any other member of the British cabinet ever seemed to reprove him.) He said that he had had to appoint a fourth judge to the Court of Common Pleas and had selected Cramahé. With four, he could divide the court into two sections, so that two judges could sit continuously in Montreal and two in Quebec. He had added £50 to the salary of each judge as compensation for the extra workload, but he felt that the extra expense to the British treasury was well justified.

In the context of eighteenth-century thought, Carleton's legal reforms were radical. At that time, imprisonment for debt was extremely common. Once imprisoned, the debtor was unable to

earn money to pay off his debt; thus his arrest was sometimes
the equivalent of a life sentence. As a general rule, most politicians initiate reforms to appease their critics; they respond to
pressure from the public and from special interest groups.
Carleton, however, was acting out of compassion and for the
public good. The *habitants*, widely dispersed, were unorganized
and unrepresented. They had no means of exerting pressure on
Carleton, who nevertheless saw it as his duty to protect them.

Do Carleton's legal reforms make him a liberal? They do not.
In England, Dr. Samuel Johnson, a stout Tory, had inveighed
against the English penal system, all to no effect.[4] Carleton
was the product of his age, but, like Johnson, ahead of his age.

Governor Murray's recall had been a tacit admission that something was wrong with Britain's administration of the Province of
Quebec. However, for nine months, there was no corrective
action. In May 1767, Secretary of State the Duke of Richmond
made a speech in the House of Lords attacking the ministry for
its inaction. On June 2nd, the House passed a motion to the
effect that the Province of Quebec needed changes in its form of
government.

In August 1767, London decided to send an emissary to Quebec to confer with the governor and other officials. The emissary
was to return with recommendations for an improved judicial
system and for other desirable changes in the form of government. Shelburne chose his former private secretary, Maurice
Morgann, to be the emissary, and Morgann arrived in Quebec
August 2nd, 1768. He and Carleton became close friends and
Morgann, almost hypnotized by Carleton's personality, became
a convert to Carleton's vision of Quebec.

What did Carleton want? He wanted an Act of Parliament that
would be the equivalent of a constitution for Quebec (although
he would never have used the word "constitution"), an Act that
would give French Canadians the same rights that they had
enjoyed under French rule. Carleton resisted any attempts to
anglicize the Province. To him, Quebec would always remain
French. As early as 1767, he advised Shelburne that "barring
catastrophe shocking to think of, this Country must, to the end
of time, be peopled by the Canadian race, who already have

taken such firm root . . . that any new stock transplanted will be totally hid, and imperceptible amongst them, except in the Towns of Quebec and Montreal."[5] Carleton was utterly convinced that the surest way to win over the allegiance of French Canadians was to reinstate French law in civil cases.

In 1764, the British government had stipulated that a civil suit was to be determined under English law and hence before a jury. The *Canadien*, Carleton knew, did not like this ruling because he could not speak English and because his attorney was unfamiliar with English civil law. Carleton wanted to retain English law in criminal cases and the law-abiding *habitants* had no objection to this system, which was in fact more humane than the French code. At first, Carleton wanted the Québécois to have the right of *habeas corpus*, as did Hey and Maseres. Carleton, however, seems to have vacillated over this question and, in the end, decided that this right should not be granted. He felt that protection against illegal imprisonment would be unnecessary while he was governor.

Carleton believed that Catholicism should be established as a state religion. For one thing, he wanted a legal obligation placed upon Catholics to pay tithes to the Catholic Church (and upon Protestants to pay tithes to the Protestant Church). Since the conquest of Quebec, most Québécois had continued to pay tithes voluntarily but the clergy was pressing for compulsory payment of tithes.[6] He also felt strongly that Catholics should have the same political rights as Protestants. To be precise, Carleton wanted Roman Catholic French Canadians on his council. At that time, no Catholic could hold public office in Britain unless he swore allegiance to the King as the temporal and spiritual ruler of the land and unless he acknowledged that no foreign person, prelate or potentate had any authority ecclesiastical or spiritual within the realm.[7] However, as early as 1765, British legal authorities had debated and finally decided that the penalizing laws of Britain against Roman Catholics should not apply in Canada; nevertheless Catholics were still being politically restricted.

Carleton wanted the boundaries to the southwest, west, and north of Quebec extended. If these wilderness regions became part of Quebec, he would have greater authority over the Indians and the fur trade. Similarly, he wanted the boundaries of

39

the Province extended so that the seal-hunting industry of the Gulf of St. Lawrence would be under his control.

When Carleton had come to Quebec, he was faced with a deteriorating seal industry, which significantly hurt the economy. For years, several hundred Québécois had made a living catching seals in the Gulf along the southern shore of what is now Labrador. Sealing was a specialized occupation that could only be practised successfully in spring and fall, when the animals migrated from open waters to those surrounding the many islands along the Labrador coast. A seal hunter had to find narrow passages between islands where schools of seals regularly swam. Placing the nets and concealing their presence was difficult. The seals quickly detected any indication of humans, and would change their course to escape the nets. Quebec sealers produced some £8,000 worth of oil each year and perhaps fifteen thousand skins. In 1765, Hugh Palliser, the governor of the English-speaking province of Newfoundland, ordered all French fishermen to leave Labrador waters under the threat of imprisonment and the seizure of their nets. Palliser was in his rights to do so, since territorial authority over the waters off Labrador had been given to Newfoundland in 1763, but the English in Newfoundland were not skilled in sealing, and the industry was languishing. In 1767 Carleton had appealed to London for redress without success.

Last, but by no means least, Carleton was strongly opposed to an elected assembly, which London had been advocating and urging. The Canadiens had had little or no experience of democracy. They had never elected anyone to represent their interests and, according to Carleton, had no desire to do so. Knowing how governors in the Atlantic colonies were squabbling with elected representatives, Carleton had no wish to share his authority.

Nearly everything that Carleton wanted for Quebec was anathema to Englishmen of all classes. Carleton favored retention of the French language, culture and civil law. France had been at war with England off and on for hundreds of years. Only a few years earlier, the Treaty of Paris had ended the Seven Years' War. Canada had been captured from France, and Englishmen, to the extent that they thought much about it, assumed that the new colony would be anglicized. They might resign themselves to the continuance of the French language for a while, but to install French civil law was repugnant to them. And most Englishmen were totally opposed to Carleton's pro-Catholic stance. The King himself and each of his ministers had to swear to uphold the Protestant Church of England; it was inconceivable that one of His Majesty's colonies should allow Catholicism as a state religion.

Carleton intended to continue to rule the Province through an appointed council. He had written that the British form of government would not work in Canada "where all men appear nearly on a level."[8] In another letter, Carleton remarked that "the British form of government transplanted into this continent never will produce the same fruits as at home, chiefly because it is impossible for the dignity of the throne or peerage to be represented in the American forest."[9]

Carleton's rejection of an elected assembly, on the other hand, was more comprehensible to his compatriots. In mid-eighteenth-century Britain, little popular conception of democracy existed. Thomas Paine had not yet published his ideas. The French Revolution, with its burning new vision of mankind, was yet to come. To the average Briton democratic government was an ideal in the same category as Sir Thomas More's *Utopia*. True, the House of Lords and the House of Commons had been established for generations, but Britain was not a democracy. The House of Lords was an hereditary body, composed primarily of rich landowners. The House of Commons was not elected on a popular basis because the majority of Britons could not vote. If they were not disqualified by geography (industrial cities such as Manchester, Birmingham and Leeds had no representatives in the House of Commons), sex or religion, they were disqualified by poverty—only a property owner or a substantial rent payer had the right to vote. In practice, most of the members of the House of Commons were selected by the Crown or by influential peers.

Sometime in 1769 Carleton made up his mind that he must go to London to plead for the form of government he wanted for the Province, believing that to talk, to persuade on the spot, would be more effective than writing letters, which always arrived weeks behind at best. Morgann had returned to London and would plead Carleton's case, but how influential or effective would he be? Two allies, Hey and a prominent *seigneur*, Chartier de Lotbinière, were going, but neither agreed *in toto* with Carleton. Maseres, who was already in London and would be considered an authority on the situation in Quebec, had developed a strong anti-Catholic bias, and a coldness had grown up between him and Carleton.

Carleton wrote Hillsborough to request a six-month leave of absence from Canada, "In order to confer with the British authorities and for personal reasons."[10] What the personal reasons were—if they existed—are not known. Hillsborough at first refused on the ground that a new form of government for Canada would soon be put in force and that Carleton would be needed on the spot to implement it. When importuned a second time, Hillsborough consulted the King and relayed consent for Carleton to return to England. Carleton had earlier appointed Henry Keller, a local lawyer, as attorney-general to replace Maseres. Now Carleton appointed Cramahé, the oldest councillor in point of service, as acting governor. Carleton was sure that his policies would be followed by this loyal friend.

On August 9th, 1770, Carleton sailed for England, expecting to stay eight or ten months. It would be four years before he again saw Quebec.

CHAPTER 6

The Quebec Act

When Carleton reached London late in September 1770, he did not encounter opposition to his views about the form of government that Quebec should have. What he did encounter was apathy and inactivity. It was to be a little over three years before anything happened. Lord Hillsborough was Secretary of State for the North American Colonies until August 1772. At first he seemed diligent, but by the time of Carleton's arrival his interest in Quebec had waned. When Hillsborough resigned, Lord Dartmouth was his replacement. A pious, affable man, Dartmouth had not the pertinacity to see a complicated, contentious piece of legislation through to its realization. Lord North, the King's chief minister and Lord Dartmouth's superior, was preoccupied with affairs in the restive Thirteen Colonies. In any case, North was completely subservient to King George III's wishes, and the monarch seemed uninterested in the Province of Quebec.

We know little of what Carleton did during these years in London. He corresponded regularly with Cramahé, sending instructions about the day-to-day business of running the Province, but there is little mention of his own activities. We know that he tried to revive one of his pet projects, the construction of a citadel for the defence of Quebec City. Carleton talked with Hillsborough about this idea and at Hillsborough's request prepared a long memorandum on the subject, but the secretary of state did nothing in response.[1] When Lord Dartmouth became secretary, he sent Carleton's memorandum to Viscount George Townshend, who had served under Wolfe at Quebec. Townshend wrote back to Dartmouth, "Building a citadel at Quebec would be beneficial, better, and probably cheaper than covering fortifications with artillery. Governor Carleton is best judge and would be best conductor of such work."[2] However, Carleton could not persuade the British government to spend the money. It was not until 1820 that the Quebec Citadel, the great fort that majestically overlooks the St. Lawrence, was completed.

In order to benefit trade, Carleton wanted a wilderness road built connecting the Chaudière River with the Kennebec River in what is now the State of Maine (at that time these lands were part of Massachusetts). Hillsborough consulted the governor of Massachusetts, Thomas Hutchinson, who replied that "the road proposed from river Chaudière to river Kennebec would be advantageous to both Quebec and Massachusetts."[3] But again, the British government was unwilling to provide the funds.

In one minor matter, Carleton was successful in prising funds out of the tight-fisted British treasury. In 1769, he had negotiated a treaty with some Mohawk Indians and had granted them a tract of land four leagues above Montreal on the south side of the St. Lawrence.[4] Carleton had promised to compensate the owners of the land. London did not object to this treaty, but as far as payment was concerned, nothing happened. The estate of Francis Mackay, the owner of the land, was pressing for a settlement of its claim. Carleton persuaded the executors of the estate to accept £1,000 compensation and somehow badgered the British government into paying this sum.[5]

Carleton must have dragged through many days in England with little to do and even less accomplished. If the idleness was wearisome to him, at least it gave him time to attend to a personal matter. As a vigorous and prominent forty-seven-year-old, Carleton saw the advantages of marriage. A wife would be useful as a companion and hostess. Not only would she warm his bed, but she would relieve him of the burden of running the Château St. Louis. Women married young—usually in their teens—in England in the eighteenth century, and marriages were seldom dissolved except by death. Could Carleton, a gruff and taciturn middle-aged man, find a suitable young woman, from a leading family, to marry?

Carleton had been a friend of the second Earl of Effingham, who was the head of one of the great families of England. Effingham had been a lieutenant-general, and presumably he and Carleton had first met in the army. The Earl had died in 1763, leaving five children, three of whom concern our story, namely his heir, the third Earl of Effingham, and two of his sisters, Lady Anne and Lady Maria. In the summer of 1771, the two unmarried daughters, Lady Anne, nineteen years old, and Lady Maria, seventeen, were living in the family's London town house with their brother, the twenty-eight-year-old Earl. One day in the early fall of that year, Carleton went to dinner with the children of his old friend. Present were the third Earl, Lady Anne, Lady Maria, and a friend of the girls, Miss Seymour. For Carleton to be a guest was not extraordinary. As children, the girls had known their father's friend, and he must have seemed to them like a kindly, if aloof, uncle.

On this particular occasion, the three girls retired after dinner, leaving the two men in the dining room with a bottle of Madeira between them. A half an hour or so later, a servant brought word that Lord Effingham requested the presence of Lady Anne in the dining room. Maria and Miss Seymour wondered what this was all about and had not long to wait. Back came Anne in a distraught state, and in tears. When asked what was the matter, she burst out: "You would be crying if you had to turn down Mr. Carleton, such a kind, wonderful man." "You are a fool," said Maria, "I only wish he had proposed to me. I would have shared my life with him."[6] Maria and Miss Seymour did not know that Anne was in love with Carleton's nephew, Christopher Carleton, whom she subsequently married.[7]

A few weeks after Anne's refusal, Miss Seymour again met Carleton and managed to whisper to him how Maria felt. Carleton was delighted over this new prospect. Maria was a petite blonde with blue eyes and golden hair.[8] She was a precocious girl who had learned flawless Parisian French at Versailles. He quickly asked Maria to marry him, and happily she had meant what she had said to Miss Seymour and accepted. On May 22nd, 1772, a beautiful sunny day,[9] General Guy Carleton and Lady Maria Effingham, twenty-nine years his junior, were married in the chapel of the Bishop's Palace in Fulham, London.[10]

Miss Seymour was proud that she had had a hand in the personal life of Guy Carleton and told this account of Anne and Maria over and over again to successive generations of Carletons. The present Baroness Dorchester and her daughter, the Countess of Malmesbury, direct descendants of Carleton, still recount this family legend.

Carleton's long bachelorhood has been attributed to an unfortunate love affair during his twenties. It is said that he was spurned by a distant cousin. Perhaps so, perhaps not. A more likely reason for Carleton's long bachelorhood was financial. His father was a man of small means. There is no evidence that Carleton ever received or inherited any substantial sum of money, except for £1,600, his share of the ransom of Havana,[11] and Wolfe's bequest of £1,000. As a colonel, Carleton's salary would have been about £500 a year, as a brigadier £600. Such an income was insufficient to support a wife in the style that society demanded. Wolfe had asserted that he could not marry unless his wife brought with her a dowry of £30,000 to £40,000, which would produce an income large enough to take care of a house, servants, horses, and various other amenities so necessary to the life of a gentleman in English society.[12]

As governor of Quebec Carleton was paid £2,000 a year. He expected shortly to be promoted to major-general, for which he would receive just over £900 a year.[13] (Actually, Carleton's commission as major-general received the King's signature three days after the marriage ceremony.) Carleton could now expect a total income of almost £3,000 a year. In other words, he could afford a wife.

Carleton was also a landowner, although this made little difference to his financial position. In the fall of 1767, when Carleton had been in Quebec for a year, he received the deed to a considerable amount of wilderness land, something that probably came as a complete surprise to him. Three hundred miles east of Quebec in the Gulf of St. Lawrence as the crow flies—and nearly twice as far by ship—was the Island of St. Jean, now Prince Edward Island. The British had seized it from the French shortly before Wolfe captured Quebec. In the next eight years, most of its French settlers left, so that the population of this island consisted of a few Indians, some fishermen, and a small British garrison. In 1767, the British government divided this island into sixty-seven townships, each approximately twenty thousand acres. These townships were assigned to prominent members of Parliament and to certain army and navy officers who had taken part in the capture of Louisbourg and of Quebec. For example, Admiral Saunders, General Townshend, and General Murray, the former governor of Quebec, each received a township. And so did Guy Carleton. Each landowner was supposed to build wharves, churches, etc., colonize the land, and develop the fisheries. They would pay a small annual fee to the British treasury and collect rents that would go into their own pockets. It was all a pipe dream, an unrealistic scheme of colonization at little or no cost, which would somehow provide a rich return. As time went by, most of the owners sold their townships for a pittance to land speculators, who, in turn, did little or nothing to improve the island's economy.[14]

In London, Carleton rented a house in Mayfair in the fashionable parish of St. George's for himself and his bride. Here, on February 9th, 1773, Maria gave birth to a boy, who was named Guy after his father. A year later she gave birth to a second son, called Thomas, after Carleton's younger brother.[15]

At this time, Carleton held the honorary position of colonel of the 47th Foot. In peace time, a lieutenant-colonel administered the regiment and Carleton's duties were nominal. In the summer of 1773, the Earl of Chatham purchased for his eldest son, John Pitt, seventeen years old, a lieutenantcy in the 47th Foot. Chatham wrote Carleton and asked if John Pitt could serve on his staff. "My son's ambition is to become a real officer," Chatham wrote, "and I trust that he already affixes to the appellation all the ideas that go to constitute a true title to that name."[16] The Earl was sixty-four years old and in poor health. Because of his opposition to King George III's policy of repressing the Thirteen Colonies, he was out of office, and there was no reasonable likelihood of his ever coming back into power. However, he had enormous prestige as the prime minister who had won the Seven Years' War. Carleton, of course, assented with alacrity.

By 1773 the Thirteen Colonies had become bellicose. Committees of Correspondence were being formed to unite the colonists in their opposition to British rule. Inflammatory speeches were being made and revolutionary articles were being published. Rhode Islanders burned a British naval schooner. On December 16th, 1773, during the "Boston Tea Party," some £10,000 worth of tea that had been taxed by the British was destroyed. In retaliation, Parliament passed in March and April 1774 what came to be called the "Intolerable Acts." One of these closed the port of Boston. The others reduced Massachusetts' power of self-government and permitted the quartering of British troops in private houses. George III and his ministers were aware of the resentment and possible defiance that these acts might cause. However, as far as Quebec was concerned, what the ministers most feared was a revolt by its inhabitants, stimulated or perhaps even aided by the Thirteen Colonies. King and cabinet alike thought it expedient to do something reconciliatory for the Québécois.

All parties agreed that an Act of Parliament which would define the form of government and stipulate the rights of the residents of the Province of Quebec was now a priority. The problem was to determine what rights should and should not be granted. The British law lords, it was felt, must quickly frame and write the necessary legislation. However, Advocate-General James Marriott, Attorney-General Edward Thurlow, Solicitor-General Alexander Wedderburn and Lord Chancellor Apsley could not agree on the contentious matter of the administration of civil and criminal law. Likewise the jurists from Canada—Hey, the chief justice, and Maseres, the former attorney-general—held differing views. When all these experts could not agree as to what should be done, the politicians naturally turned for advice and guidance to the governor of Quebec. The bill that was eventually drawn up went through four versions, and the fourth contained ninety-nine per cent of what Carleton wanted.

The Quebec Bill was introduced in the House of Commons on May 26th, 1774. Lord North acted as the leader for the government and Edmund Burke and Thomas Townshend, both of whom hated the proposed legislation, as leaders of the Opposition. Hey, Maseres, Marriott and various others testified before the House, but Carleton was the one whose testimony was most often sought. Carleton's understanding of his French-Canadian subjects and his wry humor are apparent in the following exchanges:

Question: Does the General know the proportion of old subjects [English-speaking inhabitants] to those of new ones [French-speaking inhabitants]?

Carleton: The Protestants in Canada are under found hundred, about three hundred and sixty. But the French inhabitants, who are all Catholics, amount to one hundred and fifty thousand.[17]

Question: Do they [the French inhabitants] disapprove the trial by jury?

Carleton: Very much. They have often said to me that they thought it very extraordinary that English gentlemen should think their property safer in the determination of tailors and shoemakers than in that of the judges.[18]

A Frenchman named Le Brun testifying before the committee seemed to be representing the English-speaking merchants in the province. He had favored an elective assembly and the use of English law in civil suits. Lord North asked Carleton if he knew of Le Brun. "Yes," said Carleton, "I know him very well. He was a blackguard at Paris, and sent as a lawyer to Canada where he gained an exceedingly bad character in many respects, was taken up and imprisoned for an assault on a young girl eight or nine years old, was fined twenty pounds but not being able to pay it . . . " Here Townshend interrupted, asking that Carleton's statement be withdrawn as an argument *ad personem*. Lord North replied that he wanted to know how reliable a witness Le Brun was. Carleton did not continue his diatribe. He had said more than enough to discredit Le Brun.[19]

Carleton was repeatedly questioned about the desirability of giving Quebec an elected assembly.

Question: Are the Canadian inhabitants desirous of having an assembly?

Carleton: Certainly not.

Question: Would they not greatly prefer a government by the governor and legislative council to such an assembly?

Carleton: No doubt they would.

Question: Is that the only idea of the assembly that you ever knew suggested to the Canadians?

Carleton: I put the question to several of the Canadians. They

> told me assemblies had drawn upon the other colonies so
> much distress, had occasioned such riots and confusion, that
> they wished never to have one of any kind whatsoever.
> Question: Would they have any objection to a seat in such an
> assembly in which they might have an opportunity of deliv-
> ering their opinions?
> Carleton: They never had an assembly or anything like an assem-
> bly nor have they the least desire to have one. But if there
> should be one, they ought to have a share in it.

When asked why the Bill did not give the Canadians the right of
habeas corpus, Carleton replied that Canadians had no knowledge of *habeas corpus*, and that he had consulted several French
lawyers to find that they did not know what it was.[20]

The Commons took evidence for eight days, and on June 11th
debate commenced. The House was not half full, the average
attendance being one hundred and twenty to one hundred and
thirty, but the Opposition was extremely vocal, displaying
much demagoguery. It assumed that the Quebec Bill was a measure of oppression after the fashion of the Intolerable Acts.
Edmund Burke claimed that it restored the French Canadians to
Bourbon absolutism—the difference being that George III was
taking the place of Louis XVI. Some of the other speakers were
even more virulent. For nine days, the Bill was debated, almost
every clause was criticized, and the House often sat until one
o'clock in the morning. It was generally known that the Bill
incorporated Carleton's ideas and desires, but the Opposition
refrained from attacking Carleton personally. One of them,
Thomas Townshend, bitterly opposed as he was, remarked:

> With regard to the Governor, as a military man, I entertain for
> him great respect; as a gentleman everybody respects him; and if
> despotic government is to be trusted in any hands—I will not say
> it will be safe in those of General Carleton—I am persuaded it will
> be as safe in his as in anybody's. This is only doing justice to his
> character. When I recollect the complexion of his evidence, I am
> convinced that he is determined to do right; and I wish to throw
> as few obstacles in his way as possible.[21]

On June 13th, the third reading of the Bill was carried in the
House, fifty-six to twenty. On June 16th, the legislation went
back to the House of Lords. Lord Chatham, rising from his sick

bed, made his personal condemnation very plain, describing the Bill as "the worst of despotism, a most cruel, oppressive, and odious measure, tearing up justice and every good principle by the roots . . . The bill is the child of inordinate power. I desire to know if anyone on that bench [pointing to the Lords Spiritual] will hold it out for baptism."[22] But the Bill passed the House of Lords twenty-six in favor, seven opposed. Among the seven nays was Carleton's brother-in-law, Lord Effingham.

Critics of Carleton and the Quebec legislation insist that it was railroaded through Parliament, and it is true that Lord North had the votes to do almost anything that he and the King wanted. Further, the Opposition had demanded the reports of the English and Canadian jurists concerning the kind of government Quebec should have; however, Lord North had refused to disclose these reports on the grounds that this would cause inordinate delay. The Commons upheld North's decision by a vote of two to one. This refusal of North's was perhaps high-handed. Nonetheless, he and his cabinet were trying to prepare legislation that would satisfy the wishes and aspirations of the French inhabitants of Quebec. Even Edmund Burke, for all his hatred of the Bill, could be objective. He wrote to the New York Committee of Correspondence: "They [the ministers] professed great candor in admitting alterations."[23]

At times, it was touch and go whether the Bill would contain all that Carleton wanted. For instance, during the debate Lord North persuaded Lord Chancellor Apsley to agree to insert a clause allowing suits between two English-speaking parties to go to a jury if either party so desired. The next day, Lord Apsley changed his mind. He wanted no juries. He remembered how the English-speaking mercantile minority in Quebec had made use of the jury system so that they could avoid paying duties owing on imported spirits and wines.

On only a few trivial points did the final legislation contravene Carleton's judgement. For instance, the Act did not extend the boundaries of the Province of Quebec to include a minor fort, Niagara, on Lake Ontario, as Carleton had wanted. It was decided that Niagara was in the colony of New York and must remain there.[24] However, the much more important sealing grounds off Labrador were included within the new boundaries of Quebec.

Along with the Quebec Bill, the Ministry introduced the Revenue Bill, which provided for higher duties on imported rum and molasses, plus other minor revenues to finance the government of Quebec. There was no opposition in Parliament to this legislation.

The final stage of the passage of the Quebec Bill was its presentation to George III for his approval and signature. A delegation of several aldermen of the City of London and one hundred and fifty members of the London Common Council presented the King with an address urging him to refuse to approve the Bill. Among other statements, the address reminded the King of his oath to maintain the Protestant religion. However, the King could be obstinate. He had agreed to sign the Bill into law and he refused to answer the delegation. On the afternoon of June 22nd, ignoring a mob shouting "No Popery," George III entered the House of Lords, gave his assent to the Quebec Act,* and prorogued Parliament.

Carleton must have felt great satisfaction. Toward the end of his testimony before the House, he had been asked about the merits of the Bill as a whole. He replied: "I should think it the best form desireable [sic] to give in the present state of the colony."[25] It was the obvious answer. After all, the Quebec Act was Carleton's creation.

One question naturally asked is what was Carleton's motivation for devising the Quebec Act? Why did he want to keep Quebec the way he found it? Why didn't Carleton side with the English-speaking merchants, who were strongly opposed to the Quebec Act?

The answer to this last question is fairly simple. Carleton, although himself of relatively humble origin and a self-made man, was an officer and a gentleman. And in Britain, an officer and gentleman despised the businessman, a person who engaged "in trade." Thus, the English-speaking merchants

* The complete text of the Quebec Act is reproduced in the Appendix, pages 172-179.

would not have attracted his sympathies, the more so since these particular merchants were—with few exceptions—a mixture of get-rich-quick artists and greedy entrepreneurs.

Carleton, of course, was always strongly opposed to an elected assembly. The reason he gave for this was the continual friction between governor and assembly in the Thirteen Colonies. Perhaps another reason was that all his adult life Carleton had been an officer. In the army, senior officers made the important decisions. Carleton may have instinctively felt that only the governor or his deputy was capable of making the right decisions.

Why did Carleton want the retention of French law in all civil cases? Carleton was basically a humane man. This quality may well have made him feel responsible for persons in lower social echelons, and hence may have made him want to help the *habitant*. It is true that Carleton socialized with his own class. He and Maria doubtless had many a *seigneur* and his wife to dinner at the Château and would never have thought of inviting a *habitant* to dine with them. Nonetheless, Carleton would listen to anyone who wanted to talk to him, and he seems to have had a particular sympathy for the *habitant*. These litigation-loving Québécois would have been confused and alienated by English civil law, which was radically different, in procedure and application, from the "laws of Canada."

Carleton's attitude toward the Roman Catholic Church probably stems from his pragmatism. His own upbringing and outlook were Protestant. However, he and Bishop Briand were very friendly, and perhaps Briand convinced him of the impossibility of converting the Québécois to Protestantism. Yet, Catholics had to be permitted to hold public office. It made no sense that he should have to pick council members from the Protestant one per cent of the population. It is a noteworthy example of Carleton's respect for the Catholic faith that, as Attorney-General Maseres became more and more blatantly anti-Catholic, Carleton's friendship with him faded.

CHAPTER 7

The Americans Invade

On July 20th, 1774, a month after the King signed the Quebec Act, Carleton and Maria sailed for Canada with their two infant sons. On the same ship was Carleton's new aide-de-camp, the eighteen-year-old Lieutenant John Pitt, who bore the courtesy title of Viscount Chatham. On the forty-fifth day of the voyage, Carleton celebrated his fiftieth birthday.

On the afternoon of Sunday, September 18th, the ship dropped anchor in the Louise Basin at Quebec. As the Carletons were rowed ashore, there was a roaring of cannon and ringing of church bells. They were greeted at the water's edge by Lieutenant-Governor Cramahé, members of the council, and other prominent citizens. The governor and his lady climbed into an open coach and were driven to the Upper Town, the route lined with soldiers at attention and exuberant Québécois clapping and cheering their delight at the governor's pretty young wife and two babes.[1]

It was late evening when Maria first saw the massive silhouette of her future home, the Château St. Louis. At the portico there was a pause, while Charles Louis de Lanaudière, Carleton's Canadian aide-de-camp, made a brief speech of welcome. Once inside the building Maria must have been appalled at the coldness and starkness of the enormous structure. Its two British occupants, Murray and Carleton, had been bachelors little interested in the amenities of comfortable living.[2] The building was bare as a barracks.[3] Luckily, she was distracted that evening by such duties as meeting the servants, feeding her children,

54

and trying to get them to sleep while church bells continued to ring and guns continued to boom. If she had time to look outside, she would have seen a candle burning in just about every window of the houses in the Upper and Lower towns.

On the morning of his first day back in Quebec, Carleton had to listen to further congratulatory addresses and make gracious replies. In the afternoon, a letter arrived from General Gage, now stationed in Boston, requesting Carleton to send two foot regiments, the 10th and the 52nd, to Boston. Carleton had four regiments in all and Gage, fearing armed revolt in Massachusetts wanted the two best. The letter was polite but definite and conlcuded: "These regiments may be replaced in the spring."[4] Feeling sure that Carleton would acquiesce, Gage had dispatched two transports to bring the troops to Boston.

Although he would soon come to regret his decision, Carleton did not hesitate to issue orders for the troops to join Gage's command. This left him with only eight hundred soldiers to protect the entire Province of Quebec. Carleton could have refused to send the two regiments. Although Gage, a lieutenant-general, outranked Carleton, each had an independent command; each reported to London.

The Quebec Act, which was published in the Quebec *Gazette* while Carleton was at sea, elicited an enthusiastic response from the clergy, and the *seigneurs,* and certain other Québécois. The clergy were elated that their church had been established in law as a state religion. The *seigneurs* were relieved that their traditional system of land holding was retained. Most Québécois were delighted that Roman Catholicism would no longer be a bar to public office and that their homeland was to be administered in general accordance with its traditions.

The response of the English-speaking mercantile community was very different. From the beginning, they had disliked the arbitrary, militaristic government of the Province. Now they had confirmation that the Province was going to continue to be administered for the benefit of French Canadians.[5] In October, English-speaking residents drew up three petitions: one—the mildest—was addressed to the King, another to the House of Lords, and the strongest one to the House of Commons. All three requested a revision or repeal of the Quebec Act. The King's "old subjects" wanted an elected assembly, the right of *habeas corpus*, the requirement that civil suits be settled by juries, and the use of English law, at least in matters of personal property. One hundred and eighty-six persons signed the petitions, and few were Québécois. One petition said: "Citizens are subject to arbitrary fines and imprisonment and are likely to be tried in civil cases and matters of a criminal nature not by known and permanent laws, but by ordinances and edicts which the Governor and Council are empowered to make void."[6] There was little truth in this statement but one can sense the bitterness and fear behind the wording of the petitions. Carleton wrote Lord Dartmouth on November 11th, referring to the signatories as having held "town meetings" and "nocturnal cabals" and said he had assured the King's French-speaking subjects that such proceedings would never succeed.[7] The British cabinet paid no attention to the petitions, and in May of 1775, both houses of Parliament rejected motions for the repeal of the Quebec Act.

On October 24th, 1774, the Continental Congress, a group of delegates from most of the Thirteen Colonies, addressed a letter to the "Oppressed Inhabitants of Canada" denouncing the Quebec Act. They called it undemocratic, as it did not provide for an elective assembly, for juries in civil suits, or for the right of *habeas corpus*. Thomas Walker of Montreal, who was now one of the leaders of the anti-Carleton Montreal merchants, had the letter circulated widely in English and in a French translation. The Continental Congress also sent a letter addressed to the inhabitants of Great Britain, protesting against the legal establishment of Catholicism in Quebec: "A religion that has deluged our island in blood, and dispersed impiety, bigotry, persecution, murder, and rebellion in every part of the world."[8] Priests in Quebec got hold of a copy of this letter, translated it, and circulated it, with the result that many Québécois became wary of "*les Bostonnais*," as they called the English in the Atlantic colonies, and even more wary of those English-speaking residents of Quebec who were espousing the revolutionary cause.

The propaganda continued. Various articles denouncing the Quebec Act were published in newspapers in the Thirteen Colonies. Alexander Hamilton published a two-part tract entitled "Remarks upon the Catholic Bill" that denounced the form of government in Quebec and the establishment there of the Roman Catholic Church. Parts of these articles were distributed in Canada as handbills. In February, a smart young lawyer, John Brown, agent for the Boston Committee of Correspondence, arrived in Montreal with pamphlets and letters of intoduction. His purpose was to persuade the Québécois to revolt. Thomas Walker and his Montreal friends aided him. Brown's pamphlets warned the *Canadiens* that Carleton would draft them into the army, would have them fighting for years, and that the Americans would desolate the province if the *habitants* offered any resistance.

Carleton, of course, knew all about the propaganda and Brown's presence in Montreal. As the *habitants* not only could not speak English but could not read French, Carleton felt that the propaganda was unimportant. At any rate, he issued no statements, did not prosecute Thomas Walker or any of his compatriots, or order Brown out of the country. He did, however, prevent the Quebec *Gazette* from publishing American propaganda such as the letter addressed to the Québécois from the Continental Congress. Nonetheless, bitterness between the French Canadians and the merchants increased.

The tension between the two groups reached a peak on May 1st, 1775. Some time in the early hours of the morning, a marble bust of George III on a street corner in Montreal had been painted black, and a rosary of old potatoes, from which dangled a wooden cross, had been hung around its neck. A bishop's mitre had been placed on the monarch's head. Under the bust was a label reading, "Voilà le pape du Canada, le sot Anglais." (This is the Pope of Canada and the fool of England.) This act of desecration threw Montreal into a ferment. Its French-speaking inhabitants held protest meetings, and the English-speaking citizens engaged in much oratory and demagoguery. Carleton offered a reward of £200 for information leading to the capture of the offender but the culprit was never found.[9]

Carleton was ruling Quebec in the same way he had four years earlier; that is, through a subservient council. The Quebec Act was to come in force on May 1st, 1775, when a new and enlarged council was to be sworn in. In the spring, Carleton received a sealed packet from London containing instructions specifying how he was to rule as governor under the Act and how he was to implement it. This document, about fifteen thousand words in length, drawn up after Carleton had left London, had been signed by the King on January 3rd, 1775. It contained many matters vital to Carleton. For instance, the instructions named the men who were to serve on the new, enlarged council—and in every case they were those that Carleton had requested.[10] One councillor was to be Judge Adam Mabane, the man whom Carleton had dismissed from the council in 1766. As noted earlier, Mabane had become a convert to Carleton's views, and Carleton had included his name in the list of men he wanted on the new council.

In some important respects, these instructions clashed with the provisions of the Quebec Act. The Act stated that, as an assembly was "inexpedient," the country was to be ruled by a governor and legislative council. Yet the instructions ordered Carleton to consult the council about the possibility of organizing an elective assembly. The council could do nothing without the governor's approval and everyone knew that Carleton opposed an elected assembly, so why would he consult the council about one? Again the Quebec Act stated that "in all matters of controversy relative to property and civil rights" resort would be had to the laws of Canada. And "laws of Canada" meant French law. Now, the instructions to the governor, the chairman of the council, read:

> It will be the duty of the Legislative Council to consider whether the laws of England may not be, if not altogether, at least in part, the rule for the decision in all cases of personal actions grounded upon debts, promises, contracts, and also of wrongs proper to be compensated in damages; and more especially where there are natural born subjects of Great Britain, Ireland, or our other plantations residing at Quebec, or who may resort thither, or have credits or property within the same, or may happen to be either Plaintiff or Defendant in any civil suit of such nature.[11]

Here was the King instructing Carleton to consider an elected assembly and the use of English law in civil cases, two matters that Carleton and his handpicked new council would strongly oppose. The cabinet, or perhaps the King, must have had a change of heart since Carleton had left London, because the instructions also more or less ordered Carleton to intoduce the right of *habeas corpus* by council ordinance.

Carleton must have been perplexed, amazed and crestfallen. Not knowing how to handle the situation, he decided to delay the implementation of the Quebec Act and the installation of the new council. He probably wanted to consult his friend and frequent legal advisor, Chief Justice William Hey, who might have information as to what had been going on in London in the last eight months. Hey, now the member of Parliament for Sandwich, had chosen a political career in England, but he was still chief justice of Quebec and had promised to return for a few months in order to help Carleton implement the Quebec Act. The earliest Hey could arrive was early May; as it happened, he did not appear until June 11th.

On the morning of May 19th, Carleton received a letter from Gage containing alarming news. Hostilities had broken out in Massachusetts between colonists and British soldiers (the exchanges of fire at Lexington and Concord), and the rebellion was expected to spread. All regular forces in Quebec were to take up defensive positions along the line of the Richelieu River, the historic invasion route that led to the St. Lawrence River, and thus to Montreal and Quebec City. This meant sending what troops there were up the Richelieu River and across the long length of Lake Champlain to the forts at Crown Point and Ticonderoga.

Carleton was completely surprised. He knew there was unrest in the colonies to the south but he had no reason to expect rebellion. The citizens to the south had greater freedom than existed almost anywhere in Europe, but were nevertheless willing to fight for more. The next day Carleton received even worse news. In order to obtain much-needed artillery and ammunition, Americans had captured both Ticonderoga and Crown Point. In both places, the caretaker garrisons had been taken by surprise.

Carleton immediately decided to make Montreal his headquarters, which required complex preparations. Troops at Trois-Rivières and other posts had to be contacted. Food, guns and ammunition had to be collected and their transportation arranged. Bishop Briand had to be persuaded to urge the *habitants* to resist the invaders. There were councils of war with Cramahé, who, with sixty-seven soldiers, was being left in command at Quebec. It must have been a harassing time for Carleton, but he was always at his best in a crisis.[12]

On May 23rd, Carleton, accompanied by most of the 7th Foot, left for Montreal. Maria, seven months pregnant, remained with the children in the Château St. Louis. In Montreal, Carleton learned that the Americans had followed up their surprise attacks at Ticonderoga and Crown Point by capturing the only vessels of war the British had on Lake Champlain, an armed schooner and sloop. The invaders had then continued a hundred miles north and overwhelmed the small garrison of ten soldiers at St. Jean. This success was shortlived. Colonel Templer, the officer in charge at Montreal, had immediately dispatched Major Charles Preston and one hundred and twenty soldiers to recapture St. Jean, which was done without bloodshed. The weary invaders, short of food and rest, withdrew up the Richelieu River and across Lake Champlain to Ticonderoga.

When the Americans attacked Ticonderoga and Crown Point, they were attacking forts in the colony of New York. In attacking St. Jean, they were invading the Province of Quebec. The Continental Congress had not ordered this action and as yet there was no commander-in-chief to head it. Eager rebels had invaded on their own authority. The seizure of Ticonderoga and Crown Point had given them needed powder and guns. They wanted to continue to attack and why not Quebec? They felt sure that French Canada, wrested from France fifteen years ago, would be ripe for revolt from England.

To attack Montreal, the Americans had to come down the highway of the Richelieu River or march through the wilderness. St. Jean was the ideal place to command the river approach to Montreal. Here were several acres of high land on the edge of the Richelieu, bordered on three sides by swampy land. Carleton enlisted the aid of ship's carpenters and skilled French-Canadian workmen, directed his soldiers to do manual labor, and began, in a fervor of activity, to make St. Jean a stronghold. Two redoubts, each one hundred feet square, were erected and connected by a strong palisade, on which were mounted pieces of artillery. Within three months, Carleton had managed to send to this stronghold some five hundred and fifty veterans from the 7th and 27th Foot and forty trained gunners of the Royal Artillery. (One of the officers of the 7th Foot at St. Jean was Lieutenant John André. Five years later, as Major André, he achieved posthumous fame when he was hung as a spy.[13]) Added to these were about one hundred French-Canadian militia, who acted as scouts and rangers under their leader, François Marie de Belestre.

A supply of guns, ammunition and provisions was divided between St. Jean, which was north of the Richelieu rapids, and Chambly, a fort south of the rapids. The supply at St. Jean, was, of course, for the men there. The supply at Chambly, however, was an emergency hoard that could be taken down the Richelieu to the St. Lawrence and delivered to garrisons at Sorel, Trois-Rivières and Quebec.

Although supplies were not an immediate problem, troops were. Carleton was desperately short of fighting men. He convinced himself that numbers of French-Canadian militia could be raised and commanded by the *seigneurs*, but this scheme was not successful. Most of the *seigneurs* had had no military experience. Some were too old, and almost none had the influence over their tenantry that Carleton had anticipated. At times, the *habitants* offered violent resistance to orders to form a militia. When a *seigneur* called Deschambault, who farmed land along the Richelieu River, summoned his tenants to arms, they refused. He drew his sword. The *habitants* gave Deschambault and his men a thrashing, then distributed guns among themselves, fully expecting Carleton to send his soldiers against them. Carleton immediately dispatched an officer to disavow the action of the *seigneur* and to assure the *habitants* that, if they returned to their farms, they would not be molested.[14]

This kind of extreme opposition occurred in quite a few parishes. In many others, there was no enlistment of fighting men. As the *seigneurs* were of little use as leaders, Carleton tried using as captains men who had been officers of militia fifteen years earlier under Murray, but many of these were too old or apathetic. Carleton needed officers whose loyalty he could depend

61

on; otherwise he might be relying on militiamen who, when trained, would go over to the Americans.

When the policy of voluntary enlistment failed so badly, Carleton took extreme measures. He issued a proclamation establishing martial law and ordered the militia to defend the Province. It was printed and sent, via Bishop Briand, to every priest, asking them to order their parishioners to join their local militia unit. Martial law and the influence of the Church helped, and some troops were raised in this manner. Carleton was able to review two or three hundred Montreal militia on July 9th, and on July 13th some companies at Longue Pointe and Pointe-aux-Trembles.

Carleton was assiduous in his efforts to raise militia. On a visit to Trois-Rivières, he spent the night with a friend, a French trader named Tonnancour. Outside Tonnancour's house, Carleton noticed an armed guard on sentry duty, a man who looked like a *habitant*. Tonnancour confirmed that the guard was a *habitant* who had enlisted in the militia. Carleton immediately dashed out of the house, went up to the guard, saluted, and handed the astonished man a gold guinea.[15] Then he gave a guinea to the second militiaman, who served as night guard.

The few English-speaking residents of the Province were as apathetic as the many Québécois. Some did join Carleton's army, but a larger number were openly pro-American in their sympathies. The majority was not prepared to take sides. While they hated Carleton and everything he stood for, their livelihood was linked to Britain, and they did not want to jeopardize their businesses and families.

There was one source left to Carleton to augment his fighting forces—Indians. Guy Johnson, an Indian agent, had received £2,500 from London to buy gifts for the Iroquois and induce them to take the warpath against the invaders. Johnson went to a large conference of the Six Nations at Oswego. There he distributed fowling pieces, bullets, gunpowder, hatchets, kettles, blankets, paint, pipes and gold-laced hats. As a result, these Indians were unanimous in wanting to fight alongside the British. In July, Johnson arrived in Montreal with some three hundred chiefs and warriors, plus women and children.[16] He asked Carleton to come and speak to them.

There was an old church belonging to the Jesuits, which was vacant because the Pope had suppressed this religious order three years previously. Here, on July 30th, a meeting was arranged. At six p.m., Carleton was escorted to the choir room, in the middle of which was a large armchair. The Indians, sporting head-dresses or the gold-laced hats that Johnson had given them, were seated on surrounding benches. Carleton, wearing his general's uniform, seated himself in this armchair.[17] For a couple of hours, the Indians orated while an interpreter translated their words into French. Among other things, they called Carleton their father and George III their grandfather. They expressed themselves as eager to attack *"les Bostonnais."* Finally, Carleton arose. He spoke in French, pausing after each sentence for the translator to translate it into the Iroquois tongue. Carleton praised his Indian friends to the skies, emphasizing that the tribes around him were the greatest tribes that had ever existed. He expressed great appreciation of their willingness to go on the warpath. However, he regretted that he did not need their help at present, except for fifty scouts, whom he could use at St. Jean. He forbade any Indian, except the fifty scouts, from crossing the border. He said he would give each tribe silver coins. He reiterated that they could not go to war, said the gifts would stop if they disobeyed his words, which were really the words of their grandfather, George III.

At the conclusion of the speech, Carleton was given a necklace. Then, one by one, every Indian came up and shook his hand. Then Carleton left: he would never eat with the Indians.[18] But for the Indians the night had scarcely begun. Food and wine were distributed, and they feasted and danced until daylight.

The Iroquois sided with the British mainly because of their relations with, and dependence upon, the fur traders in Montreal. Added to which, the British were not advancing westward and invading their hunting grounds as American frontiersmen were doing. Also, the Indians were impressed by Johnson's gifts. Carleton, of course, did not want the Iroquois to side with the Americans, but he did not want them to fight the invaders. He was convinced that they would attack non-combatants, would scalp women and children.

Carleton's decision not to use Indians may have been a

humane one. From a purely military point of view, it is a debatable one. Major-General Philip Schuyler, the commander of the invading Americans, feared that Carleton would let Indians loose upon his men.[19] It is at least possible that if they had attacked in large numbers, Schuyler and his second-in-command, Brigadier-General Richard Montgomery, would have been so preoccupied protecting themselves against Indian raids that they would have deferred or even abandoned attacking Montreal and, later, Quebec.

London kept importuning Carleton to use Indians. In response, he tried to explain the limitations of Indians as fighters: "They [the Indians] were easily dejected and chose to be on the strongest side; so that when they were most wanted, they vanished," he wrote.[20] To Gage, who also desired to have the Iroquois harass the Americans, Carleton wrote: "What is or can be expected from them further than cutting off a few unfortunate families whose destruction will be but of little avail towards a decision of the present contest."[21]

Privately Carleton expressed his feelings more strongly. At a later date he explained: "I would not even suffer a Savage to pass the frontier, though often urged to let them loose on the Rebel Provinces, lest cruelties might have been committed, and for fear the innocent might have suffered with the guilty."[22]

On July 31st Carleton left Montreal. He had done all he could to prepare against an American invasion of the St. Lawrence Valley. He sailed down the St. Lawrence, stopping off at Longvue and Sorel to review militia units, and arrived back at Quebec on the evening of August 2nd. [23]

CHAPTER 8

Carleton's Humiliation

On Sunday, July 23rd, between two and three o'clock in the morning, Maria had given birth to their third son.[1] A month later, the baby, named Christopher for Carleton's father, was baptized, the ceremony taking place in the Recollets' Chapel right after the regular Church of England Sunday morning service. Maria, the baby in her arms, stood before the pastor, with a uniformed Carleton at her side, towering over her.[2]

Sometime that summer, Carleton made up his mind that he must send Maria and their three children back to England. He knew that he might be killed defending Quebec, in which case his wife should be close to her family. If Carleton survived but the Province fell, he would be a prisoner of war, and how would his young family fare in an American-occupied Quebec? Maria and the children sailed for England on September 22nd.[3] Her husband was not on hand to kiss her goodbye. Due to a threat to St. Jean two weeks earlier, Carleton had been obliged to rush back to Montreal. Boarding the ship for the long weary voyage, Maria must have wondered whether she would ever see her husband again.

Carleton had returned to Quebec partly because of Maria and partly because something had to be done about a new government. He was ruling under martial law, but there were civil appointments and other decisions to be made that martial law might not cover. The new council was summoned to meet on

Thursday, August 17th. In the meantime, Carleton caught up on his paper work, drew up plans for the organization of a militia in Quebec, and examined and re-examined the walls of the city with Cramahé to see how they could be strengthened. There were also, even in wartime, certain official appearances a governor was expected to make. For instance, a week after his return to Quebec, Carleton handed out the prizes to the top scholars of the Quebec Seminary. (The prizes were not solely for excellence in theology. Excellence in Latin, English, French literature, geography, physics, and chemistry was also rewarded.[4])

On the appointed day, all twenty-three members of the new council assembled in the council chamber of the Château St. Louis, with Governor Carleton in the chair. Eight of the twenty-three members were Roman Catholic. One by one, each man repeated before the governor the one-hundred-and-twenty-word oath incorporated in the Quebec Act, an oath of loyalty to the King, but with no repudiation of the Pope, no statement that King George III was their spiritual leader. Two other meetings were held, and bills were prepared to create new law courts and to prohibit the sale or gift of liquor to the Indians, but no further progress was made. On September 7th, word was received that Americans had landed on the Ile-aux-Noix, about twelve miles south of St. Jean and within forty of Montreal. Meetings of the council were suspended indefinitely. The war situation had become too serious.

Carleton went dashing off to Montreal. At first, the news there was good. Americans trying to approach St. Jean had been driven back by a small contingent of Preston's soldiers and Indian scouts. Then more enemy troops had arrived, the Indians had deserted, and Preston had had to withdraw behind St. Jean's fortifications. On September 17th, led by General Montgomery, the enemy commenced to lay siege to St. Jean. General Schuyler had returned to Albany for health reasons.

In laying siege to St. Jean, Schuyler and Montgomery thought they were acting under the orders of the Continental Congress. The congress ordered an attack on Quebec—if the attackers were assured they would be welcomed by the French Canadians. George Washington, now commander-in-chief, assented. Schuyler and Montgomery assumed that the Québécois would revolt and once they had beaten the British regular soldiers, the rebel forces would be welcomed.

Now enters on the scene Ethan Allen, a flamboyant character who became unduly famous for accomplishing little of historical significance. The leader of several hundred frontiersmen called the Green Mountain Boys, he had attacked Fort Ticonderoga one morning before dawn, found the solitary sentry on duty asleep, and captured the fort without having to fire a single shot. Shortly after, his leadership of the Green Mountain Boys was repudiated, and Allen joined Montgomery's army as the commander of forty or fifty Connecticut volunteers.

Allen was not the kind of man who could follow others' orders. He craved personal glory, and Montgomery was probably glad to get rid of him. At any rate, Allen and his Connecticut followers left Montgomery while he was besieging St. Jean, and moved on to Montreal, ostensibly to try and persuade French Canadians to join his force. He offered any *habitant* who would enlist thirty *sous* a day—twice what Carleton was offering. Furthermore, Allen promised each enlisted man a share of the booty when Montreal fell, another share when Quebec fell, and more still when London, England, was taken. Quite a few *habitants* joined him. When Allen reached Longueuil, on the other side of the St. Lawrence from Montreal, he was ready to take Montreal the way he had taken Ticonderoga. On the evening of October 24th, he crossed the river with his Connecticut volunteers and about eighty *Canadiens*. Then he waited in some farm buildings for word from Thomas Walker, who had promised to cause enough confusion within the city to aid Allen in his bold venture.

Carleton had organized a force of a hundred and twenty militiamen, a handful of English-speaking volunteers and thirty-four regular soldiers. Commanded by Major Carden, they sallied forth and attacked their would-be conquerors. Most of Allen's *habitant* followers fled: they liked their pay and the prospect of looting Montreal, but did not relish being shot at. In all probability, they did not want to shoot anyone, especially their fellow countrymen. Half of the Connecticut volunteers also deserted. Allen, after losing six men, surrendered what was left of his force—twenty Connecticut volunteers and eleven enlisted

Canadiens. The British loss was two, one of whom was Major Carden.

The next day, the governor of Quebec marched Allen and the other prisoners down the main street of Montreal at gunpoint. Carleton wanted to give proof of victory and use his success to stiffen French-Canadian morale. As a direct result, 900 *habitants* in the Montreal district answered the call of the recruiting drums. Allen was imprisoned in the hold of a small man-of-war, and Montgomery wrote Carleton, damning him for keeping Allen in irons in the hold of a ship. Carleton did not bother to reply but explained to Dartmouth that "we have neither prisons to hold them [the prisoners] nor troops to guard them so that they have been treated with as much humanity as our safety will permit."[5] Later, Allen and his followers were shipped to England. The eleven *Canadiens* were kept in custody for a time and then set free. Carleton pitied these forlorn men more than he blamed them. He firmly believed that the propagandizing of some of the Montreal merchants had led them astray.[6]

Carleton followed up his Gilbert-and-Sullivan victory over Ethan Allen by sending an officer with twelve regulars and thirty militiamen to attack the American camp at Longueuil. The presence of professionals must have encouraged the militia to warlike efforts, because the enemy was put to flight and his stores were seized.[7]

Another threat to security was dealt with at this time. Thomas Walker had been corresponding with the enemy, entertaining American agents, and preaching sedition to Montreal's inhabitants. Once in posession of letters that compromised Walker, Carleton sent several soldiers to arrest him at his potash plant in L'Assomption, some thirty miles from Montreal. Walker and members of his household opened fire on the soldiers, who succeeded in setting his house ablaze. Walker and his wife were taken prisoner; he was put in irons in the hold of a ship and she was set free.

These minor successes improved the recruitment of militia, but could not resolve the basic military problem. With barely fifty regular soldiers in the Montreal area, Carleton lacked the trained manpower with which to augment militia units. Unless led and directed by regulars, militiamen would rarely fight. They could be used as scouts, but for little else.

The siege of St. Jean continued but was making little progress. The size of the American force kept increasing but the men were plagued by dysentery and other diseases. By early October, Montgomery was finding it harder and harder to provision his army and was also running low on ammunition. Morale was poor; the desertion rate was high. A local Chambly merchant advised Montgomery that the fort there was well stocked, and was commanded by an ineffectual officer. A handful of Americans and seventy *Canadiens* who had enlisted with Montgomery were therefore sent to take it. Slipping past St. Jean in bateaux at dead of night, they managed to drag several nine-pounders around the rapids, and on October 15th they put the fort to siege. In Chambly were ten officers and seventy-eight soldiers, thirty women, and fifty-one children. The commander was Major the Honorable Joseph Stopford, the son of an Irish peer. On the 17th, fearing that a stray shot might cause the magazine to blow up, the timid Stopford surrendered, although not a single person on either side had been killed or wounded. The stone-walled fort would not have withstood a long siege but Stopford's surrender was premature. What is utterly incomprehensible is that Stopford turned over to the Americans six tons of gunpowder, three mortars, one hundred and fifty muskets, six thousand five hundred hand grenades, three hundred swivel shot, and two hundred and thirty-eight barrels of edible provisions.[8] As the waters of the Richelieu lap one wall of the fort, it would have been easy to dump all the armaments, ammunition and most of the foodstuffs into the river, making them useless to the invaders.

The fall of Chambly not only improved American morale but gave the invaders the essential supplies, food and ammunition to continue the siege of St. Jean. (Carleton did not criticize Major Stopford for the surrender of Chambly and its stores. He probably blamed himself for having left the witless Stopford in charge.) When Carleton heard of this sudden turn of events, he realized that an attempt to relieve St. Jean must be made. Colonel Allan Maclean was ordered to see what militia he could enroll in Trois-Rivières, Nicolet, and Sorel and then ascend the Richelieu. Carleton would join him with militia from Montreal, and jointly they would try to raise the siege of St. Jean. But Maclean had little success with the *habitants,* many of whom deserted shortly after enlisting. From the parishes around the mouth of the Richelieu quite a number of men joined, were given muskets, and then walked off with their new weapons, a few to enlist with the Americans, most to return to their farms. Maclean had to suspend his recruitment efforts.[9]

On October 30th, Carleton set out with some nine hundred militia, thirty or forty regulars, and a contingent of Indians. They embarked in fifty small boats, expecting to cross the St. Lawrence and land above the camp of an American advance guard. As the boats were rowed near the shore, three hundred Green Mountain Boys, now led by Lieutenant-Colonel Seth Warner, opened fire with muskets and a light cannon.[10] Carleton retreated to Montreal. His force outnumbered the enemy so one wonders why did he not land and give battle? In all probability, the militia refused to land. It takes fidelity to orders and considerable courage to jump out of a small boat and wade ashore under fire. Carleton made no further attempt to relieve St. Jean. The militia was far too unreliable.

On November 2nd, with his ammunition practically exhausted and rations sufficient only to feed his garrison for a couple of days, Major Preston surrendered. Montgomery took prisoner five hundred and thirty-six officers and men, seventy-nine militiamen, and nine English-speaking volunteers. Carleton now knew that he must retire to Quebec. An attempt to defend Montreal would be hopeless. Moreover, there was disturbing news from Indian scouts that Americans were descending the Chaudière River to attack Quebec itself.

Anchored off Montreal were three small armed vessels and eight even smaller transports. Into these, Carleton loaded as many guns and as much ammunition as possible; the rest he destroyed. Any other craft—schooners, sloops, bateaux, and whaleboats—that could be found nearby were destroyed or sunk. He disbanded the militia, ordering the men to return to their homes. In Montreal, there were two so-called King's Buildings, which had been used as military headquarters and barracks and were now ordered destroyed. Several citizens appealed to Carleton on the ground that burning these buildings might set the city on fire. Carleton countermanded the order, and the buildings were saved—for eventual use by Montgomery and his men.

On the evening of November 11th, Carleton boarded the *Gaspé*, in the hold of which was the imprisoned Thomas Walker. Carleton's few regulars boarded the various ships, and that evening all set sail. When they got downriver near Sorel, an easterly storm arose, which created headwinds for Carleton's tiny fleet. Opposite Sorel, the river channel narrows between an island and the bank of the St. Lawrence. The Americans had already placed cannon on this island and also on the river bank, which made it dangerous for any ship fleeing Montreal to pass, even with the aid of a favoring wind. With a headwind, passage through the channel was impossible, and Carleton anchored. The Americans fired on him, and his ships were forced to move a bit upriver and re-anchor.

On the 16th of November, the winds were still unfavorable, and Carleton, impatient and nervous, was wondering how he would ever get through to Quebec. The skipper of a riverboat, Jean-Baptiste Bouchette, known as La Tourte (a French-Canadian word meaning "wild pigeon") for his ability to make speedy time, suggested that a longboat could be rowed at night through the channel past Sorel and on to Trois-Rivières. The governor agreed to try Bouchette's scheme.

Carleton and Bouchette, plus two aides, de Lanaudière and the Chevalier de Niverville, set out late in the evening of the 16th. Each of the four was dressed like a *habitant*. Carleton himself wore a woollen cap and a heavy blanket coat, belted with the customary sash, the *ceinture flèche* of the Québécois. Abreast of Sorel, the quartet could see the lights of the town and hear American sentries pacing their beats on the shore. To avoid any noise, they let the longboat drift with the current, paddling with their bare hands. Landing at Trois-Rivières around noon the next day, the four men went to Tonnancour's house. Carleton had intended to borrow a carriage and drive to Quebec, but Tonnancour warned him that Arnold's men were already on the north side of the St. Lawrence and would intercept any carriage.

71

In addition, Americans were said to be on their way to Trois-Rivières from Montreal and might arrive at any moment. Tonnancour gave the hungry men a hearty meal. Then they got back into the longboat, rowed up and across the river to the *Senaut Fell*, an armed brig commanded by Captain Napier.[11] By this time, there was a mild southwest wind, and the *Fell*, without mishap, carried a defeated Carleton to Quebec.

Carleton didn't know what happened to his eleven boats at Sorel. The day after Carleton left, the wind had shifted to the southwest, and some, if not all, of the vessels could have risked the American guns and reached Quebec. However, the officer in charge threw all the guns and ammunition into the water, then surrendered the little fleet and all its personnel.

Until 1775, Carleton's life had been an almost continuous success story. Lacking wealth or connections, he had managed to climb the army's ladder of promotion and was now a major-general. He had married into one of the great families of England. He was governor of a colony won by a feat of arms in which he, himself, had played a part. Surmounting many difficulties, he had been a successful administrator, at least in the eyes of the London government. His reputation was such that he had been able to persuade King and cabinet to give Quebec a form of government devised by him, one that promised much for the future. Now, his world was falling to pieces. Why?

Carleton had failed to stop the Americans because he could not raise an army to repel the invaders. He had not foreseen armed confrontation; he had not allowed for the possibility that, once hostilities broke out, the rebellious colonists might try to take over Quebec. He had made a big mistake in sending Gage eight hundred infantry—half his military strength—in the fall of 1774. He kept hoping that Gage would return these soldiers, but the embattled general was in no position to do so. To be fair to Carleton, the summer of 1775, he had written London pleading for reinforcements. As a result, several regiments had embarked at Spithead. Unfortunately, the order for their dispatch was rescinded. By September he was writing Boston again, pleading for troops. His letter was received by General Howe, who had just replaced Gage. Howe immediately ordered one battalion to proceed to Quebec on two transports, but Admiral Graves said that his captains would not venture up the treacherous St. Lawrence in mid-October.[12] Actually there was plenty of time before ice blocked the channel, but Howe, having no control over the Navy, was powerless.

Carleton had tried to raise a Québécois militia and struggled to turn them into a fighting force—to little or no avail. (Once he had decided that five hundred of his professionals must defend St. Jean, he had only some fifty veterans left in Montreal, not nearly enough to give the militia a backbone.) The militia had fought fairly well against Wolfe in 1759, but the situation in 1775 was markedly different. In 1759, for the defence of Quebec, there had been not merely the militia, but also Montcalm's three thousand regulars. Some of these mingled with the militia, acting as examples to enliven and spur their *Canadien* cousins to greater efforts. In 1759, when Wolfe's guns were destroying the city of Quebec, a member of the militia felt that he was defending his homeland. In 1775, American guns were not destroying homes; they were pounding Quebec's new masters. In 1759, French Canadians were fighting an invader with a different language, religion, and culture. In 1775, one group of Englishmen was feuding with another group.

As noted, Carleton made no attempt to censor or supress American propaganda. By personality and temperament, he was incapable of running a police state. Agents of revolution were permitted to enter Quebec without let or hindrance. With the exception of Thomas Walker, none of their contacts was arrested. In June, Carleton talked to Walker's fellow conspirator, James Price, when Price returned from Philadelphia carrying pro-American propaganda.[13] Carleton did not imprison Price. He wanted to persuade him to change his ways. Carleton firmly believed that time would lead the residents of Quebec back to obedience and wayward Americans back to loyalty to their King.

To what extent American propaganda influenced the *habitants* is hard to determine. It must be remembered that the average Québécois not only did not speak English, but received almost no formal education and usually could neither read nor write French. Despite this, some propaganda may have reached a few

73

habitants and turned them pro-American. But the basic situation was that the *habitants* did not realize that their way of life had been in jeopardy from English and American interests, and that Carleton, via the Quebec Act, had preserved their culture and customs. In a letter to Gage, Carleton expressed the opinion that the one defect of the Act was that it had been created too late to help.[14] If the Quebec Act had been enacted in 1770, its beneficial effects might have filtered down to the *habitants*. If Carleton had had four years in which to gain the confidence of the average Québécois, perhaps an army of militia could have been trained to fight, and the entire colony would have rallied behind Carleton.

The best way to understand Carleton's greatest disappointment is to quote from letters written by two of his closest associates, Cramahé and Hey. Cramahé advised Dartmouth on September 21st that "no means have been left untried to bring the Canadian peasantry to a sense of their duty and engage them to take up arms in defence of the Province, but all to no avail."[15] On September 18th, Hey informed Lord Chancellor Apsley:

> Hardly a Canadian will take up arms to oppose them [the Americans]. Everything seems to be desperate and I cannot fear that before this reaches your Lordship Canada will be as fully in the possession of the rebels as any other province upon the continent. I shall stay until every hope is gone which I fear will be a short time.[16]

Hey did sail November 11th, eight days before Carleton reached Quebec.[17]

When major events dishearten a man, minor matters only add to his discouragement. Early in September, Maria received news that her brother, Lord Effingham, had made a speech in the House of Lords to the effect that, as an Englishman, he could not fight the residents of the Thirteen Colonies and that he was resigning from the army.[18] In September, Carleton received a letter from Lady Chatham (her husband was too crippled with the gout to write himself),[19] stating that Lord Chatham so disapproved of English soldiers fighting "with our fellow subjects of America" that he requested that Carleton relieve his son, Lieutenant John Pitt, of his duties as aide-de-camp and let him return to London.[20] It was Chatham who had organized Wolfe's assault and capture of Quebec. To have Chatham imply that Carleton's desperate struggle to retain Quebec was wrong must have been a bitter blow. Carleton, of course, acquiesced and Pitt sailed for England four days later.[21]

In early November, when St. Jean fell, Carleton was thinking not merely of the defence of Quebec but was looking ahead into the next year. He had earlier written Dartmouth that ten to twelve thousand troops should be sent to Quebec as early as possible in 1776. There would also be naval problems too difficult to describe by letter, so Carleton sent to London a naval officer, Lieutenant Thomas Pringle, to effect several matters.

Pringle was instructed to urge the necessity of an army of ten to twelve thousand men reaching Quebec early in May and take with him ten river pilots. They would be used the following May to guide troop transports up the St. Lawrence to Quebec. (Carleton must have remembered how Admiral Durell in 1759 had captured Canadian pilots and, at gunpoint, forced them to lead his vessels safely upriver. Britain might not be so lucky a second time. Without pilots, the British could lose vessels crossing the Traverse, a notorious graveyard of ships.) Then there were the logistics of driving the Americans out of Quebec. To do so the British would have to ascend the Richelieu and then cross Lake Champlain. Pringle was to obtain flat-bottomed transports to carry troops, cannon and provisions, and warships to protect the transports. However, on the Richelieu just below St. Jean, there were almost ten miles of rapids, through which no large craft could navigate. So Pringle was to ask London to build all these craft in sections and ship them across the Atlantic. These sections would be hauled around the rapids to St. Jean. There transports and escorts would be "built" and launched.

It was in Montreal that Carleton had written these instructions to Pringle. Pringle found ten pilots and sailed with them from Quebec in the middle of November.

CHAPTER 9

The Defeat of the Americans at Quebec

In September 1775, Montgomery had taken St. Jean and Montreal. The next step was to descend the St. Lawrence and capture
Quebec. To aid Montgomery's move, General George Washington had approved a plan for Colonel Benedict Arnold to lead a
second military expedition. Arnold's troops were to travel in
almost a straight line via the Kennebec, Dead, and Chaudière
rivers across what is now the state of Maine to the outskirts of
the city of Quebec. Montgomery's and Arnold's combined
forces would then capture the capital of Britain's northernmost
colony.

Why did Washington approve the Arnold expedition? The
British Army under General Gage was in Boston, and Washington could not persuade his chief officers to agree to attack these
forces. Washington hated his troops to be idle, which he felt was
bad for morale. He feared that the British would use Quebec as a
jumping-off place to besiege the New England colonies, and
above all he was under the common misapprehension that the
Québécois would revolt in enthusiastic support of the American
invaders.

Leading eleven hundred soldiers, Arnold left Cambridge,
Massachusetts, on September 11th and reached the mouth of
the Kennebec River nine days later. At what is now Augusta,
Maine, his soldiers embarked in two hundred and twenty-four
rowboats, four or five men to a boat, each packed with guns,
ammunition and food.

From the start, there were troubles, difficulties and obstacles.

They were rowing and paddling against a strong current. There were portages that involved incredible exertion. One was a twelve-mile, wilderness march to the Dead River, the men hauling boats and supplies up and down hills, often having to cut a path through bush and scrub. It rained almost continually; then it snowed. Men contracted dysentery or fell victim to pneumonia. They deserted and they died. Finally. on November 11th, Arnold and what was left of his army, about seven hundred men, reached the south bank of the St. Lawrence River and the outskirts of Quebec. It was an heroic exploit of enterprise and endurance.

The impetuous Arnold, unwilling to wait for Montgomery, decided to storm Quebec's walls on the night of November 13th. His troops crossed the St. Lawrence to Wolfe's Cove, but were discovered by a British naval patrol. Changing his tactics, Arnold led his men up onto the Plains of Abraham. For six days they remained outside the city walls, hoping to draw the defenders out and fight a pitched battle. (Arnold had no artillery to blast an entrance through the walls.) However, when Arnold finally checked his serviceable muskets, he found that he had an insufficient number and also that he was low on ammunition. Now worried that a British sortie might overwhelm him, he decided to withdraw upriver eighteen miles to Pointe-aux-Trembles and wait for Montgomery's troops to arrive from Montreal.

As Arnold's men marched back along the north bank of the St. Lawrence, a British schooner passed them. This was the *Senaut Fell*, transporting Carleton to Quebec. As it rounded Cape Diamond, guns on the walls of Quebec boomed a salute. When the governor stepped ashore in the Lower Town, Cramahé, Maclean, and a number of friends met him and escorted him to the Château St. Louis. There, he recounted Captain Bouchette's skilfulness, and expressed his certainty that the Americans would be beaten. He admitted no possibility that Quebec would fall. Outwardly, he exuded optimism.[1]

Cramahé had been getting the city ready to withstand a siege. The militia had been put to work repairing walls and mounting guns. Barricades had been built across streets in the Lower Town and also shut off the approaches to the Upper Town. Provisions had been collected to feed the citizens during the coming

77

winter. With luck, the city would hold out, although firewood, oats and hay were very scarce.[2]

Carleton's first question to Cramahé was: "How many fighting men do we have?" The roster was 1,326.[3] To lead them, there were three veteran officers: Colonel Allan Maclean—who had slipped past Sorel before the American gunners had arrived there; Major Henry Caldwell, who had fought with Wolfe; and Colonel Noël Voyer, a trustworthy militia captain, even though he had fought against Wolfe. The men these officers had to lead were a motley groups of French-speaking and English-speaking militia with little experience of working together and almost no military training, plus seventy British regulars.

Quebec was a hotbed of dread, doubt and dissension. It needed a cleansing, which Carleton effected in two moves. First, he ordered every known malcontent to leave the city under penalty of being treated as a rebel and a spy. These men were ordered to take their wives and children with them. Some joined relatives or friends living on farms at a distance from the city. Some joined Montgomery. Among the latter was Walker's partner, James Price, and a lawyer from New Jersey named Edward Antill. Montgomery made Antill the chief engineer of his army.[4] Secondly, Carleton issued an edict that all able-bodied men who had not joined the militia were to quit the city with their families within four days, "leaving an inventory of their provisions and stores with George Allsopp, Commissary, who will pay them a just and fair price." Those who failed to depart would be treated as spies. The Quebec *Gazette* had ceased publication November 23rd, so Carleton had his edict printed in French and English and distributed as a handbill.[5] It was also read by the priest in every church. As there were sentries on duty night and day at every city gate and at the two entries to the Lower Town, anyone who left the city was unable to return. By these two actions, Carleton eradicated the danger of enemies in his midst and improved the morale of those who remained.

There were two warships, HMS *Lizard* and *Hunter*, anchored in the harbor and quite a number of smaller cargo vessels. Earlier, Carleton had placed an embargo on ships leaving the city.[6] He now issued a further directive. All ships were to be put away for the winter, and their officers and crew were to join the army.

By December 1st, the roster of fighting men was quite different:

Royal Fusiliers	70
Scots immigrants	230
Fire workers (for artillery)	22
Marines	35
Artificers	120
English-speaking militia	330
French-speaking militia	543
Seamen	345[7]
Masters, mates, ship's carpenters etc.	50
	1,745

The best of these men were the thirty-five marines, the seventy fusiliers, and the two hundred and thirty Scots immigrants, many of whom were former soldiers who had taken their discharge in North America. Maclean had recruited them by offering each, with Carleton's approval, one guinea, plus two hundred acres of land rent-free for twenty years, plus an additional fifty acres for a wife and each child, such land to be theirs at the end of their sudden recall to military service.[8]

All in all, Carleton had almost twice as many combatants as his besiegers. Moreover, as far as the Upper Town was concerned, he was defending a walled city. These were his two strengths. His weakness was the questionable reliability of four-fifths of his force. He knew he could not risk a pitched battle on the Plains of Abraham. Furthermore, he did not have enough personnel to man the walls of the Upper Town twenty-four hours a day.

Carleton's tactics were simple. He placed lookouts along the walls and at the barricades in the Lower Town. If a lookout reported an attack, an alarm was to be set off by the ringing of bells and the beating of drums. Every defender was assigned a position to go to upon hearing the alarm. Two-thirds of the positions were behind the walls or at the barricades. The remaining third of Carleton's force was to report to his headquarters so that he could use them as a reserve to rush to any danger spot.[9]

The defence plan looked good on paper, but Carleton had much to worry about. Would there be too many false alarms?

Would the lookouts give the real warning in time and the defenders reach their assigned positions? Suppose he deployed his reserve force in the wrong place due to a feint or to a false report and then the city was assaulted from a different direction?

On December 1st, Montgomery's forces sailed downriver in the boats captured at Sorel, and joined Arnold at Pointe-aux-Trembles. With him, he brought provisions, muskets, powder, clothing, and small cannon. However, he arrived with only three hundred soldiers.[10] His force had been radically reduced by the expiration of enlistments, by desertion, and by sickness. He had also had to leave men to police Montreal. Smallpox and dysentery had reduced Arnold's effectives to about six hundred, so the united army under Montgomery as commander-in-chief that marched to the Plains of Abraham on December 5th was barely nine hundred strong.

From what deserters told him, Montgomery was convinced that the occupants of Quebec did not want to fight and would hastily surrender. Thus, his first act was to send a flag of truce to the St. John's Gate, one of the entrances through the walls to the Upper Town. There his emissaries asked for permission to see Carleton and deliver to him a letter demanding the surrender of Quebec. A runner was sent to the governor at the Château St. Louis. Carleton's reply was that he would neither talk with the rebels nor read any communications from them.

Montgomery then tried a ruse. He gave a letter to an old woman, who went to another of the gates, told the sentry that she wanted to see General Carleton on an important matter, was admitted, and taken to the Château. Carleton was working at a table before an open fire. The woman told him that she had a letter from General Montgomery. Carleton told her to lay the letter on the table. He then summoned a drummer boy, bade him take the tongs from the fireplace, pick up the letter and deposit it in the flames. This done, Carleton had the woman escorted out of the city.[11]

On December 15th, Montgomery had issued general orders to his troops, promising them booty when Quebec fell. The orders included the following: "The General is confident [that] a vigorous and spirited attack must be attended with success. The troops shall have the [personal] effects of the Governor, garrison, and of such as have been acting in misleading the inhabitants and distressing the friends of liberty to be equally divided among them . . . "[12] Hoping to scare the besieged, Montgomery arranged for an Indian to attach these orders to arrows and shoot them over the walls and into the city. The next day, Montgomery wrote yet another letter to Carleton, which he delivered in the same unorthodox manner. It began: "Notwithstanding the personal ill-treatment I have received at your hands—notwithstanding the cruelty you have shown to the unhappy prisoners you have taken—feelings of humanity induce me to have recourse to this expedient to save you from the destruction which hangs over your wretched garrison." Montgomery then proceeded to explain how strong his forces were and how weak Carleton's position was. He ended his letter: "Should you persist in an unwarrantable defence, the consequence be on your head. Beware of destroying stores of any sort as you did at Montreal in the river. If you do, by heaven, there will be no mercy shown."[13]

Carleton waged his own brand of psychological warfare. While inspecting the walls of the city, he noticed an elevated sentry box on the ramparts of Cape Diamond. The governor had somehow acquired a good-sized wooden horse, presumably a toy for one of his sons. He had the sentry box filled with hay and the wooden horse firmly secured to a board, its head turned toward the box. Carleton then announced: "Je ne rendrai point Québec jusqu'à ce que le cheval ait mangé le foin!" (I shall not surrender Quebec until the horse has eaten the hay!) Carleton understood the folksy humor of the Québécois. His challenge was all over the city within forty-eight hours, and men, women and children climbed Cape Diamond to view "Carleton's horse."[14]

During the latter part of December, Carleton made his headquarters at the seminary of the Recollets. Here, like the other officers, he slept each night in his clothes.[15] As we have seen, Carleton was always at his best when under duress. "Misfortunes animated him to doubled exertions. He always made the utmost of his resources and had the valuable quality of adapting small means to the achievement of great ends."[16] Now, with the decisive time close at hand, he was a dynamo of energy and inspiration. He supervised the training of men every day. By December 1st, a foot of snow had fallen; by the end of the month there was at least another foot. Carleton had paths dug after every snowfall. He even had the snow drifts against the walls outside levelled. He was afraid these drifts might form ramps to support enemy scaling ladders. Extra barricades were built in the Lower Town and on the ascent to the Upper Town. Houses outside but close to the walls were burned so that Montgomery's men could not use them as fire points. Some were burned because they blocked the view of British gunners on the walls.

Montgomery and Arnold were in a quandary. Their best cannon were only twelve-pounders and few in number. They tried setting them up on the Plains of Abraham, but the artillery on the walls soon got their range and damaged or destroyed their guns. The American commanders had little better luck in the suburb of St. Roch. Firing at the walls was useless. Cannon balls bounced off, but howitzer shells could be lobbed into the city. However, the Upper Town was thinly settled, especially the area nearest St. Roch, and the shells just dropped harmlessly in the snow. It was said that during the three weeks of occasional shelling only one person was hurt and one dog killed.

Another plan was devised. Aaron Burr, whom Montgomery had commissioned a captain, started training volunteers to climb over the walls using ladders. The idea was that, under cover of night, these men would scale the walls at some unprotected place, seize one of the gates, and Montgomery's men would pour through to capture the city. This plan was given up, possibly because one of Burr's volunteers deserted to the British, and Montgomery was certain that the scheme would have been made known to Carleton. Also, there were doubts as to whether the plan was practicable. For a soldier to climb a ladder in the middle of the night, carrying a musket or with one tied to his back, would be a difficult undertaking. The British had flares which, even in driving snow, could light up the outside of the walls. A hand grenade, musket shot, or gun used as a club—or even just pushing the ladder sideways until it toppled over—would be an effective means of defence.

Montgomery and Arnold decided that they must attack the Lower Town. Antill and Price assured Montgomery that if he could capture the Lower Town, the citizens would force Carleton to surrender the Upper Town. The plan adopted in the latter part of December was for Montgomery, with some two hundred to two hundred and fifty soldiers, to attack from the southwest by breaching the barricades across a narrow roadway that led from Wolfe's Cove around the high cliff of Cape Diamond into the unwalled Lower Town. Arnold, starting from his encampment in the suburbs of St. Roch, with five to six hundred men, would come round from the northeast, forcing other barricades, until he reached the warehouse area of the Lower Town. One force would await the arrival of the other. Then, together, they would fight their way into the Lower Town. The two-pronged attack was to be made at night during a snowstorm.

The nights of December 27th, 28th and 29th were clear, but on the evening of the 30th, a northeasterly wind began to blow and a heavy snow began to fall.[17] Between three and four o'clock on the morning of the 31st, some of Montgomery's men made feints at the St. John's Gate and at Cape Diamond. Major Caldwell galloped to St. John's Gate and Maclean to Cape Diamond, but extra troops were not sent to the walls.

Montgomery set out from Wolfe's Cove around three a.m. His soldiers were dragging a sled on which was mounted a cannon. They came to a place on the roadway where enormous ice blocks had been thrown up by the river. The men could crawl and clamber over the ice, but pulling the sled past it proved impossible, and the cannon was abandoned. They reached the first barricade, which was undefended.[18] Using axes and saws, posts were cut off and timber knocked away so that they could get through. Montgomery then set off three rockets to signal Arnold that he was on his way.

Around four a.m., they came to a second barricade, again an undefended one. Once more a passage was cut through. They were now at a place called Près-de-Ville. The roadway here was scarcely wide enough for four men to walk abreast. On the left was a high perpendicular cliff; on the right was the river, which was partially iced over. Montgomery and three of his captains—Burr, McPherson, and Chessman—plus a few soldiers, were the first to walk past the second barricade. Blinding snow was blowing into their faces. Ahead fifty yards or so was a faintly lit structure next to the cliff.

Unknown to the Americans, this house had been turned into a blockhouse with cannon in the windows. The defenders were some sailors commanded by a Captain Barnsfair. There were also some militiamen under the command of Captain John Coffin. Barnsfair had heard the Americans coming. His sailors were standing behind the guns with lighted tapers. When the shadowy advancing figures were thirty to forty feet away, Barnsfair gave the order to fire. The guns spewed grapeshot. Montgomery, Chessman and McPherson were killed instantly, along with a few soldiers. Burr and the remaining attackers tumbled back through the barricade.[19]

With Montgomery's death, command passed to Colonel Campbell. Deciding that it was hopeless to try and pass the blockhouse, he ordered the troops to retreat to Wolfe's Cove. From there, they climbed the cliff, tramped across the Plains of Abraham, and marched to St. Roch. Had Montgomery lived, perhaps a second attempt would have been made at Près-de-Ville to get through to the Lower Town, but it is hard to fault Campbell's decision. To advance on a narrow road, in the dark, against grapeshot was simply to walk into the jaws of death.

What of Colonel Benedict Arnold and his troops? The main force, led personally by Arnold, set out between two and three a.m. (For some reason, Captain Henry Dearborn, with seventy-five to one hundred men encamped to the north of the main force, did not get started until much later.) In the pitch darkness, Arnold and his men had to wade through several feet of snow, with a strong, bitterly cold gale blowing falling snow around them. As was the case with Montgomery, they had one cannon on a sled. Close to the Lower Town the snow drifts seemed higher. Dragging the sled became a back-breaking business and delayed the advance, so this cannon too was abandoned. As the troops came near the Palace Gate on the northeast corner of the Upper Town, they were encouraged to see Montgomery's rockets. Then they were spotted by the defenders. Church bells started ringing, drums started beating. Guns on the Upper Town walls began firing. As the Americans approached the first barricade at the entrance to the Lower Town, Arnold was wounded in the calf of his left leg by a musketball.

Arnold had given orders that wounded men were to be disregarded, to be left where they fell. This seems inhumane, but militarily it was necessary. There were no stretchers or stretcher-bearers. To try to carry the wounded back to St. Roch would have taken able-bodied men away from the attacking line. Arnold wanted to continue marching with his troops, but his aides persuaded him that he must retire, and he went hobbling back, a soldier supporting him on either side. Arnold met Dearborn's sluggish troops and urged them to hurry forward.

Captain Daniel Morgan took command. He successfully overran the first barrier, capturing some militia. However, there was a delay due to the necessity of occupying houses, putting the prisoners into them, and detailing guards to look after the captives. As the Americans approached the second barricade at Sault-au-Matelot, there was a half an hour or more of waiting; they apparently hoped to hear that Montgomery was attacking from the other side. Then the advance continued. It had stopped snowing, but the sky was dark. Houses were taken and retaken by the Americans, by the British, and then again by the Americans. Then two things happened.

First, dawn broke. By now a large number of the attackers' muskets could not be fired because snow had ruined the powder in their priming pans. Some muskets taken from the militia prisoners were in good condition, but there were not enough of these to go around. The failure of the muskets made little difference in the darkness and in the snowstorm. Under such conditions, hitting the enemy was a matter of luck. A musket was more valuable as a club or bayonet. Once dawn broke, however, musketry became effective, and the British had dry weapons. To protect themselves against fire, the Americans crowded into houses they had captured or hid behind houses where they could not easily be seen and shot at, which slowed their advance.

Second, Carleton sent an engineer officer, Captain Lawes, with two hundred soldiers—promptly followed by two hundred more—through the Palace Gate and down to the Lower Town to

85

take the besiegers in the rear.[20] Dearborn's men, who had lost their way, stumbled into the path of Lawes' men. Many of Dearborn's muskets would not shoot. He thought he was surrounded, which he was not, and doubtless his morale had been hurt by seeing Arnold wounded and retiring. At any rate, Dearborn promptly surrendered.

Lawes' troops now advanced towards Morgan's men, who were caught between two fires, one from the barricades at Sault-au-Matelot and other fortified houses, and one from Lawes' men. Morgan did not know where many of his troops were. Men had lost their way in the strange, narrow streets. Communications were difficult, and Morgan could not organize any co-ordinated attack or defence. Moreover, most of the attackers were exhausted from the six-hour ordeal of marching and fighting in deep snow and biting cold. Lawes' troops were the best Carleton had. They were fresh, and their muskets were dry. Their officers directed them to surround and clear one house after another. Before a house was attacked, an officer shouted two or three times that Carleton personally promised "good quarters and tender usage" to anyone who surrendered. The Americans, in a hopeless position, became demoralized. A few surrendered, quickly followed by more. Morgan fought to the last, was the hero in the debacle, but finally he, too, capitulated, handing over his sword to a priest.

By ten a.m., all the Americans who had entered the Lower Town were prisoners, with the exception of a few who escaped across the frozen Charles River. (Perhaps because it was shallow, it froze more quickly than the St. Lawrence.[21]) The shivering prisoners, numbering four hundred and twenty-six, climbed, shuffling and stumbling, up to the Upper Town. The thirty-two officers were imprisoned in the Recollets' building; their men in the seminary. In these two buildings, the men were warmed by a belated breakfast of biscuits and rum.[22]

After the battle, Arnold estimated the American dead at sixty, but some of the wounded died later and some corpses were not found until the snow melted in April. The total of American dead probably reached seventy-five. Carleton reported his losses as seven killed and thirteen wounded. Again, the final figure was probably slightly higher.[23]

Shortly after nine a.m., when there was no doubt as to a British victory in the Lower Town, Carleton sent a small detachment, his last reserve, into the outskirts of St. Roch to seize the enemy's artillery battery, the one that had been intermittently lobbing shells into the Upper Town. These were captured with no casualties, the gunners having run for their lives.

On the afternoon of December 31st, the day of victory, a militiaman noticed a hand sticking out of the snow at Près-de-Ville. When the snow had been dug away, the body of Major-General Richard Montgomery was revealed. (He had been promoted from brigadier-general by the Continental Congress on December 9th.) Thirteen years earlier, at the siege of Havana, Montgomery had been a captain in one regiment and Carleton a colonel in another. The two may or may not have met, but Carleton must have been aware of Montgomery's career. Here, at Quebec, lay a former officer of the British army, a man who had taken an oath of loyalty to the King. This officer had retired from the army, selling his commission, had emigrated to North America, and at the time of his death was a rebel, fighting his former comrades. To Carleton, Montgomery must have seemed a most reprehensible turncoat. Nonetheless, Carleton asked his chief of engineers, James Thompson, to have a "genteel coffin" prepared.

At sundown on January 4th, a burial service was conducted by the military chaplain, with Thompson and five other men attending. Several weeks later, Mrs. Montgomery wrote Carleton asking if she could have her husband's watch and seal. Carleton acquiesced. The watch and seal, addressed to her, were sent via a flag of truce to the American encampment.[24]

The four hundred and twenty-six prisoners that Carleton had captured had nothing with them except the clothes they were wearing. Three days after the attack Carleton put on parole one of his prisoners, Major Jonathan Meigs, and sent him to Arnold under a flag of truce.[25] Meigs carried a letter from Carleton saying that if Arnold would transmit the prisoners' "baggage" to the city, Carleton would see that this was distributed to its owners. Meigs reported the complete defeat of the Americans and he convinced Arnold that the prisoners of war were being treated well. In a letter to his wife, Arnold commented: "The prisoners are treated politely and supplied with everything the garrison affords."[26]

On the morning of January 10th, a line of six sleighs arrived at the Palace Gate. The driver of the first sleigh was waving a stick to which was tied a white handkerchief. This signalled that the prisoners' "baggage"—clothing and personal effects—was following them into the city.

CHAPTER 10

Driving out the Americans

The first four months of 1776 were grim for those American soldiers encamped in the vicinity of St. Roch. A third were laid up with smallpox; it was a sick and pessimistic army. The attack on Quebec had ended in disaster; discouragement was rife and rapidly demoralized new enlistees as they arrived in small groups from Montreal. Four months of idleness hurt morale, too. The men had little to do except battle the bitter cold during a winter more severe than Quebec had experienced in a decade. (One night, the thermometer registered -28 Fahrenheit.) Had Arnold been up and about, affairs might have been different, but the brave colonel was flat on his back, recovering from his leg wound. Late in March, General David Wooster assumed command, and Arnold left reluctantly for Montreal. Wooster, who was lazy and had no notion of leadership, only made matters worse. Some of his officers believed that they were still besieging Quebec, but there was no serious thought of trying, a second time, to take the city by assault.

Carleton on his part made no effort to attack. For this he has been bitterly criticized. What is the explanation? Carleton was a cautious man, perhaps overly cautious. He knew that those militiamen who had fought well behind barricades would not be dependable in a pitched battle. If, by some chance, he was beaten, Quebec would fall. If, as seems more probable, he won, he would have more prisoners to feed, more wounded to take care of, plus men sick with the dreaded smallpox. Carleton wanted none of this. Moreover, to conquer the enemy at Quebec would not improve the basic situation. In the midst of winter, he could not retake Montreal. His meagre forces could not march, transport supplies and cannon, and bivouac in the snow and ice—at least not without great difficulty. His course was to stay inactive for four months and let "General Winter" further weaken his foes. He hoped an army would arrive from England in May.

For those within Quebec, the winter months were also tedious and hard. Food was scarce, yet there were extra mouths to feed—the prisoners of war. Fresh meat and eggs were soon exhausted; the principal diet became salt pork, salt beef and salt fish. It had been the custom each December to bring into the city on sleds the firewood so essential for heating as well as cooking. The advent of the Americans had prevented this, and the shortage of wood was serious. During January and February, Carleton used his militia, not to attack the Americans, but to forage for provisions and firewood.[1]

The governor's first priority was to deal with the prisoners. In the latter part of January, all but the officers had been transferred from the seminary to the dilapidated Dauphin Jail. The bars on many of the jail's windows were so corroded that they could easily be removed; hinges and padlocks on gates could be wrenched loose. In addition, the prisoners were guarded very casually, visitors coming and going at will. Some had smuggled into the prison a few pistols and some powder and the prisoners plotted a break-out. They planned to seize their guards on the night of April 1st, overpower the sentries at the St. John's Gate only one hundred yards away from the jail, and then turn the cannon at the gate on the city. At the same time, they were going to set the guardhouse on fire and halloo a signal to their comrades on the outside that the St. John's Gate was open. The prisoners hoped their comrades would dash through and storm the city.

The first task was to communicate with those in St. Roch. A veteran non-commissioned officer, Sergeant Martin, managed to escape from the jail, reached St. Roch, and informed General Wooster of the prisoners' plan. Martin's disappearance seems to have gone unnoticed by the prison guards. However, winter also conspired against the escapees. Ice had formed on the floors and blocked the opening of a heavy door that led out of the prison. A couple of nights before the break-out, two men, trying to cut the ice with knives and a tomahawk, made too much noise. One of the guards became suspicious, the ice cutters were discovered, and a thorough search of the prison disclosed the pistols and the powder in the prisoners' possession. One prisoner, doubtless trying to curry favor, confessed the plan, which others corroborated.

The discovery of the break-out seems to have jolted Carleton. He realized that he had been too lenient with the prisoners and remiss in the conditions under which they had been guarded. He reacted promptly; in fact, he overreacted. He had iron bars, twelve feet in length and two or three inches in diameter, taken to the prison. Those considered the leaders of the would-be escapees were chained to these bars with handcuffs and foot-irons, ten or twelve men to a bar. For the next six weeks, they suffered this humiliation and misery.[2]

On the night of April 1st, Carleton stationed extra troops and cannon at the St. John's Gate. Trying to simulate the prisoners' plan, he had a large fire lit as if the guardhouse were in flames and had his soldiers halloo, hoping that the Americans would attack. Perhaps General Wooster suspected a trap, or felt that the morale of his troops was too low for any fighting.[3] At any rate, nothing happened. On May 4th, General John Thomas took over command of the besiegers, who numbered about twenty-five hundred.[4] The next day, Thomas held a council of war and decided to abandon the siege and withdraw to Montreal. Doubtless, Thomas had received information that reinforcements from Britain were approaching.

At six a.m. on May 6th, a British brig, the *Surprise*, hove into sight near the Ile d'Orléans, followed by another, the *Iris*, and a sloop-of-war, the *Martin*. Three or four hours later, two hundred marines were being rowed ashore. The inhabitants of Quebec City were excited. Victory was in the air and every citizen, bored by the long winter of confinement, wanted to be part of it. Carleton threw caution to the winds and organized an impromptu army consisting of the newly arrived marines, plus regulars and militia from the garrison, about nine hundred fighting men in all. At noon, he personally led them to attack Thomas' encampment in the neighborhood of St. Roch. A few shots were fired. No one seems to have been hurt, but the Americans—soldiers and officers—panicked and started running in the general direction of Montreal, jettisoning their equipment as they went. Carleton's men captured all the Americans' supplies—guns, ammunition, provisions—including a substantial lunch that had been prepared for General Thomas. Everything had been left intact.

By midnight, some of the besiegers had reached Pointe-aux-Trembles. The next day, some had arrived at Deschambault, fifteen miles farther on.[5] Here, General Thomas was able to stop the rout and impose some discipline. At a leisurely pace, Carleton followed the enemy as far as Sillery, where he called a halt. Leaving a small guard, the governor and his impromptu army returned to the city. The next morning, Carleton visited the Dauphin Jail and ordered the irons removed from the prisoners of war. With their comrades in flight, these men were no longer a danger to the city.[6]

Many of those who had fled were ill. Twenty or twenty-five of these had been picked up by the British and, under Carleton's orders, had been taken to the Hôpital-Général. He suspected there were others whom his men had not found. Thus, on May 10th, the following proclamation was printed as a handbill and distributed to militia captains and to priests in nearby parishes:

> Whereas I am informed that many of his Majesty's deluded subjects of the neighboring provinces, laboring under wounds and diverse disorders, are dispersed in the adjacent woods and Parishes and in great danger of perishing for want of proper assistance: all captains and other officers of militia are hereby commanded to make diligent search for all such distressed persons, and afford them all necessary relief, and convey them to the General Hospital where proper care shall be taken of them. All reasonable expenses which shall be incurred in complying with this order shall be paid by the Receiver of Taxes.
>
> And lest the consequences of past offences should deter such miserable wretches from receiving that assistance which their distressed situation may require, I hereby make known to them, that as their health is restored, they shall have free liberty to return to their respective provinces.[7]

British reinforcements arrived slowly; by May 22nd, only two regiments had reached Quebec. Carleton sailed with these up the St. Lawrence to an encampment a little below Trois-Rivières. Scouting parties searched far and wide but never saw an American. The troops were ordered to follow the road past Trois-Rivières to Rivière-du-Loup. Here, a stream with a bridge across it flowed into the St. Lawrence. Carleton placed a contingent of redcoats under a Major Grant to guard the bridge, using cannon borrowed from the Royal Navy. Everything being under control, Carleton returned to Quebec to await the advent of further reinforcements.

On June 1st, sixteen British transports carrying some eight thousand men anchored at Quebec. Carleton met Major-General John Burgoyne, his second-in-command, and Major-General Baron von Riedesel, the commander of the German mercenaries, some four thousand in number. All of these remained on board until June 4th, when they were rowed ashore and celebrated the King's birthday with a parade and much firing of cannon.

What were the fleeing Americans doing? They had retreated across the St. Lawrence to Sorel, which was situated on the southern bank at the mouth of the Richelieu River. The invaders were suffering from an old complaint; nearly a quarter of them were incapacitated by smallpox. General Thomas fell prey to the disease and died, and Major-General John Sullivan succeeded to the command.

The Americans were told that Trois-Rivières, a town of fifty houses on a bluff overlooking the river, was lightly held by the British. A plan was made to cross the St. Lawrence and attack this centre. Trois-Rivières had no military importance, but Sullivan approved the plan. He felt that he must have any sort of victory to improve the morale of his soldiers. Many British soldiers were now still at Quebec, and he would have a greater chance of success if he could attack before the entire enemy force moved upriver. Sullivan put his second-in-command, Brigadier-General William Thompson, in charge of the assault force and gave him two thousand of the best troops.

Thompson marched down the southern bank of the St. Lawrence to Nicolet. Here, about fifty large flat-bottomed boats had been collected. On the night of June 7th, the assault force crossed the river without incident, landing in the early hours of the morning at Pointe-du-Lac, seven miles west of Trois-Rivières. Thompson felt certain the road along the river would be watched and guarded. He decided to move his army inland, circling around to the northern edge of Trois-Rivières and attacking at dawn to take its inhabitants by surprise. He forced a local *habitant*, Antoine Gautier, to guide his men through the countryside to Trois-Rivières. But Gautier led Thompson's troops on detours into swamps, and it was well into the morning before the Americans, tired from their excessive marching, came in sight of Trois-Rivières. The British, warned of Thompson's expedition by a Pointe-du-Lac militia captain, were ready. Troops and, above all, cannon had been landed at Trois-Rivières and trenches had been dug. Thompson led the attack and found himself between two fires; one from the defenders of the town, and one from British warships anchored close to the river bank. Lacking cannon, rarely did he get within musket shot of the British. Even then his men were firing in the open, the British from behind trenchworks. The result was that Thompson was taken prisoner with some two hundred of his men. The rest of his command straggled back along the road to Pointe-du-Lac.

A few miles west of Pointe-du-Lac was Rivière-du-Loup, where Major Grant was positioned. He started moving his men up the road past Pointe-du-Lac towards Trois-Rivières, taking the cannon with him. In addition, British warships started picking up the flat-bottomed boats. The Americans were in a trap. They were saved by Providence—in the person of General Guy Carleton. He reached Trois-Rivières and immediately ordered Grant's contingent to withdraw and the warships to leave the Americans and their boats alone. Carleton had opened the trap. The Americans walked to Pointe-du-Lac, climbed into their bateaux, rowed across and up the St. Lawrence, safely reaching Sorel. Carleton could have captured every one of them, more than a fourth of the American army, and more than a third of its effectives.[8]

Carleton did not want any more prisoners. He had, in fact,

made up his mind to free all prisoners of war in his custody. When he visited the prisoners in the Dauphin Jail, he promised them he would send them back to New York City—which was still in American hands—if they would swear allegiance to the King. The prisoners objected, and Carleton worked out the following compromise oath: "We, whose names are underwritten, do hereby solemnly promise and engage to his Excellency General Carleton not to say or do anything against his Majesty's person or government."[9] Officers signed a parole promising not to fight again unless they were exchanged for captive British officers of similar rank.[10] Carleton's order dated August 7th read:

> All prisoners from the rebellious provinces who choose to return home, are to hold themselves in readiness to embark on a short notice. The commissary, Lieutenant Murray, shall visit the transports destined to them, to see that wholesome provisions, necessary clothing with all conveniences for their carriage, be prepared for these unfortunate men.[11]

Five of the prisoners opted to remain in Quebec. The rest set off for New York City on the 11th of August.[12]

Carleton's parting gifts to his prisoners on the day before they sailed were not limited to food and clothing. He gave some officers and men £100,[13] and linen shirts to others[14]—all paid out of the British treasury.

Carleton's release of the prisoners made him seem to some circles in London not merely eccentric but perhaps a madman. However, there were several reasons for his behavior. The city of Quebec had some six hundred houses and a population of five or six thousand people, not including British troops. Montreal was almost the same size. The rest of the Province was farmland. To house, feed and guard several thousand Americans was practically an impossibility. Carleton could probably have shipped them to England, but this seemed to him cruel and, moreover, pointless. The British Army was accustomed to fighting professionals. In Europe, the British took prisoners because that meant there were fewer of the enemy left to fight. The American soldiers were citizen soldiers. Nearly every young farmer in the Thirteen Colonies used a gun for hunting and learned to be a sharpshooter in order to repel Indian raids. Capturing a thousand or more of such men meant little. There were thousands more where they came from.

The third and most important reason for Carleton's benevolent treatment of prisoners was his belief that killing or incarcerating colonial rebels accomplished nothing. He thought that their revolt was misguided and could be overcome by reasonableness and kindness. He was convinced that his policy would ultimately persuade the rebels of the true value of the British connection. He had followed much the same philosophy in governing the Québécois. On August 7th, when Carleton released the prisoners, he addressed a proclamation to his own troops, which ended as follows:

> It belongs to Britons to distinguish themselves not less by their humanity than their valor. It belongs to the King's troops to save the blood of his deluded subjects, whose greatest fault perhaps is having been deceived by their leaders to their own distraction. It belongs to the Crown and it is the duty of all faithful servants of the Crown to rescue from oppression and restore to liberty the once happy, free, and loyal people of the continent.[15]

Carleton was not acting as a general, whose sole weapon is force. He was acting as a statesman—although whether he was being sensible or hopelessly idealistic is debatable.

On August 10th Carleton wrote London that the release of the prisoners on parole "surprised them not a little. If they fulfill their engagements, they will become good subjects; if not these can never turn the scale."[16] His attitude is exemplified in a letter to General Howe in New York, on August 8th.

> I have sent the rebel prisoners taken in this province (except such as have chosen to remain here) to New York, that they may from thence return to their respective homes; in hope that the confinement they have undergone may have brought them to a sense of their past crimes and this proof given to the rebels still in arms that the way to mercy is not yet shut against them, the contrary be inculcated by their chiefs, and those who have an interest in fomenting the disorders of the country, may tend to work a favorable change in their minds and contribute to restore the peace of America.[17]

The chief American encampment of about seven thousand men remained at Sorel, under the command of General Sullivan. There were also some three hundred soldiers under Arnold at Montreal. Carleton ordered Burgoyne to move on Sorel with some four thousand troops. Carleton, with five thousand others, would go on to Montreal, capture the city, and then march some fifteen miles to Chambly on the Richelieu River. Once he had taken Chambly, he would move down the Richelieu. Thus Sullivan's Americans would be caught in a trap. They would not be able to retreat up the Richelieu because of Carleton, or escape down the St. Lawrence because of Burgoyne.

On June 13th, Sullivan, sighting Burgoyne's fleet off Sorel, abandoned the town and retreated up the Richelieu. Burgoyne occupied Sorel and then followed Sullivan upriver, but made no contact. His orders were not to press or attack until Carleton had closed the trap.

Carleton approached Montreal on June 15th. Arnold, incapable of putting up any opposition with only three hundred soldiers, evacuated the city, marched to Chambly, and then moved past the rapids to St. Jean, which he reached on June 16th. Carleton now delayed. He probably could have taken a substantial number of his troops to Chambly by the evening of June 16th, certainly by June 17th. The distance was only fifteen miles, although the wilderness road was very bad. Carleton finally reached Chambly on June 19th. Sullivan's troops had already passed through and reached St. Jean, where they embarked on the 19th. Carleton was thirty-six to forty-eight hours too late. He had planned a trap but he had not sprung it. It seems that he no more wanted to capture Sullivan's army than he wanted to capture Thompson's troops at Trois-Rivières.

The Americans had now crossed Lake Champlain to Crown Point and Ticonderoga, and further British pursuit was impossible. On the St. Lawrence, the British had the upper hand. Their warships controlled the river. On the Richelieu and Lake Champlain, the situation was reversed. Here, the Americans had four warships and they had seized every passenger or freight vessel they could find on the Richelieu. Carleton perhaps could have taken thousands of prisoners; he never could have captured the American warships.

The British could not use their warships and transports because of the ten miles of rapids between Chambly and St. Jean. And there was no road around Lake Champlain. Troops could have hacked a way through the wilderness along the shore, but they would have been unable to haul cannon to Crown Point and Ticonderoga. In addition, moving supplies around a lake controlled by the enemy would have been highly dangerous. Carleton's advance was stopped until he could build vessels and transports at St. Jean, on the south side of the rapids.

Carleton had foreseen this problem. The previous fall he had sent Lieutenant Pringle to London to ask for bateaux. However, only ten flat-bottomed boats, each with a gun in the bow, had arrived, along with materials for building fourteen others. Sir William Howe, the British commander-in-chief in North America, had needed landing boats for his proposed invasion of Long Island, and his request had been given priority.

CHAPTER 11

Vice-Admiral Carleton and the Battle of Lake Champlain

For the next three months, there was no pursuit of the enemy, no armed activity. Carleton's men were too busy building transports and creating an inland navy. During these months Carleton attempted to restore conditions in the Province to normal. He appointed three commissioners to visit each parish around the city of Quebec, inquire about the conduct of captains of militia, disarm any suspected of disloyalty and, where desirable, appoint new captains.[1] In June, five days after the Americans had left Montreal, he appointed a similar commission of inquiry in the area. Carleton was lenient toward men who had helped, or even served with, the Americans, provided they were now prepared to obey his rules and regulations. Anyone who disobeyed these was promptly imprisoned under martial law. As matters turned out, few had to be incarcerated.

The Province began to return to normal within a very short time. In the first place, the Americans had alienated many of the Québécois who, at first, had espoused their cause. The invaders had soon run out of cash and had printed worthless paper money. At gunpoint, they had seized food, carts, boats, and other materials. To make matters worse, in his stupidity, General Wooster continually exhibited contempt for the *habitants*. He did not hesitate to put in irons any Québécois who ignored his orders or whom his soldiers reported as failing to co-operate.

During the previous year, business and commerce had been

badly interrupted. The fur trade and much of the import-export business had come to a standstill. Naturally, everyone longed to get back to what they considered the "good old times" as quickly as possible. With the invaders on the run, with many Québécois no longer being conscripted as militiamen or laborers, the economy picked up rapidly.

As always, Carleton would listen to anyone, talk to anyone. It was reported that when a *Canadien* had a complaint, the common expression was: "Je vais le dire au Général Carleton" (I shall tell it to General Carleton).[2] There was a further reason why Carleton was popular. He was winning, and people like to be on the winning side. Carleton, however, was not misled by his popularity. In September 1776, he wrote London: "As to my opinion of the Canadians, I think there is nothing to fear of them while we are in a state of prosperity, and nothing to hope for when in distress. I speak of the people at large; there are some among them who are guided by sentiments of honor, [but] the multitude is influenced by gain or fear of punishment."[3]

While the grave, formal-mannered Carleton was admired by many, some of his under-officers had another opinion of him. One lieutenant described Carleton as "one of the most distant, reserved men in the world. He has a rigid strictness in his manner which is very unpleasant and which he observes even to his most particular friends and acquaintances."[4] Another called him "a man of sour, morose temper."[5] Likewise there were *habitants* who remained hostile toward Carleton's regime, especially the army officers, as illustrated by the following story.

Colonel Thomas Carleton was driving with a lady on the river ice in a two-wheeled cariole. A *habitant* deliberately drove his sleigh against the cariole, thus upsetting it. Fortunately no one was hurt. The colonel, a big, powerful man, extricated himself and his companion from the overturned carriage and then proceeded to whip the *habitant*. The *habitant*, complaining over his treatment, said, "I shall tell it to General Carleton." The colonel replied: "Do that and tell him that it is his brother who is whipping you and is now going to whip you all the harder."[6]

Governor Carleton revived civil government. Three "Conservators of the Peace"—Mabane, Thomas Dunn, and Jean Claude Panet—were appointed judges of a court of civil jurisdiction for the Quebec district. For the Montreal area, Carleton appointed as judges two men sent from England, Peter Livius and William Owen, and a third, Gabriel Elzéar Taschereau, a well-known French Canadian. Carleton also appointed justices of the peace and bailiffs.[7]

Carleton hesitated to summon a meeting of the full council. Of the seven councillors who were pro-Québécois in outlook, four were prisoners of the Americans, two had returned to England, and one was ill. Of the remaining members, half or more were as anti-Québécois as the English-speaking mercantile community. In other words, it was doubtful that Carleton could command a majority of the remaining councillors. Certainly he would not have a subservient council.

The Quebec Act stated that "the Council shall have power and authority to make ordinances for the peace, welfare, and good government of the said Province." And further, "that no ordinance shall be passed at any meeting of the Council where less than a majority of the whole Council is present." However, in the King's instructions to Carleton was the following provision: "That any five of said Council shall constitute a Board of Council for transacting all business in which their advice may be requisite. Acts of legislation only excepted in which case you [Carleton] are not to act without a majority of the whole."[8] Carleton decided to rule under the authority of this instruction. He appointed Cramahé, Hugh Finlay, Thomas Dunn, John Collins, and Adam Mabane—men who were devoted to him and would follow his leadership without question—to be the board of council. For a second time, Carleton was ruling through an executive committee.

Carleton's first proclamation of a legislative nature was a board of council ruling forbidding the sale of rum and other spirits to Indians. The second dealt with foodstuffs. The presence of British reinforcements had increased the population of the Province and hence the number of mouths to be fed. Would there be enough food to go around? Carleton asked the board of council to investigate. It made inquiries and concluded that there was a surplus of wheat and that the crop outlook for 1776 was good. However, the number of cows had been substantially reduced; the Americans had slaughtered many for food. Also the supplies of flour and biscuits were not large; the war had curtailed milling operations. On August 30th Carleton, acting through the board of council, issued a proclamation permitting the export of wheat, but banning the export of livestock, flour and biscuits.[9]

Both of these proclamations were legislative decrees and their enactment violated the Quebec Act and the King's instructions. Carleton's ethical and legal position was shaky, to put it mildly. Certainly the British government never envisioned him governing through a board of council. But then, London never envisioned that the council itself would be so reduced in membership and there was no legal authority, such as a supreme court, to nullify what Carleton did. London could criticize his actions, but it was powerless to stop them.

Carleton made his Royal Navy aide, Lieutenant Thomas Pringle, now back from London, a captain. He put him in charge of the shipyard at St. Jean and made him supervisor of the entire naval construction program. Skilled men of all sorts were drafted and every soldier became a laborer. With fantastic energy, Pringle's work force built and dragged in sections around the rapids to St. Jean the following vessels: the *Inflexible*, a full-rigged, three-masted schooner, armed with eighteen twelve-pounders; the *Carleton* and the *Maria*, each mounting twelve six-pounders; the *Thunderer*, a huge raft carrying six twenty-four-pounders; the *Loyal Convert*; a thirty-ton gondola with six nine-pounders; twenty-four small gunboats, each with a cannon in its bow; and six hundred and eighty small flat-bottomed boats, enough to transport the army. Of these, the *Carleton* and the *Maria* had come in sections from Britain, as did ten of the flat-bottomed transports. To build the *Inflexible* took exactly twenty-eight days from the laying of the keel to the launching. This vessel of about three hundred tons was equipped, manned, and victualled in twenty-four hours.[10]

On October 5th, Carleton's navy set forth. The governor, a self-styled vice-admiral, was on the *Maria*, less powerful than the *Inflexible*, but the better sailor. At the other end of Lake Champlain, Benedict Arnold's principal strength was three eight-gun schooners, and a ten-gun sloop, all captured the previous year. He had also constructed ten sixty-foot gondolas, flat-bottomed, open craft each with a twelve-pounder in the bow and two nine-pounders amid-ships; three galleys, each with six to eight cannon, some being eighteen- or twenty-four-pounders. Arnold lacked a large number of carpenters, tools were scarce, and seasoned wood unavailable. To build these vessels at all was a magnificent achievement.[11]

Arnold had anchored his vessels almost halfway down the lake, in a channel between the west coast of Lake Champlain and Valcour Island. This was, in effect, a cul-de-sac because the northern end was blocked by reefs and shoals. The channel was so narrow that the enemy, other than small gunboats, could only enter in a line, one following another. Arnold's ships, each held by bow and stern anchors, formed a crescent shape so that the fire of the entire fleet could be concentrated on the British as they came into the channel, one by one. This tactic compensated for the fact that his firepower was inferior to that of his opponents.

On October 11th, the British sailed up the east coast of the lake, passing the channel without sighting the Americans. The wind was light, and progress was slow. Arnold sent out the *Royal Savage* and his three galleys, the *Washington, Trumbull* and *Congress*, in the hope of catching some of the laggards. Sighting the enemy, the British turned around and headed for the channel. The American galleys retreated into the channel under oars. The *Royal Savage*, which could not be rowed, was slow in making any way. When fired on by the British gunboats, the crew ran the sloop aground.

The *Carleton* was the first to reach the channel and received a terrific pounding. Out of control, it would have sunk had not two British longboats towed it out of range. Toward evening, the *Inflexible* reached the channel, and its cannonades were devastating. The *Philadelphia* was soon awash, and the *Washington* was partially dismantled. The *Congress* began to take in water steadily, although the crew kept firing, Arnold himself helping to aim the cannon.

By now it was twilight. The British withdrew and anchored off the coast of Valcour Island, expecting to resume the engagement the next day. Arnold realized that if he stayed in the channel, he would lose every one of his ships. Fortunately for him, a mist arose in the evening, and he was able to row his vessels out of the channel without being seen or heard by the enemy. When the British stood to at dawn, there was no American fleet. Carleton was furious.[12] He got under way, intending to follow Arnold up the lake. But the wind was southerly and light, so that there was no contact between the contestants that day.

On the morning of the 13th, aided by a strong northeasterly wind, Carleton caught up with Arnold's crippled fleet some fifteen miles beyond Valcour Island. The *Washington* had to strike its colors, the captain, Brigadier-General David Waterbury, and his soldier-sailors surrendering. Some American ships were sunk. Others were driven ashore and set on fire. Arnold personally burned the *Congress*. Altogether, fourteen of his seventeen vessels were sunk, burned or captured. One schooner, one sloop, and the *Trumbull* reached Ticonderoga, carrying Arnold and the survivors. The British loss, aside from severe damage sustained by the *Carleton*, was one gunboat blown up.[13]

After the annihilation of the American fleet, General Riedesel, on board the captured *Washington*, wrote his wife: "General Carleton fought with the fleet like a hero. He spared the married men as much as possible."[14] In his memoirs Riedesel wrote about the naval battle: "General Carleton received a slight wound in the head from a splinter torn up by a ball."[15]

Anburey writes:

> On board the *Maria* was General Carleton, who had a very narrow escape, a cannon shot passing close by him as he was giving directions to an officer, and which the General with the coolness and intrepidity that so much distinguished his character, took no notice of, but turning round, gave his orders with as much composure as if he had been in the most perfect state of security.[16]

During the first thirty years of Carleton's army life he had led his troops in battle, taking as much risk as any of his soldiers. This accounts for his being three times wounded. In the fighting during 1775, Carleton remained safely behind the battle lines. Probably he realized that if he were killed, no one could take his place and Quebec would fall. It was his duty to avoid danger to himself. However, Carleton did lead the troops at St. Roch and in the Battle of Lake Champlain he risked his life just as much as any sailor or soldier did. There were good army officers like Riedesel and Burgoyne with him. He was no longer alone and irreplaceable; others could step into his shoes. Also Carleton loved to inspire his men and enjoyed the thrill of battle.

Colonel Trumbull, one of Arnold's senior officers, wrote of the aftermath of the battle:

> As soon as the action was over, Carleton gave orders to the surgeons of his own troops to treat the wounded prisoners with the same care as they did his own men. He then ordered that all the prisoners should be immediately brought aboard his ship, where he first treated them to a drink of grog, and then spoke kindly to them, praised the bravery of their conduct, regretted that it had not been displayed in the service of their lawful Sovereign, and offered to send them home.[17]

The British fleet sailed on to the southern end of Lake Champlain and anchored within three miles of Fort Ticonderoga. A few days later a number of rowboats approached Ticonderoga under a flag of truce. They carried one hundred and six American prisoners whom Carleton was releasing on parole. According to Colonel Trumbull, the prisoners, warm in their praises of Carleton, were not permitted to mingle with their fellow Americans. Trumbull and General Horatio Gates were afraid that the morale of the soldiers at Ticonderoga would be impaired if they talked with the jubilant parolees. The released prisoners were sent immediately to their homes.[18]

Carleton wrote Lord George Germain, the new secretary of state for the colonies, a concise description of the battle, with a list of ships captured or destroyed. It was the middle of October, and the long, cruel Canadian winter was not far away. Carleton ended his letter: "The season is so far advanced that I cannot pretend to inform your Lordship whether anything further can be done this year."[19]

Carleton reconnoitered Ticonderoga. The fortress was manned by about seventy-five hundred troops, some of whom were new recruits, some the remnants of Sullivan's defeated army.[20] The garrison consisted solely of effectives; the sick had been transported south.[21] Due to the approach of winter, Carleton was unable to undertake a lengthy siege; either he captured Ticonderoga right away, or he left it alone. He consulted his senior officers—Burgoyne, Riedesel and Phillips—but none was confident that the fort could be taken by storm. Thinking the defending force larger than it was, Carleton decided to retire.[22]

Farther north, the Americans had burned every building at Crown Point, until only stone walls were standing. Carleton toyed with the idea of rebuilding this fort, but gave up that idea. He did not have the time to make it a stronghold, and the supply problem would have been difficult. Carleton withdrew to Montreal, leaving a garrison, strong and well supplied, at St. Jean.

Late in May of that year, Carleton had written Maria and asked her to come back to Quebec as soon as possible.[23] Early in August, she and her three children sailed for Canada on the *Diamond*. Travelling with Maria was her elder sister, Anne, whom the reader will remember had married Major Christopher Carleton, now an aide to his uncle. The long tedious voyage came to an end with the *Diamond*, faced with contrary winds, anchored off Kamouraska, on the south bank of the St. Lawrence some one hundred and fifty miles from Quebec. Maria, impatient at the further delay, persuaded the captain of the *Diamond* to put herself, her three children, and her sister ashore. They then drove over a primitive road through the desolate countryside to Lévis, where they crossed the river to Quebec.[24] There was no husband to greet her at the Château; Carleton was still on Lake Champlain. Maria, who had not seen her husband for over a year, promptly drove to Montreal. There, in early November, the two were reunited.[25]

Maria had brought with her a new honor for Carleton. He was now Sir Guy. In June, the cabinet had recommended to George III that, for his successful defence of Quebec, Carleton be made a Knight of the Bath, at that time a most esteemed order of knighthood. On July 6th, the King had given Maria an audience, conferring the knighthood upon her husband *in absentia*. He then handed Maria the red ribbon and insignia, telling her that he would dispense for the present with the ceremony wherein he tapped with his sword the kneeling subject.

It was not until late on Friday, November 15th that the Carletons returned to Quebec and the Château. There, waiting for Maria, was a surprise. Carleton had bought her a welcome home gift: a bright new carryall, seating four, drawn by one horse.[26] Maria could drive this carriage herself, or she could have the coachman drive her, she and a friend sitting on the back seat.[27]

Sir Guy and Lady Maria celebrated New Year's Eve by giving a dinner for sixty guests at the Château St. Louis. This was followed by a grand ball. They were also celebrating the anniversary of the successful defence of the city.[28]

CHAPTER 12

Governor Carleton versus
Lord George Germain

In November 1775, Lord Dartmouth resigned as secretary of state, his place being taken by Lord George Germain.[1] A bitter feud soon developed between Carleton and Germain.

Carleton's antipathy for Germain went all the way back to August 1759, and the battle of Minden, when a British army of forty-five thousand fought a French army of some sixty-five thousand. When the French eventually began to retreat in disorder, Germain was ordered to advance his cavalry and ride down the enemy. The order was repeated, but Germain still made no move. In all probability, had Germain obeyed orders and promptly attacked, the French would have been either destroyed or taken prisoner. As it was, a good many of them got away.

In a court-martial, Germain was convicted of disobedience, adjudged "unfit to serve his Majesty in any military capacity whatever," and cashiered. Why Germain refused to obey orders is, even today, unclear.

The conduct of Germain at Minden would have been known to Carleton from the Duke of Richmond, who had fought in the battle, and also from General Albemarle, under whom Carleton had served at the siege of Havana, and who had been one of the judges who had convicted Germain. Carleton may well have thought it was demeaning to be supervised by Lord George Germain, a man whom many referred to as the "Coward of Minden." The distaste, however, was mutual. Germain first exhibited his disapproval of the governor of Quebec by being the one member of the cabinet who was against Carleton's being created a Knight of the Bath. Germain's bitterness toward Carleton increased. The King wrote his prime minister, Lord North, on December 13th, 1776: "That there is a great prejudice perhaps not unaccompanied with rancour in a certain breast [Germain's] against Governor Carleton is so manifest to whomever has heard the subject mentioned that it would be idle to say any more than that is a fact."[2] Carleton received notice of Germain's appointment in May 1776, and shortly thereafter the first clash occurred between the two.

On June 1st, a Lieutenant-Colonel Gabriel Christie arrived in Quebec with a commission as quartermaster-general of the army in Canada. Christie was a friend of Germain's, had been his supporter at the Minden court-martial, and Germain had arranged for Christie to have the post. However, a few weeks previously, Carleton had appointed as quartermaster-general his younger brother, Thomas. This appointment had been made with the approval of Lord Barrington, secretary of war, and with at least the tacit approval of the King. Germain was doubtless unaware of this appointment. Carleton wrote Germain that he would not discharge his brother and would not accept Christie "until his Majesty's pleasure thereupon should be satisfied."[3] Germain had to accept the situation: the King was not going to overrule his secretary of war and his commander-in-chief in Canada. Germain did appeal to Burgoyne to use his influence with Carleton so that Colonel Christie would have employment of some kind in the army. Burgoyne wrote back: "I find Major Carleton acting as Quarter-Master General. I perceived also in my first conversation with the General [Carleton] that he was determined not to employ Colonel Christie. The General, I understand, means to request that they never serve in the same army."[4] The unemployed Colonel Christie returned to England.

Carleton's motives in selecting his brother were mixed. Certainly he wanted to help Thomas' career. Carleton also wanted as quartermaster-general a man whose integrity was beyond question. Carleton, who had been both Wolfe's and Albemarle's quartermaster-general, knew full well the graft possibilities of the position. Even if Carleton had been satisfied with Christie, it is hard to imagine him discharging his own brother. The governor would not have been embarrassed by the nepotism involved. In the eighteenth century, nepotism was considered a virtue, and a man in power was expected to favor members of his family.

The altercation between Carleton and Germain over Colonel Christie was followed by continual wrangling over other appointments. Germain expected to select judges, which was his right. Carleton wanted to make his own recommendations and expected Germain simply to accept them. One man Germain appointed as judge, Edward Southhouse, Carleton described as "totally ignorant of the laws, manners, customs, and language of the Canadians."[5] Here, Germain seems to have made an unfortunate appointment, but it was an exception. Most of his choices were suitable, even admirable. Carleton objected to the appointment of Peter Livius as chief justice for a different reason. "This gentleman," wrote Carleton, "is commissioned to be judge of the Vice-Admiralty court of the Province and thereby supercedes the surrogate I had appointed. And as by the former of his offices [judge of the Court of Common Pleas] that gentleman is under the necessity of residing at Montreal, he must execute the Admiralty jurisdiction by his deputy at Quebec."[6]

The system of deputy judgeships was subject to abuse. The deputy sometimes received only part of his salary, the man whose place he was taking getting the balance. There is no evidence that Livius was dishonest or that Germain was trying to promote corruption. As always, Carleton was trying to limit or abolish fees but Germain was not interested in reform. His response was that "abolishing fees had not been agreed upon and it would have slowed up the course of justice."[7] Carleton's letters to Germain were bitter. Germain's correspondence was, on the whole, even-tempered; he seems to have been trying to mollify Carleton—without giving an inch.

Carleton's and Germain's quarrels were not merely over which of them should make decisions as to appointments. They contested the conduct of the war. Carleton had written Germain on May 14th, 1776, giving an account of the siege and the relief of Quebec. On June 21st, Germain acknowledged this letter politely, but then made the following remarks:

> I must necessarily regret that you have neither specified the actual force of the rebels, nor communicated the intelligence which you may have received, or the conjectures which you have formed relative to their intentions. Your silence also as to your intended operations and the present disposition of the Canadians is much to be lamented, because the ignorance in which you have left me, concerning these matters, renders it impossible for me to convey to you at present any further instructions.[8]

Germain was implying, somewhat tactlessly and superciliously, that Carleton needed instructions from London. Carleton took at least the second sentence as insulting. He caustically replied:

> I must beg leave to observe that I could have had but one great object in view when I wrote the letter your Lordship alludes to, the expulsion of the rebels from the Province in the most rapid manner possible, which was happily executed long before I could profit by any instructions your Lordship might think necessary to favor me with.
>
> The next operation was to establish a naval force on Lake Champlain, to command the navigation of that lake and render the passage of troops in batteaux secure, in order to pursue the rebels into their own provinces; neither in this could your Lordship have afforded me any assistance, had I required it in the letter.[9]

Germain was technically in the right. A governor—or a general—serving in a colony had to follow the orders of the secretary of the colonies. The alternative was to resign. In practice, however, the situation was entirely different. The distance between London and Quebec was too great, the time lag in receiving instructions too long, and London's ignorance of Canadian conditions too extensive, to make supervision by Germain—or by anyone—efficient or effective. Moreover, Carleton had been making policies and appointments on his own for the last ten years. The earlier secretaries—Shelburne, Hillsborough, and Dartmouth—had taken the attitude that they should try to help carry out Carleton's wishes rather than give him orders. Carleton expected Germain to do likewise. Regardless of Minden, the two men would never have got along amicably.

111

Against the background of this feud is the rise of John Burgoyne, who was serving as major-general under Carleton. Now in his fifty-fourth year, "Gentleman Johnny Burgoyne" had had a distinguished career in the army. He was also the author of a play, *Maid of Oakes*, produced by the great David Garrick in the Drury Lane Theatre in London. He was a member of Parliament, belonged to all the best clubs, and loved to gamble, in the tradition of an English gentleman. His acquaintances probably included the entire cabinet and half the peers of the realm. In 1775, Burgoyne had served in Boston under Gage. There, he had had no opportunity to distinguish himself. Disgusted, he returned to London and secured the position of second-in-command under Carleton. Again, Burgoyne had no opportunity to win glory. Burgoyne now wanted an independent command. With it, he believed, he could win both battles and renown.

At the beginning of November 1776, Burgoyne sailed for England. The first person he called on was Germain, who had startling news for him. The cabinet had decided that Quebec was to be the jumping-off point for an invasion of the American colonies, an invasion directed at Albany, New York, and, ultimately, New York City. Further, the cabinet had suggested that Burgoyne lead this invasion, not Carleton. Letters so instructing the governor of Quebec had been entrusted to a packet, the *Swallow*, which, due to extremely bad weather, had been unable to reach the St. Lawrence and had returned to England.[10]

It was Germain who had persuaded the cabinet to nominate Burgoyne. Germain had argued that it was necessary for Carleton, as governor, to remain in Quebec, pacify the Province, and implement the Quebec Act. Furthermore, Germain was adamant that Sir William Howe must not be replaced as commander-in-chief in New York City. Carleton outranked Howe, so if Carleton turned up in New York City, he would automatically become commander-in-chief in North America. (Howe had reminded London that he was outranked by Carleton and had stated that he would be glad to serve under Carleton.[11]) These two were acquaintances of long standing, both having taken part in the struggle to win Canada, the capture of Belle-Ile-en-Mer, and the taking of Havana. They respected each other. There is also evidence suggesting that Howe did not feel up to his command.[12] Be that as it may, Howe was a popular personality. The cabinet that had replaced Gage with Howe did not now want to replace Howe with Carleton.

Germain had succeeded in preventing Carleton from leading a military expedition into New York. In February 1777, he thought he had the power to replace Carleton as governor of Quebec. The King put a stop this, writing Lord North on February 24th: "He [Germain] wants Carleton to be recalled and I have thrown cold water on that and Lord Suffolk and Lord Gower will oppose it at your meeting."[13]

Burgoyne had an audience with the King and called upon various cabinet members. He does not seem to have criticized Carleton. He did not have to. The leadership of the American expedition was his. He discovered that Carleton's prestige had dropped due to the failure to capture Ticonderoga. Ticonderoga was an emotional symbol. In early 1775, the garrison of redcoats at Ticonderoga was a reminder to the Indians of the British presence, which protected Canadians and Americans alike. To the British, the seizure of Ticonderoga was an act of banditry. They were ashamed that the fort had been taken so easily, that not a shot had been fired in its defence. There was a strong feeling that Carleton should at least have made an effort to recapture Ticonderoga and thus restore the nation's honor.

Burgoyne had brought with him a plan, prepared by Carleton, for the capture of Ticonderoga early in 1777, followed by a move into New England. Burgoyne showed this plan to Germain and others, who were enthusiastic. On February 28th, Burgoyne presented his war strategy—based upon Carleton's plan—to Germain. There was, however, one important difference. Albany was the ultimate objective. Howe was to send an army from New York City up the Hudson River to Albany, where the two invading forces would unite. Any American forces between them would be crushed, and the rebellious colonies would be split in half. King and cabinet approved this simple strategy.

On May 6th, 1777, the *Apollo* reached Quebec, bringing Major-General John Burgoyne and, in the care of the ship's captain, fourteen letters for Carleton. (Four of the fourteen were Germain's letters, dated August 22nd, 1776, which could not be delivered the previous year.) One letter, dated March 26th, 1777, ordered the governor to remain in Canada with three thousand seven hundred troops.[14] Carleton was informed that General Burgoyne, his junior in rank, had been given command of seven thousand troops and ordered to invade the colony of New York. Further, Burgoyne was not to be under Carleton's command; he was to answer for his actions to Howe. The order giving Burgoyne command of the punitive expedition was, for Carleton, a *fait accompli* because Burgoyne was to start off the following month. If, by some miracle, Carleton's letters persuaded the cabinet to change its mind, it would be impossible to reverse the orders. Any letter reversing the orders would reach Quebec far too late.

In another letter of March 26th, Germain criticized Carleton for not having besieged Ticonderoga, for not having established a base at Crown Point, and for withdrawing from Lake Champlain. Carleton replied: "Any officer entrusted with supreme command ought, upon the spot, to see what was most expedient to be done better than a great General at three thousand miles distance." The "great General," of course, was a barbed reference to Germain's behavior at Minden.[15]

Germain also charged that Carleton's failure to capture Ticonderoga had released troops to attack Howe. To this, Carleton replied:

> If your Lordship means the affair of Trenton [New Jersey], a little military reasoning might prove the rebels required no reinforcement, from any part, to cut off that corps, if unconnected and alone; the force they employed upon that occasion clearly demonstrated this. Without my troubling your Lordship with any reasoning upon the matter, a little attention to the strength of General Howe's army will, I hope, convince you that, connected and in a situation to support each other, they might have defended themselves tho' all the rebels from Ticonderoga had reinforced Mr. Washington's army.[16]

Acidic though Carleton's words were, his argument was unassailable. Washington had crossed the ice-strewn Delaware River with twenty-four hundred farmers turned soldiers and taken prisoner nearly one thousand Hessian professional soldiers.[17]

Howe had, in nearby New York City, over twenty-five thousand veterans. Carleton continued:

> In spite of every obstruction a greater marine was built and equipt; a greater marine force was defeated than ever appeared on Lake Champlain before; two brigades were taken across and remained at Crown Point until the 2nd of November, for the sole purpose of drawing off the attention of the Rebels from Mr. Howe and to facilitate his victories during the remainder of the campaign. Nature had then put an end to ours. His winter quarters, I confess, I had never thought of covering; it was supposed, 'tis true, that was the army favored by your Lordship and in which you put your trust, yet I never could imagine while an army to the southward found it necessary to finish their campaign, and to go into winter quarters, your Lordship could possibly expect troops so far north, should continue their operations lest Howe should be disturbed during the winter. If that great army near the sea-coast had their quarters assaulted, what could your Lordship expect would be the fate of a small corps detached into the heart of the rebel country in that season? For those things I am so severely censored by your Lordship, and this is the first reason assigned why the command of the troops is taken from me.[18]

Carleton was making strong accusations. In another letter to Germain, he was quite blunt: "When your Lordship was announced minister and distributor of all favors, it was then rumored your Lordship's intentions were to remove me from this command the first opportunity, in the meantime you would render it as irksome to me as possible by every kind of slight, disregard and censure, occasion and events might render plausible."[19]

Carleton read Germain's letters, presumably the day they arrived. When he knew he could not change anything, why did Carleton write such antagonistic replies? Coupled with his pride and haughtiness, Carleton had an inability to mask his personal feelings. He was mortified and bitter that London had bypassed him in favor of a subordinate officer. His sarcastic replies certainly read as if they were written immediately, in a white heat of anger. If this surmise is correct, Carleton delayed dating them and mailing them until two weeks later. He probably hesitated to send the letters until he had made up his mind whether or not he was going to resign.

When he did decide to resign, his decision was undoubtedly influenced by deep disappointment. He surely felt that he was hated by Germain, that all these insults were but the first steps in an effort to discredit him, and that it would be only a matter of time before he would be dismissed from the governorship. On July 1st, George III received word that Carleton had resigned. However, Lord North insisted that Carleton continue as governor until a successor reached Quebec. The King, who punctiliously noted time as well as date, wrote Lord North on July 2nd "at 56 minutes past 5:00 p.m.": "Anyone that will for an instant suppose himself in the situation of Sir Guy Carleton, must feel that the resigning the Government of Quebec is the only dignified part, though I think as things were situated the ordering him to remain in the Province was a necessary measure, yet it must be owned to be mortifying to a soldiers."[20]

Germain picked Lieutenant-General Frederick Haldimand as the new governor of Quebec. He was an experienced officer and possessed some knowledge of Canada, inasmuch as he had served under Amherst when Montreal was captured in 1760. Late in September, Haldimand sailed on a frigate leaving for Canada. Contrary winds forced the vessel to turn back, and it was not until 1778 that he reached Quebec. Carleton had to remain at his post as governor of the Province for another year.

Carleton ordered General Riedesel to be Burgoyne's second-in command. In making this appointment, he wrote London: "It is my intention to provide everything for this detachment with the same care and attention to the good of the service as if I was to command it myself."[21] One of the ways to help Burgoyne was to raise a militia force. In March 1777, Carleton had had the council pass an ordinance making service in the militia obligatory for every male between the ages of sixteen and sixty. Only *seigneurs*, government employees, clergy, and *voyageurs* were exempted from such service. Those who refused to serve were to be punished: for the first offence, a fine; for the second, a month in jail. The *habitants*, of course, did not want to serve in the militia, but there was no organized or armed resistance; they just grumbled endlessly. They were drilled and they labored on corvées (unpaid work on roads or fortifications), but getting them to fight was another matter. Finding men to join Burgoyne, men who would invade the American colonies, who might be away from Quebec for a year or more, became a near impossibility. *Habitants* refused to serve; or they joined up and then deserted. Carleton enlisted, drafted and organized some eight hundred militiamen. By the time Burgoyne reached Saratoga in New York, desertions had reduced this number by half. Three months later, there were scarcely three dozen militiamen still with Burgoyne. When he needed a thousand drivers for his supply carts, Carleton could only supply a hundred and seventy-five.

Burgoyne and his senior officers were aware of Carleton's overwhelming difficulties. In August 1777, Lord North wrote to Carleton: "All the letters from General Burgoyne and other officers of the northern army are full of the warmest acknowledgement of the cordial, zealous, and effectual assistance they have received from you." [22] Anburey reports:

> People in England, whose rapidity of ideas keeps pace with their good wishes, little imagine that the distance from this place [Crown Point] to Canada is ninety miles, therefore the time it takes to bring forward stores is necessarily considerable. To the great praise of General Carleton, however, very little delay has yet occurred, for he forwards the stores very expeditiously, and however ill treated many people suppose he is, or however he may conceive himself so, in not having the command of this army, after being the Commander in the last campaign, he lets no pique or ill will divert him from doing all the real service in his power to his King and country. [23]

Carleton may only have been doing his duty in helping Burgoyne, but the two men remained friends. Carleton's ire was vented on Germain, never on Burgoyne.

The plan for Burgoyne to invade from the north, sailing up the Richelieu and over Lake Champlain and then marching to Albany, had been contingent upon Howe's sending an army up the Hudson River to Albany. On June 10th, Carleton received a letter from Howe stating that he could not detach a corps to operate up the Hudson, as he would be in Pennsylvania at the time that Burgoyne reached Albany. [24] Here was a dangerous

117

mix-up, a fatal misunderstanding that Carleton immediately relayed to Burgoyne. Burgoyne, however, was so optimistic about his plan, so confident of his own abilities, that he was unconcerned by Howe's decision not to help. What Carleton's reactions were we do not know. He had done everything he could to assist Burgoyne.[25]

Burgoyne set sail from St. Jean using the same fleet that Carleton had built the year before, and also two vessels that Carleton had captured from the Americans, the galley *Washington* and the gondola *Jersey*.[26] The fleet moved slowly, reaching Ticonderoga on July 1st. On July 5th, its American occupants prudently evacuated the fort. Carleton's failure to capture Ticonderoga the previous fall delayed Burgoyne only four days.

On July 11th, Burgoyne wrote Carleton, asking him to garrison Ticonderoga. Carleton replied July 19th, 1777:

> I received your letter of the 11th instant in which you submit the expediency to me of supplying from Canada a garrison for Ticonderoga.
>
> I cannot think it has been left in my power to send any more troops out of the Province and I am persuaded in reading Lord George Germain's letter to me of the 20th of March last, marked separate, you must be of the same opinion. He not only orders those I am to send and those I am to keep, but points out where the latter are to be posted, and you must observe the Ile-aux-Noix is the most advanced on your side.
>
> As to the great division of the troops, his Lordship leaves no room for our reasoning, but issues orders, and I might with as great propriety have disregarded the whole as part of his letter. Whatever I may think of his Lordship as an officer or as a statesman, I must respect his office as Secretary of State signifying to me the King's pleasure, he must be obeyed . . . .
>
> I am very ready to acknowledge that I think the whole of our minister's measure, civil and military, very strange. Indeed to me they appear incomprehensible unless they turn upon private enmity and resentment. I was so convinced of this that I lost no time in entreating the King's permission to resign and return home.[27]

Burgoyne left eight hundred and fifty of his soldiers under General Powell to garrison Ticonderoga, which reduced his army by just over ten per cent.

A couple of months later, there occurred an exchange of letters of no importance, except that they show how Carleton's mind worked in military affairs. Powell wrote asking Carleton for advice. Powell knew by now that Burgoyne was in trouble and he feared that the Americans would attack Fort Ticonderoga. He wanted to know whether he should abandon the fort and retreat. Carleton replied that "he was too ignorant of the strengths and weaknesses of the post" to advise and that Powell must use his own judgement. Then Carleton continued:

> I can only recommend to you not to balance between two opposite measures whereby you may be disabled from following the one or the other with advantage, but that either you prepare with vigor to put the place in such a situation as to be able to make the longest and most resolute defence, or that you prepare in time to abandon it with all the stores while your retreat may be certain. Your own sense will tell you that this latter would be a most pernicious measure if there be still hope of General Burgoyne's coming to your post.[28]

Carleton never believed in half measures, whether in attack or defence. Actually, Powell abandoned Ticonderoga before the snows settled in, retreating with his stores intact.

Burgoyne, plunging through wilderness country to Albany, encountered fourteen thousand Americans under Gates and Arnold, was surrounded, and outfought. The news sifted back to Carleton. On November 6th, he advised Germain that he had receive no official information, but from all the intelligence he could gather, Burgoyne had had to surrender his entire army. Carleton, of course, took the usual potshots at Germain. He ended his letter with the hope that his successor would arrive soon, since Lord George Germain had manifested to all the world that he no longer trusted his governor to execute the duties of his appointment.[29]

Six days later, Carleton had confirmation that Burgoyne had surrendered at Saratoga all that was left of his army. Carleton wrote him, offered sympathy, and ended his letter: "This unfortunate event, it is to be hoped, will in future prevent ministers from pretending to direct operations of war in a country at 3,000 miles distance, of which they have so little knowledge as not to be able to distinguish between good, bad, or interested advice, or to give positive orders in matters which from their nature are ever upon the change."[30]

As 1777 drew to its close, there were only two events that gave Carleton any satisfaction. In August, Maria gave birth to their fourth child, a girl, who was named after her mother.[31] On August 29th, the King promoted Carleton to the rank of lieutenant-general.[32]

The Carletons marked the passing of the old year by attending, at Minuit's Tavern, a supper and ball given by the officers of the Quebec militia. In a militia uniform, and wearing his insignia as Knight of the Bath, Sir Guy arrived at six-thirty, with Maria on his arm.[33] At this low point in his career, we may wonder what Carleton had to look forward to in the coming new year.

CHAPTER 13

Out of Office

In January 1777, Carleton had called the first of what was to be a series of meetings of the full council and, altogether, eighteen ordinances had been passed.[1] (Carleton's fears that he might not have a majority were needless. If a member proposed something that Carleton did not like, the threat of a veto disposed of the proposal.)

The ordinances were mostly re-enactments of earlier ones that had been superseded by the Quebec Act. However, in many cases, the re-enactments were improvements. For instance, it was stipulated for the first time that every writ of summons had to be made in the language of the defendant. Hence, as a practical matter, it was printed in both French and English. A new ordinance was passed regulating the public markets in Quebec and Montreal. These opened at six a.m. in the summer and eight a.m. in the winter. The problem was to prevent wholesalers from buying up in advance all of a particular product, say chickens, and then charging an exorbitant price. The ordinance stipulated that no produce could be purchased before the market opened and that no wholesaler could make any purchase during the first three hours after the opening. The penalty was the imposition of a £5 fine on the buyer. (The seller, who was usually a *habitant*, was not considered liable.)

Another ordinance dealt with the repair of public highways and bridges in the Province. In their retreat, the Americans had destroyed many bridges, and the roads were in bad shape anyway. Corvées of militiamen were organized to expedite the road work. Where a road ran alongside or through a farm, the owner was theoretically responsible for its upkeep, but one running at some length through a farm could make the burden too great for any one man, and a corvée had to help out. By this ordinance, the main road had to be thirty feet wide, and a minor crossroad twenty feet. Each had to be fenced, with ditches alongside to aid drainage. The fences were intended to keep carriages from sliding into the ditches, and also to restrain hogs—often wild ones—from damaging the road. There were continual complaints over the havoc the hogs caused. As one historian noted, "The pigs of Canada were considered a vile degenerate race."[2] As winter neared, the sides of roads had to be marked with long poles. Then, after every snowstorm, a passage between the poles, wide enough for two sleighs to pass, had to be made. In the interests of public safety, there were detailed instructions covering the construction of bridges. For example, the main beams had to be of cedar, and the width of the bridge had to be eighteen feet. Bridges were not covered, but they had to have a three-foot-high fence on either side.

Earlier meetings of the council had been held at the Château St. Louis, with Carleton in the chair. By 1778, the procedure had changed. Carleton would deliver an address of welcome at the opening formal session, now held in the chamber of the Bishop's Palace. Then Lieutenant-Governor Cramahé took the chair for later meetings. Although Carleton retired to the background, he kept, through Cramahé, a firm control over everything the council did.

All the ordinances were passed by the full council, as the Quebec Act required, but Carleton continued to use the board of council for such executive functions as appointments and the auditing of public accounts. It would have been cumbersome to have used the whole council for such functions. He also used the board of council to consider all proposed ordinances before they were introduced at council meetings. In other words, Carleton used the board of council as an executive committee. In using the board of council, Carleton was acting legally—as far as the King's instructions were concerned. He was, however, acting illegally in terms of the Quebec Act, which made no mention of such a board.

Carleton's contact with London took on a new dimension in the person of Peter Livius, who had been a judge in the colony of New Hampshire. While there, he had accused the governor of financial irregularities in his administration, with the result that Livius lost his judgeship. In this Livius was probably in the right. Livius, a Germain nominee, had been appointed judge of the Court of Common Pleas in Montreal. In May 1777, Livius was appointed chief justice, replacing Hey. This automatically gave Livius a seat on the council. At first, Carleton seemed to get along satisfactorily with the new councillor. During the early summer of 1777, when Carleton was in Montreal trying to help Burgoyne, Cramahé, the acting governor, got into an altercation with the chief justice. Cramahé had ordered army authorities to arrest a tanner named Giroux and his wife, both of whom had been accused of making seditious utterances. Cramahé put the couple in a military prison so that they could not be released on bail and thus would be unable to continue their activities. The arrest and imprisonment by military, rather than civil, authorities aroused Livius. He demanded that the two prisoners be brought before him on the ground that their alleged crime was a civil one. In an exchange of acrimonious letters, Cramahé refused Livius' demand. When Carleton returned, he decided that Livius was right, that the offence was a civil not a military one, and that the accused should appear before Livius.

Livius, honest and beholden to no one, was a good judge, but he was a pernickety lawyer—egotistical, stubborn, unwilling to compromise, and lacking in tact. He was not afraid to speak his mind and, once on the council, became the leader of those opposed to Carleton's benevolent despotism. Toward the end of 1777, Livius called on Carleton at the Château St. Louis. Livius wanted him to suggest to the full council that there should be a discussion of, and a vote on, whether the English minority should have trial by jury in civil cases. In addition, Livius proposed a discussion of and vote on an elected legislature. (The King's instructions had told Carleton to do just this.) Finally, Livius asked Carleton to cease running the council through the board of council. He claimed that this was illegal. Carleton categorically refused Livius' requests. Livius accomplished nothing except to make a bitter enemy of the governor.[4]

On April 8th, 1778, at a full meeting of council, Livius introduced a motion: "That as the council has not hitherto had communication of his Majesty's instructions for the making and passing of laws in the Province, his Excellency be humbly requested to communicate to them such royal instructions as he might have received relative to the legislation of the Province." This motion was discussed on April 11th and, when brought to a vote, was defeated eleven to five.[5]

On April 23rd, Livius introduced a motion stating that the meetings of "the Privy Council" (the board of council) were illegal and humbly prayed that "His Excellency, the Governor, would be pleased to order convenient remedy."[6] Discussion of this motion was postponed until the 25th. On that date, the councillors gathered. Cramahé in the chair called the meeting to order, and then prorogued the meeting upon the orders of the governor. Five days later, Livius received a note from the governor's office to the effect that he, Livius, had been removed from his position as chief justice. Astounded, Livius asked to be informed as to the accusation. He received a verbal message that there would be no answer to his request.

Carleton was dealing with Livius as he had dealt with Irving and Mabane twelve years earlier. However, as Livius' seat on the council resulted from his position as chief justice, the only way of dismissing him from the council was to discharge him as chief justice. Carleton wrote candidly to Germain about the matter. The governor made no citicism of Livius as a jurist or as chief justice. He simply reported that Livius was a troublesome fellow whom he had to dismiss to preserve discipline in the colony and ensure peace for his successor.[7]

Burgoyne's surrender at Saratoga raised the spectre that the Americans might attempt another invasion of Canada. Carleton had thirty armed vessels on Lake Champlain and the Richelieu River and felt confident that he could command that route during the coming spring and summer. However, a winter campaign could not be entirely ruled out. After all, Montgomery and Arnold had attacked Quebec City at the beginning of winter. Carleton ordered Brigadier-General Allan Maclean to adopt a scorched-earth policy and burn every house between St. Jean and the Ile-aux-Noix to make it difficult for the Americans to provision any troops that might, in one way or another, get beyond Lake Champlain.

Despite Carleton's failure to obtain for Burgoyne militiamen who would fight, he continued to enforce the law that all qualified men must join the militia, undergo training, or work on corvées. In applying the law, he was as considerate as possible. Corvées of city dwellers were kept to a minimum, and were sometimes subsidized. Blankets and shoes were issued to militiamen. Carleton also paid bonuses to those who had served loyally during the previous campaign: £16 to sergeants, £12 to wounded men, £8 to combatants, £4 to non-combatant drivers or laborers. Widows received £40, wives of prisoners £16. Each widow or wife also received a pair of shoes, a pair of mittens, and three and a half yards of bed blanket.[8] (The wives of *habitants* usually made their own clothes, but shoes, mittens and blankets usually came from Britain.) These bonuses made joining the militia more attractive, and Carleton's efforts showed signs of success. By the end of the year, militia captains were reporting that a substantial number of Québécois would fight in defence of the Province.

Toward the end of February 1778, Carleton received information that Major-General the Marquis de Lafayette was going to head an invasion of Canada in the early spring. How would Quebec react to a Frenchman leading an army of liberation? On March 5th, two months before he expected to be relieved of his command, Carleton went to St. Jean to satisfy himself that it was defensible and to confer with his officers and militia captains as to how best to turn back Lafayette. As it happened, Carleton's inspection of St. Jean was unnecessary. The Continental Congress had authorized an attack on Canada, but when Lafayette reached Albany in February 1778, he discovered that General Gates had failed to organize an army, and the invasion was cancelled.

In May, Carleton was notified that George III had appointed him governor of Charlemont in Ireland. This position, with its nominal duties, brought a pension of £1,000 a year that would continue through the lives of his wife and two eldest sons. Germain threatened to resign when he heard that the King proposed to give Carleton this lucrative sinecure. The King explained to Lord North on March 3rd that

> I should never have recommended his [Germain's] removal unless with his own goodwill now he will save us all the trouble. The laying it [Germain's possible resignation] on my bequeathing the government of Charlemont is quite absurd and shows the malevolence of his mind. Carleton was highly wrong in permitting his pen to convey such asperity to a Secretary of State but his meritorious defence of Quebec made him a proper object for a military award and as such I could not think of providing for any other General 'till I had repaid the debt his services had a right to claim.[9]

Germain did not resign.

To Carleton, the pension was extremely welcome. It relieved him of any financial burden that might have resulted from the loss of his salary as governor of Quebec. It also meant that he was in the good graces of his sovereign, and could hope for some further career in the service of his country.

On the evening of Friday, June 26th, the frigate *Montreal* carrying the governor-elect, Frederick Haldimand, anchored at Quebec. Haldimand, although an older man and an officer senior to Carleton, seems to have been almost hypnotized by his host's personality. For five days, the two men talked and talked. They spoke in French because Haldimand, Swiss by birth, could scarcely speak English. (As governor, Haldimand followed in Carleton's footsteps. For three years, he governed Quebec through the board of council and only desisted when peremptorily ordered to by London.[10] He refused to be browbeaten by Livius, and denied him access to Carleton's papers.[11]) On July 2nd, when the *Montreal* was ready to return to England, Haldimand came on board and had dinner with Carleton.

The passage of the *Montreal* to Britain was uneventful. Maria, who had boarded the ship a day early to get her four children settled, had become an old hand at shipboard life. In her party was Charles Bailly, a Catholic priest, whom Carleton had obtained as a French tutor for his five-year-old son Guy.[12] Carleton's brother, Lieutenant-Colonel Thomas Carleton, and his nephew and sister-in-law, Major Christopher Carleton and Lady Anne Carleton, remained in Quebec.

Carleton reached London to find that Burgoyne, paroled by the Americans, had been in the city for three months. In the summer of the preceding year, the ruling classes were singing the praises of "Gentleman Johnny Burgoyne." If Carleton had come to London that year, he would have encountered coldness everywhere. But popular opinion is fickle, and in September 1778 all was different. Burgoyne, who had lost his army, was an embarrassment. The King, reacting to public opinion, would not receive him at his levees. People began comparing Burgoyne with Carleton. Carleton had saved Quebec and driven the Americans out of Canada. In his impassive, stiff way, Carleton looked and acted as people expected a general should look and act. Questions began to be asked. Should not Carleton have headed the expedition against Albany? Would not Carleton, perhaps, have won? British officials now had qualms over the way Carleton had been treated. Lord North suggested to Carleton that perhaps Parliament would vote him a pension as compensation for his having been superseded by Burgoyne. Carleton refused to accept any pension that Lord North or the House of Commons might grant him.[13] Carleton's sense of injustice could not be erased by any offer of money. The governorship of Charlemont was in a different category. This had been given by his sovereign as an award for his successful defence of Quebec.

The Opposition tried to lionize Carleton for their own purposes, but his conduct was discreet. He called upon his friends in the Opposition, but he would not permit them to give any receptions or dinners in his honor. He called upon Lord North and others in the cabinet. He had an audience with the King and regularly attended royal levees. Carleton refused to criticize Burgoyne, Howe—who had failed to send troops to Albany to meet Burgoyne—or Lord George Germain. (Carleton did not call upon Germain; he ignored him.) He would not discuss his resignation, although he did say that he would decline to serve in any capacity under the present colonial secretary.

In May 1779, a parliamentary committee was appointed to

inquire into the conduct of General Burgoyne. During his four-hour testimony, Carleton neither criticized Burgoyne nor defended him. Here are some extracts from his testimony:

> Question: "Do you know any circumstances of General Burgoyne's military conduct, while under your command, that you disapproved?"
> Carleton: "I had no reason to disapprove any part of his conduct while under my command."
> Question: "After he had received the letter from General Howe informing him that Howe's aid to Burgoyne would be at most very limited, whether on that information you considered that you had any discretionary power to detain General Burgoyne after that information?"
> Carleton: "I could not change General Burgoyne's orders one tittle, that was my opinion."
> Question: "Should you, if you had been in General Burgoyne's situation and acting under the orders which you knew he received, have thought yourself bound to pursue them implicitly, or at liberty to depart from them?"
> Carleton: "I should have certainly thought myself bound to have observed them to the utmost of my power. What I should have done I really don't know."
> Question: "Do not the orders from the Secretary of State go to the details of the smallest posts within the Province?"
> Carleton: "The letter is before the committee."[14]

Whether Burgoyne's expedition would have been successful under Carleton is problematic. Major-General Riedesel who, along with Burgoyne, had served under Carleton in 1776 and who, under Burgoyne, had served on the ill-fated expedition in 1777 wrote that " . . . a great mistake was undoubtedly made by the British Ministry. Carleton had hitherto worked with energy and success; he knew the army thoroughly and enjoyed the confidence of the officers and men. It was a great risk to remove a man, who was so peculiarly fitted for so important a position with a better cause."[15] These words are somewhat equivocal and must be discounted because of Riedesel's friendship for Carleton. Canadian historian Sir Charles P. Lucas argues:

> Of Carleton's merits as a soldier there can be no question. No one ever gauged a military situation better. No one ever displayed more firmness and courage at a time of crisis, made more of small resources, or showed more self-restraint. But he was more than a

good military leader; he was a statesman of high order, and, had he been given a free hand and supreme control of the British forces and policy in America, he might well have kept the American colonies as he kept Quebec . . . . Above all he had a character above and beyond intrigue. Had he not been ousted by malign influence . . . . [16]

Yet the fact remains that Carleton had recommended the expedition into New York. If Carleton had been given the command, perhaps all the mistakes that Burgoyne made would have been avoided. But, in the opinion of most students of the campaign, the expedition, no matter how well conducted, would have failed. Germain, in depriving Carleton of the command, had unwittingly done him a great favor.

In England, Carleton was confronted with a continuation of the Peter Livius case. On reaching London in September, Livius immediately prepared a memorandum to the King stating that he had been removed from office illegally and without just cause and should be reinstated. The Board of Trade, after considering this memorandum, asked Carleton his reasons for dismissing Livius. Carleton referred the board to his letter to Germain of June 25th in which he had called Livius a "trouble maker." The Board of Trade then suggested that both Carleton and Livius might come before them. Carleton wrote back: "I have not a wish to know what that gentleman has or may say upon the matter, nor have I wish to offer anything further, nor do I consider myself more interested in the event than in any other of like importance to the King's service."[17]

On March 22nd the Board of Trade exonerated Livius. Germain then entered the fray. He may have been sorry for Livius. He may have wanted to harass Carleton. At any rate, he arranged for Livius' dismissal to be referred to a committee of the Privy Council. Carleton was invited to appear before this body but declined in writing:

> I am very sensible of the Lord President's attention but I submit the propriety of the measure to their Lordship's judgement; and leave Mr. Livius to explain his own proceedings in the Legislative Council of the Province, in March and April seventy-eight . . . to his own words I refer their Lordships that from them they may judge, whether it would have proved detrimental to the service,

and to the tranquillity of his Province of Quebec, had Mr. Livius continued Chief Justice during General Haldimand's administration. If not, I can only wish for nothing more ardently than his being immediately reinstated.[18]

On March 29th an order in council cleared Livius of any wrongdoing and ordered his reinstatement. In all of this, Carleton was, by implication, criticized, but somehow no one in the government or the Opposition seemed to blame Carleton—or to care about the matter. Strangely, Livius became a broken man. He fell into debt, suffered health problems and never returned to Quebec.

By the spring of 1782, Carleton had been idle in England for three and a half years. During this period, we only catch glimpses of him. In an attempt to limit graft and corruption, Parliament set up a commission of ten men with authority to inspect and audit the public accounts. To keep the commission non-political, it was stipulated that no member of the commission could be a member of either house of Parliament. Early in May 1780, the Commons, by a vote of 193 to 163, elected Carleton to head this commission[19] On May 19th, 1779 he went through the ceremony of being created a Knight of the Bath. (The knights-elect included General William Howe and, by proxy, General Henry Clinton, who had succeeded Howe as commander-in-chief in North America.) The knights-elect met in the Princess Chapel of Westminster Abbey. In procession, they moved to the Henry VII Chapel, where they were ceremonially installed before members of the Royal Family and various celebrities. That evening, Sir Guy and Lady Maria attended a grand ball at the King's Theatre in Haymarket, a ball given by the new knights. Some one thousand of the nobility and gentry of the kingdom were present.[20]

Carleton had no expectation of seeing Quebec again and yet his thoughts kept returning to the Province. He corresponded with Riedesel, who had remained in Quebec in command of German mercenaries. Three years after Burgoyne's surrender at Saratoga, Riedesel sent from Canada bows and arrows as presents to Carleton's sons.[21] During the years 1779-1780 Maria had given birth to two boys, who were christened William and Lancelot. Both died in infancy. In 1781, the Carletons rented a house in Richmond, Surrey, and there Maria bore their seventh child, a healthy boy named George, who survived all childhood diseases.

In 1780, Carleton could not restrain his curiosity as to how his friend Bishop Briand was getting along with Governor Haldimand. In answer to Carleton's letter, Briand replied: "Some had thought that I was afraid of the Governor. No, I never feared man in my life, and now that I am on the brink of the grave, I reproach myself for not fearing enough my dreadful judge—God. I know how to love, not how to fear; kindness renders me weak; vigor and insult find me manly and firm."[22]

Benedict Arnold reappeared in Carleton's life in a curious way. Carleton had defeated him at the siege of Quebec and had beaten him in the naval battle of Valcour Island. Five years later, Arnold changed sides. He joined the British, who gave him the rank of brigadier-general. In the winter of 1782, Arnold, making his first appearance in court, was "ushered into the Royal presence on the arm of Sir Guy Carleton."[23]

When Cornwallis surrendered at Yorktown, much of the blame, rightly or wrongly, fell upon the commander-in-chief, General Henry Clinton. The government felt that Clinton had to be recalled. The question was, who would take Clinton's place? The King wrote Germain on December 15th, 1781:

> Lord Cornwallis is now out of the case [as commander-in-chief] . . . . The country will have more confidence in a new man and I believe without partiality that the man who in general by the army would be looked upon as the best officer is Sir Guy Carleton. Besides his place in the Commission of Public Accounts makes him well known in Parliament . . . . Whatever disagreements have been between you and him, I have no doubt if on consideration you should think him a proper person, that both you and he will, by some common friend, so explain yourselves that . . . . will make the public service be cheerfully carried on."[24]

Germain ignored the possibility of any reconciliation between him and Carleton, and, in his place, Carleton would undoubtedly have done likewise.

On December 24th the King wrote Lord North: "Undoubtedly if Sir Guy Carleton can be persuaded to go to America, he is in every way the best suited for the service. He and Lord Germain are incompatible. Lord George is certainly not unwilling to retire if he gets his object, which is a peerage."[25] On February 22nd, Carleton was appointed to replace Clinton, Germain simultaneously resigning and being elevated to the peerage. However, Carleton, receiving no instructions, had to wait. On March 20th, Lord North resigned. On the 27th, Lord Rockingham became prime minister, and Welbore Ellis secretary of the colonies. Both men were delighted to have Carleton's service. Three days later, he received orders to proceed to New York City.

CHAPTER 14

Commander-in-Chief of North America

On May 6th, 1782, Lieutenant-General Sir Guy Carleton landed in New York City to replace Sir Henry Clinton as the commander of the thirty-four thousand British soldiers stationed in the Thirteen Colonies.[1]

Carleton's orders were to evacuate the troops stationed in New York City and in other centres on the Atlantic coast. He was to send whatever reinforcements he thought wise to garrisons in the West Indies. The remaining regiments were to be shipped to Halifax, Nova Scotia.[2] These orders seemed to suggest a routine job. However, Carleton received from Welbore Ellis another letter dated March 26th, 1782. This stated, in addition to his military appointment, that he had been designated, along with Admiral Digby, commissioner "for restoring peace and granting pardon to the revolted provinces in America."[3] It was this responsibility that had induced Carleton to accept the assignment.

The day he landed, Carleton faced a nasty situation of long standing. Since the surrender of Cornwallis, there had been almost no fighting between British regulars and the army of soldier-citizens serving under General George Washington. But the fratricidal conflict between Patriots, who espoused the cause of independence, and Loyalists, who supported Britain and the King, was worsening. Bands of Patriots continued to assault Loyalists, steal their money and other personal items, and sometimes confiscate their farms or businesses. In turn, groups of Loyalists raided Patriots' homes, manhandled them, and seized their possessions. Against this background, a specific incident had occurred.

During the previous winter, Philip White, the captain of a Loyalist militia band, had been captured and killed by Patriots. They maintained that their prisoner had grabbed a gun, shot at a sentry, and in the resulting fight had himself been shot. Loyalists insisted that White had been tortured to death. Whether murder or not, White's death aroused great bitterness in Loyalist circles. Richard Lippincott, the leader of a Loyalist group, decided to exact revenge. His followers were holding a prisoner, the captain of a Patriot band, named Joseph Huddy. Lippincott was able to release Huddy from imprisonment, ostensibly to exchange him for a Loyalist held captive by Patriots. Lippincott and some of his men took Huddy to heights overlooking the New Jersey shore, and there they hung him from a tree, with a placard pinned to his breast that read:

> We, the refugees, having with long grief beheld the cruel murder of our brethren, and finding nothing but such measures daily carried into execution, therefore determined not to suffer without taking vengeance for the numerous cruelties, and thus begin, having made use of Captain Huddy, as the first object to present to your view, and we further determine to hang man for man while there is a refugee existing. UP GOES HUDDY FOR PHILIP WHITE.[4]

In April, General George Washington had written Clinton, demanding that Lippincott be turned over for trial for murder. Clinton disowned the hanging of Huddy, expressed great sorrow, but refused to surrender Lippincott. Clinton started a board of inquiry, but Lippincott refused to testify, claiming that he was not subject to court-martial since he was not a professional soldier. On May 3rd, Washington ordered Brigadier-General Hazen, who was in charge of British prisoners captured at Yorktown, to designate, by lot, one whose rank was that of captain, and send him to Washington in Morristown, New Jersey. Hazen did as he was ordered. The man who drew the fatal straw was Captain Charles Asgill, the nineteen-year-old son of a wealthy baronet who had been a lord mayor of London. Captain Asgill was duly sent under guard to New Jersey. Washington then informed Carleton that, unless Lippincott was handed over

134

for trial, Asgill would be hung.[5] What Washington was proposing to do was contrary to any civilized conduct and, more specifically, to the articles of capitulation signed at Yorktown, one of which ensured British prisoners against any manner of subsequent punishment, including any form of reprisal.[6]

Carleton immediately started court-martial proceedings against Lippincott. There was a Board of Associated Loyalists, which exercised loose control over Loyalist bands. William Franklin, the illegitimate son of Benjamin Franklin, was the chairman of this board.[7] At the court-martial proceedings, evidence of a somewhat flimsy nature was introduced to the effect that Lippincott had been obeying verbal orders given by the Board of Associated Loyalists. The resulting acquittal was a parody of justice. But feelings were running so high that no group of British or their adherents would have sent Lippincott to his death for murdering a Patriot. To what extent Franklin and the other members of the board were involved is hard to determine. However, Carleton promptly dissolved the board.

Carleton wrote Washington to say that murder was contrary to British policy and that he had abolished the Board of Associated Loyalists. He pointed out that, in some cases, colonials who had joined the British army had been branded as traitors and shot. Nonetheless, Carleton maintained that, in times of civil war, treason simply did not exist. If it did, each side would be devising regulations to legalize the murder of its opponents.[8] Carleton also remarked that he was investigating in the hope of finding the individual responsible. (This statement was untrue: Lippincott was the murderer.) Carleton could do nothing further, beyond returning to Washington two dragoons whom a Loyalist band had captured.

Carleton wrote to Asgill's parents suggesting that they appeal to the King of France who, in turn, could appeal to Washington for their son's life. As is usual in diplomatic matters, many individuals became involved. The youth's mother, Lady Asgill, in a moving letter, begged Louis XVI to intervene on her son's behalf. The French foreign minister, at his king's request, wrote to Washington, pleading for Asgill's release. This letter, along with Lady Asgill's, was sent to Lord Cornwallis, then a prisoner on parole. Cornwallis forwarded the letters to Carleton. Carleton sent them under a flag of truce to Washington, and Washington duly forwarded them to the Continental Congress. Finally, on November 7th, as a result, the Congress ordered the release of Asgill.[9]

Whether Washington wanted Asgill's death in retaliation for a cold-blooded killing is not clear.[10] Toward the end, Washington may have had a change of heart. He wrote Congress that the fact that Lippincott had been tried for murder "changed the ground that I was proceeding on."[11] On the other hand, after Asgill's release, Washington told the French ambassador that "the very unsatisfactory measures which had been taken by the British commander-in-chief to atone for a crime of the blackest dye" had not justified Asgill's release.[12]

In the early fall, Carleton had another altercation with Washington. He had sent two men, Andrew Elliot and General James Campbell, to a conference with American generals Henry Knox and William Heath, the purpose being to arrange an exchange of prisoners. The Americans started off the conference with an ultimatum. They demanded a sum of money as reimbursement for what had been spent feeding British soldiers captured at Yorktown. From the British point of view this was blackmail, and the conference broke up with no agreement of any sort. Washington then wrote Carleton that Congress insisted upon payment for the prisoners' food: "If this is not produced, it will be high time to take measures however disagreeable for diminishing a burden which has become intolerable."[13] Replying on October 2nd, Carleton refused to pay a penny for the prisoners' upkeep and chastized Washington for his threat: "It has not been usual I think since the barbarious ages to use any menaces, however obscure, towards prisoners, and still less to practice towards them any barbarity."[14] Washington did not carry out his implied threat to molest the prisoners. One suspects that he had been bluffing, at the urging of Congress. If so, Carleton had called his bluff.

Events now moved rapidly in Britain. Rockingham's ministry ended with his death. Lord Shelburne became prime minister and Welbore Ellis was replaced as secretary of state by Thomas Townshend. And the desire for peace at any price now became irresistible. It seemed as if everyone at Westminster wanted to grant independence to the Thirteen Colonies.

The Continental Congress appointed Benjamin Franklin, John Jay and John Adams, all of whom were in Europe, to negotiate peace with Britain. Influenced by France, the three Americans stipulated that negotiations should take place in Paris. London agreed. France was near enough that Lord Shelburne could more or less conduct the negotiations himself.

Scarcely three months after Carleton's arrival in New York, he received a letter from Shelburne stating that the Americans were to be granted independence immediately and unconditionally; that Carleton was to so inform them; and that negotiations over a treaty of peace would be carried on in Paris.[15] Carleton immediately informed both Washington and Elias Boudinot, the president of the Continental Congress, that Britain was granting unconditional independence. At the same time, he wrote Shelburne asking to be relieved of his command in North America. Carleton's dream of restoring peace was no more. He did not want to be employed just to do a routine, tidy-up job; he did not want to be a mere "inspector of embarkations."[16]

London shilly-shallied over a replacement for Carleton. Shelburne and Thomas Townshend were both reluctant to accede to Carleton's request. Finally, early in the summer of 1783, Townshend wrote: "Let me earnestly entreat you to remain at this important moment for the evacuation of New York and distribution of His Majesty's troops . . . . The justice of your claim to return home is obvious. If His Majesty could find any man on either side of the Atlantic as much trusted, he would not press you so urgently."[17] George III had made the decision; he would not let Carleton retire. Carleton, of course, obeyed his King's command.

Soon after Carleton's arrival in New York City, he learned that many Loyalists wanted to leave the Atlantic colonies and live elsewhere. Some were families whose properties had been confiscated by Patriots. Others were men who had fought alongside British regulars and feared Patriot retaliation. Carleton had no orders from London to transport or help these Loyalists in any way. However, he felt that it was Britain's duty to aid them and hence his responsibility. He informed Shelburne and Townshend that he was going to try and resettle the Loyalists, and they agreed to support him in this endeavor. In the summer of 1782, Carleton wrote Sir Andrew Snape Hammond, the governor of Nova Scotia, advising him that upwards of six hundred people were planning to immigrate to Nova Scotia and requesting that each family and each individual be granted several acres of land. Carleton then gave orders that each immigrant be given provisions from the King's stores sufficient to sustain them for a year, plus clothing, medicines, farm tools, a musket, powder and ammunition.[18] Again, he had no orders to spend the British government's money in this way, but London never objected.

The news that Britain was granting unconditional independence to the Thirteen Colonies produced consternation among the Loyalists. They had lost the war. The redcoats would be leaving. Patriots could therefore assault and dispossess Loyalists with little fear of retaliation or punishment. Indeed, there was an increase in Patriot harassment of Loyalists. For example, a captain of the Loyalist militia, who was about to leave for Nova Scotia, went to say goodbye to his parents in a place in New York State called Walkill. In the very community where he had grown up, his onetime friends and acquaintances shaved his head and eyebrows, coated him with tar and feathers, put around his neck a pig-yoke with a cow bell attached, and ran him out of town.[19] At times, Americans committed what could be called legalized murder. When the British army evacuated Charleston, South Carolina, Patriots hung twenty-four Loyalists. Their "crime" was that they had fought on the British side.[20]

The Loyalist exodus, which started with hundreds wanting to leave, multiplied into thousands and tens of thousands. They came from New England in the north and as far south as Georgia, bringing to New York City in carts and carriages as many of their possessions as they could. Most of the men had been farmers, and some of them herded their cattle into the city. While waiting for ships to take them away, they were housed on Long Island in tents and on derelict farms. To arrange for the transportation of the Loyalists, Carleton set up an office of Superintendent of Exports and Imports. Every refugee was permitted to take whatever he or she thought would be useful. As a result beds, chairs, boxes of clothing, kitchen utensils, even horses and cattle went aboard transports.[21]

Governor Hammond of Nova Scotia wanted to be co-operative, but he could not understand the problem of six hundred immigrants, let alone a situation that now involved anywhere from ten to fifty times this number of refugees. Fortunately, Carleton realized that he could not ship people to Nova Scotia without sending agents to assess its timber reserves and arable land, the availability of water for milling operations, and to ascertain what difficulties might be anticipated in forming settlements.[22] Added to which, there was a particularly pressing need to relocate Loyalists who belonged to such regiments as Tarleton's British Legion or the New York Volunteers. In April 1783, Carleton appointed Colonels Edward Winslow, Isaac Brown, and Stephen Delancy as agents for some five thousand of these militia soldiers. They were to find suitable land around what is now Saint John, New Brunswick. If possible, settlement there was to be in a contiguous line so that all former soldiers would be together and could defend each other against Indians—or Americans. Carleton went down to the dock where the three colonels, with friends gathered around them, were waiting to board ship. He is said to have made the following short speech: "Gentlemen, you are to provide an asylum for your distressed countrymen. Your task is arduous. Execute it as men of honor. The season for fighting is over. Bury your animosities and persecute no man. Your ship is ready and God bless you."[23]

Although Nova Scotia was the destination of many of the emigrating Loyalists, a considerable number went elsewhere. A few chose to go to Bermuda, Nassau and the Bahamas. Some settled in England. Others journeyed to the Province of Quebec. One was a German saddle and harness maker named Michael Grass, who came to see Carleton. This man had been a prisoner of the French some twenty-five years earlier and had become familiar with the land at Cataraqui, a place whose name was later changed to Kingston. Grass convinced Carleton that Cataraqui possessed fine farming land and would be a good location for Loyalists. Carleton commissioned him a captain of militia. Grass then proceeded to enroll in his regiment some five hundred Loyalists, chiefly artisans. Carleton wrote to Governor Haldimand of Quebec that he was sending these "militiamen" to Quebec with tents, clothing, provisions, and tools, and that they wanted land at Cataraqui. Since these men were technically in the army, they were entitled, upon their discharge, to receive free grants of land; a captain received seven hundred acres, a non-commissioned officer two hundred, and a private one hundred. Haldimand seemed doubtful about the whole venture, but he met Carleton's request and had a township laid out at Cataraqui. Grass and his men reached Quebec in August. Most of them wintered at Sorel and moved to their plots of land at Cataraqui the next summer.[24]

Outfitting Loyalist refugees was only one of Carleton's supply problems. He had been in New York City scarcely two months when he was forced to declare his own war on corruption within the military. It was well known that the British Army in the American colonies was plagued by venality: it was riddled with thieves, superfluous employees, and graft of various kinds. If, for instance, a member of the commissariat signed a voucher for the army to pay one hundred dollars for fifty dollars' worth of hay, he could expect a kickback of twenty-five dollars, the other twenty-five dollars going as a bonus to the hay contractor. The most shocking peculation was the feeding of prisoners. The provost marshal, William Cunningham, confessed in 1791 that, while in New York, he had starved two thousand prisoners confined in various churches "by stopping their rations, which I sold."[25] In his campaign against corruption, Carleton did not charge anyone with a crime or brand anyone as guilty. He did not, as far as is known, investigate any individual, or formally punish anyone. What he did was to discharge almost every army employee involved in procurements or military expenditures. Officers and enlisted men who were involved in such work were transferred to some other occupation. According to one authority,

> In a short time [Carleton] broke, discharged, dismissed, and cashiered such a number of supernumerary barrack-masters, land commissioners, cattle feeders, wood inspectors, timber commissaries, board inspectors, refugee examiners, refugee provi-

sion providers, commissaries of American, French, or Spanish prisoners, along with a train of clerks and deputy clerks.[26]

Carleton took steps to prevent a return to graft and waste. In London, he had presided over a commission to audit public accounts, a commission consisting of laymen, not members of Parliament. In light of this experience, Carleton realized that he must use civilians to help keep the army free of corruption. An army man would not testify to the guilt of another army man. Carleton decided that all accounts and vouchers of the different military departments were to be subject to thorough examination by Major Drummond, the commissary of accounts, and then passed on for inspection by a board of public accounts, which he established. Its initial members were Drummond, Henry White, a merchant who had been equipping provincial regiments for General Howe, and Hugh Wallace, a prominent businessman. Carleton himself presided over the board. If he had to be absent from any one of its weekly meetings, Major-General Robertson took his place. All generals and officers of field rank (major and above) were entitled to attend any of the meetings of the board and were required to attend when their departments were involved.[27] It has been estimated that Carleton saved Great Britain over £2 million in the first twelve months. Undoubtedly this figure is too high, but Carleton did save the British treasury a great deal of money. In December 1781, the King, when urging Carleton's appointment to the New York command, had presciently written Germain: "His incorruptness is universally acknowledged."[28]

When Carleton discovered that American prisoners were losing rations due to graft, he naturally wondered what was the condition of American seamen taken prisoner by the British Navy. A general has no authority over naval personnel and cannot give orders to a midshipman or a seaman, let alone an admiral. But perhaps through his friendship with Admiral Digby, the commander of the British fleet based at New York, Carleton obtained permission to visit some of the prison hulks, where he found many prisoners suffering heat prostration. Carleton was familiar with Blackwell's Island (now Roosevelt Island) because he had made his headquarters at Beekman's House at the fifth milestone on the East River. This house looked across the water toward the island.[29] Carleton persuaded the navy to let these prisoners go ashore on Blackwell's Island during the summer. The following winter, he found the naval prisoners on one ship almost naked. He immediately sent each a new suit of clothes.[30] (To use army funds to clothe prisoners of the British Navy was, to say the least, somewhat irregular.)

Carleton performed other acts that were unorthodox, at least one of which was illegal. Major George Beckwith, the officer in charge of British intelligence, had taken into custody one Thomas Poole, a man who had incriminating papers on his person and confessed to being a spy. He had been collecting information about colonials who had been secretly collaborating with the British. Many of these Loyalists did not feel up to making a new home for themselves in the wilds of Canada. They hoped to conceal from fellow Americans their former pro-British activities so that they could remain undisturbed in their home communities. Carleton wanted to protect these particular Loyalists, so something had to be done about Poole. Thus, on October 20th, 1782, Carleton sent him to Bermuda. With him went the following letter (extracted and excerpted) to William Browne, the governor of Bermuda.

> Sir Guy Carleton sends by this conveyance to Bermuda one Thomas Poole, an American, who has been imprisoned some time as an acknowledged spy. The same humanity which saved him from the customary fate of that class of men when detected would probably have shortened the duration of the confinement could it have been effected without inevitable ruin to many Loyalists in the country whose names he had contrived should be made known to him and who were from their acts of attention to him when under the character of a Loyalist left entirely at his mercy. However, as he has suffered the most severe confinement and is in consequence become very decrepit, he is sent with severe injunctions not to leave the island during the war, but he [Governor Browne] is asked to ensure his continuance there for the welfare of the persons mentioned. If too difficult [the writer] recommends that he be sent to one of the West Indian Islands where the possibility of his returning to this continent would be most impracticable. Clothes and substance are to be given him.[31]

Six months later, Browne returned Poole to Carleton, saying that Poole had recovered his health, and that with the cessation of hostilities, Carleton would presumably release Poole to the Americans.[32] On May 12th, 1783, Carleton shipped Poole for the second time to Bermuda, writing the following to Browne:

> As the presence of Thomas Poole in this country, while the minds of the people continue heated against those who have shown their attachment to Government, may be productive to great distress to many who have secretly been our friends, I return him to Bermuda and request that he may be kept there, not considered as a close prisoner until he can be permitted to return to the continent with more safety to them. As he never was considered as a prisoner of war, the cessation of hostilities does not operate upon him. I therefore wish him to remain within your government until the present heats have subsided.[33]

This was too much for Browne. He replied that if Poole was a prisoner of war, he must be released with the signing of the peace treaty. If he was not a prisoner of war, then Browne had no legal reason to confine him. Browne sent Poole where he wanted to go, South Carolina, a colony from which the British had withdrawn their troops. Browne's view was unassailable; Carleton's action was legally indefensible. (Whether Poole in South Carolina did any harm to Loyalists, the record does not show.)

The resettling of the Loyalists involved an enormous correspondence. During the nineteen months that Carleton was in New York City, he dealt with thousands of communications. Many of these were warrants or routine papers but, in addition, he received many letters concerning other than military or emigrant matters. From Quebec, Governor Haldimand and General Riedesel kept regularly in touch. Carleton had brought along with him, as his official private or executive secretary, Maurice Morgann, the man London had sent to Quebec in 1768 to inquire as to the form of government best suited to the Province. However, the mail became too much for Morgann to cope with alone. Carleton persuaded the Rev. Jonathan Odell to enroll in the army as a chaplain with a chaplain's pay, but to devote his time to being a second secretary. Carleton was able to reward both of these ardent and loyal workers. He secured for Morgann a pension of £250 a year.[34] He sent Odell at the end of 1783 to Nova Scotia with a strong recommendation. There he was made provincial secretary, a post he was still holding at the time of his death thirty years later.

On April 5th, 1783, Secretary of State for the Colonies Thomas Townshend informed Carleton that preliminary articles of peace had been signed in Paris. He immediately declared a cessation of hostilities. Washington did likewise, writing Carleton that the prisoners captured at Yorktown, some six thousand seven hundred in number, would be released. Washington wanted Carleton to send transports to pick them up either in Baltimore or Philadelphia. Carleton had to answer apologetically that all his transports were being used to take troops and Loyalists out of the country and that the released prisoners would have to march to New York City.

Washington also suggested a conference between himself and Carleton to arrange for an orderly withdrawal of all British troops. The British commander-in-chief showed Washington's letter to his advisors, Maurice Morgann, Andrew Elliot, and William Smith. The three expressed doubts as to the wisdom of his conferring with Washington. They reminded him of the conference of generals over a proposed exchange of prisoners, during which the Americans had tried blackmail. They were afraid the Americans would refuse to deliver the Yorktown prisoners unless he accepted some unusual conditions. Carleton brushed aside their doubts; he agreed to meet Washington right away.

Tappan, a town on the west bank of the Hudson River some twenty-five miles from New York City, was suggested as the meeting place. Carleton could come up the Hudson by ship, while Washington could ride over on horseback from New Jersey. On May 6th, the *Perseverance*, one of the newest and finest frigates in the Royal Navy, anchored off Tappan. The next morning, Carleton, with Morgann, Elliot and Smith, plus a colonel, two majors, and a captain, were rowed ashore. General Washington greeted them while a contingent of infantry with drums beat a salute. Carleton and Washington climbed into a coach pulled by four horses and started for Tappan. Carleton, fifty-nine years old, was looking forward to retiring to England as soon as his successor reached New York. Washington, fifty-one years old, was looking forward to resigning from the army and retiring to his home in Virginia. Both were somewhat ill. Carleton had had a chill or ague the previous night and suffered from a heavy cold.[35] Washington was bothered by a periodic toothache.

Carleton and Washington had a certain facial resemblance. At a casual glance, one could be taken for the other. But their similarities went deeper.[36] They had much the same character; great common sense, a large store of patience (that was sometimes disrupted by hot bursts of impatience), courage in adversity, and a warm humanity under a cold exterior.[37] Both men had charm and magnetism that inspired others to follow them. Of Carleton, it was said that: "His charm was so impressive that had he been in America longer, he would have made Tories of all Whigs."[38]

At Tappan, they arrived at a small farm where yet another contingent of infantry saluted them. Carleton was introduced to Governor George Clinton of New York and his staff. In the farmhouse, the British—Carleton, Morgann, Elliot, and Smith—conferred with the Americans—Washington, Clinton, Jonathan Trumbull, who was Washington's secretary, John Morin Scott, the New York secretary of state, and Egbert Benson, attorney-general of New York.

When the nine were seated, Washington opened the conference by addressing Carleton slowly and in a low voice. He made three points. First and foremost, he wanted Negro slaves who had escaped from their masters and joined the British to be returned. Washington had been pressed on this point by the Continental Congress and he pointed out that the preliminary articles of the peace treaty provided that: "His Britanic Majesty should with all convenient speed and without causing any destruction or carrying away any Negroes, withdraw all his armies, garrisons, and fleets from every port, place and harbor within the United States."[39] Secondly, he wanted agreement as to the day of the final evacuation of British troops from New York City. Thirdly, he requested that Americans be allowed to

145

take over control of Westchester County and of Long Island within the next few days. Throughout, Washington's speech was temperate, gracious and conciliatory.[40]

Carleton replied that he would proceed with the evacuation with all possible speed but that it was going to take time. He said that he had just dispatched to Nova Scotia some six thousand men, women, and children, that there were many thousands more waiting to emigrate, and that he didn't know when this could be accomplished, since it depended upon shipping and weather. He said that he would evacuate Westchester within the next few days, but that he needed Long Island to protect those Loyalists waiting to leave. He did not want them to be at the mercy of Patriots.

Carleton then went into the Negro question. He pointed out that, long before his arrival, the British had promised freedom to any slaves who joined them. This was true. Thousands of slaves had joined the British in order to gain their freedom. A few had actually fought in the army. Many had become drivers or officers' servants. Many had no jobs at all. Carleton said that he would set up a registry of Negroes so that perhaps their former owners might eventually be compensated. He then remarked that he already had embarked some Negroes. Washington seemed to be startled. He interrupted, asking "Already embarked?" Carleton explained that the national honor was binding upon him and must be "kept with all colors." No Negro would be sent back into slavery, and he reiterated that the only solution was to pay for the Negroes. In this way, justice would be done to slave and owner alike.[41]

After Carleton had finished speaking, the debate was opened. It became acrimonious at times, the Americans shouting that everyone must conform to the peace terms, the British replying just as loudly that no Negroes could be returned to their masters. Washington and Carleton listened, only occasionally uttering a word or two. Finally, Washington stood up. When all was quiet, he observed that it was nearly dinner time and that he had some wine and bitters to offer. Afterward, the nine, together with some twenty other British and American officers, sat down in a tent outside the farmhouse where an elaborate dinner was served. The chef was Samuel Fraunces, "Black Sam" of Fraunces Tavern in New York City, a man whose culinary skills delighted Washington. Six years later, as President of the United States, Washington hired Black Sam as his personal chef.

The day after the dinner at Tappan, Washington and his aides were guests on the *Perseverance*. Carleton had had another attack of the ague and did not attend, although he came up from his cabin after the meal to apologize for his absence, to shake hands with Washington, and to say goodbye.

The conference between the two generals effected very little. The British prisoners were released and they marched to New York City without incident. A week after the conference, Carleton withdrew his forces from Westchester County. In the case of the slaves, Washington appointed inspectors whom Carleton permitted on the docks, but they were powerless to prevent any Negro with a British pass from boarding a ship. The inspectors saw to it that a registry of departing Negroes was maintained, but this proved to be an idle gesture. The former slaves invariably made up pseudonyms for themselves, one of their favorite names being "Prince." They also gave false names and false addresses for their former masters.

In fact, no Negro was returned to slavery by the British. No slave owner received compensation for slaves who had taken refuge with the British. Exactly how many Negroes obtained their freedom is not known, but the total is probably in the thousands. Most of them immigrated to various islands in the Caribbean, although some twelve hundred journeyed to Nova Scotia and settled near Halifax.

Both the Continental Congress and Washington kept importuning Carleton to withdraw his troops. Carleton would not be hurried. He wrote the president of the Congress: "The violence of the Americans increased the number of their countrymen who look to me for escape from threatened destruction. Almost all within these lines conceive [that] the safety both of their property and their lives depend upon their being removed by me which renders it impossible to say when the evacuation will be completed."[42] To Washington, Carleton wrote: "I should show an indifference to the feelings of humanity as well as the honor and interest of the nation whom I serve to leave any of the Loyalists that are desirous to quit the country, a prey to the violence they conceive they have so much cause to apprehend."[43] All in all, Carleton organized the emigration of some thirty thousand Loyalists and aided them to acquire land of their own and the initial equipment with which to earn a living.

November 25th arrived, the day when New York City, the last British garrison town, was ready for evacuation. At one p.m., a contingent of British soldiers, led by Lieutenant-General Sir Guy Carleton, started its march down the Bowery. At Wall Street, they turned left onto Broadway, and then onto a wharf where they boarded the *Ceres*. Carleton, appointed to supervise the dissolution of a large part of the British Empire, had completed his work.

When coming into the city, Washington was delayed by the whimsy of some British sailors. At the Battery end of Broadway was Fort George. On a flag pole in front of the fort the sailors had left the Union Jack flying. Moreover, they had cut off the halyards, removed the cleats, and thoroughly greased the pole so that no American could shinny up. There was no immediate way to replace the British Ensign with the American flag. It was two hours before cleats were found in an ironmonger's shop, and an American sailor, with halyards tied to his waist, was able to ascend, step by step, driving in the cleats as he climbed. Only when the British flag was lowered and the American one raised did Washington enter the city.[44]

For three days, the *Ceres* remained moored in New York harbor. On the afternoon of the 28th, a light breeze arose, and the ship got under way for England.

Carleton's critics fault him for many of his actions as governor of Quebec, but, almost without exception, they extoll his supervision of the New York evacuation. All the British generals of high rank who came to the Thirteen Colonies—Gage, Burgoyne, Howe, Clinton, Cornwallis—had their reputations tarnished as a result of the American Revolution. Carleton's reputation was enhanced. Many men who attain the power, position and prestige of a generalship lose their sense of values and become obsessed with their own importance. Carleton had been a kindly autocrat in Canada; he remained a kindly autocrat in New York City, never abusing his considerable power and authority as commander-in-chief. An admiring Tory contemporary wrote:

> He sees everything with his own eyes and hears everybody. He is up and about before four in the morning. Before a quarter part of the army have opened their eyelids, he has perhaps rode ten or twelve miles. He comes almost every day to the parade, which is a signal that immediately after he will have a levee, where everyone may tell their story, or request a private hour . . . and those who have had conversation with him go away very much satisfied with his patience and condescension. In short his conduct has procured him the respect of the army and the love of the Loyalists.[45]

CHAPTER 15

Governor-in-Chief of British North America

With Carleton on the *Ceres* was his New York friend, Judge William Smith. During the long Atlantic voyage, the two men must often have discussed why Britain had lost the Thirteen Colonies. Both men seem to have been persuaded that London's initial mistake had been the failure to make the colonies into a federation. Smith argued that if they had had one overall governor and one overall legislature with some power to tax, the federated colonies would have been glad to help support an army to defend them against the Indians. It had been the arbitrary imposition of taxes by Parliament to meet military expenditures that had sparked revolution. Perhaps the lesson from this was that the loyal provinces in British North America—Nova Scotia, Newfoundland, Prince Edward Island and Quebec —should be united under a "governor general" as chief executive and have one common legislature. The "governor general," whose position with regard to the provinces' lieutenant-governors would be that of *primus inter pares*, would be the link with Westminster and the Crown, "the reservoir of all information and the conduit of communication."[1] He would also be commander-in-chief of the army in British North America.

In January, 1784, Carleton reached London and joined Maria in a house she had rented in the neighborhood of Queen Anne Street.[2] Then he called on the secretary for the colonies, Thomas Townshend, who was shortly to become Lord Sydney. The British cabinet wanted advice about the Canadian colonies, whose populations had dramatically increased due to Loyalist migrations, the largest of which was to Nova Scotia. Carleton suggested that it should be divided in two, the peninsular region centred on Halifax to remain Nova Scotia and the region around what is now the city of Saint John to become the new colony of New Brunswick. He also suggested that his brother, Colonel Thomas Carleton, be the first governor of New Brunswick. Carleton urged the appointment of a governor general and commander-in-chief of all Canada.[3]

The province of New Brunswick was created in 1784, Thomas Carleton being appointed its first governor. That same year, Cape Breton Island had to be given its own government because hundreds of Loyalists had settled there and were establishing a valuable fishing industry. However, in the matter of a governor general of all of British North America, the British government would make no decision for almost three years.

In the late 1780s, the Province of Quebec experienced disturbing ripple effects from the newly established United States of America. English-speaking immigrants poured in. The lure of land grants, the provision of seed, agricultural implements and food rations by British officials drew thousands of Loyalists and other Americans from the frontier fringes of Pennsylvania, New York and New Hampshire to the northern shores of lakes Ontario and Erie. In time, this particular migration was less a movement of Loyalists and more one of experienced pioneer families moving westward. In time, like the merchants of Montreal and Quebec City in the days of Murray, these newcomers became dissatisfied with the lack of an elected assembly in which to debate their problems, with the unfamiliar workings of French law, and with the rental basis of the seigneurial land system. Thus, they joined with the city merchants and other English-speaking inhabitants of the Province in agitating for the repeal of the Quebec Act. Alarmed that their rights would be taken away from them, many Québécois started denouncing the newcomers. They claimed that an elected assembly would be used as an excuse to impose more taxes on their people. They were afraid that an assembly would amend, or perhaps cancel, the religious freedom and French property laws guaranteed by the Quebec Act. Governor Haldimand, trying to please both sides, simply got himself into an endless series of troubles. In the summer of 1784, he was recalled, although for two years no decision was made as to his successor.

As early as August 1785, Sydney, becoming alarmed by the growing turmoil, sent the following memorandum to Prime Minister William Pitt.

> The Province of Quebec in its present situation is a dominion of a very precarious tenure. I cannot help dreading that the cabinet will separate without a decision upon which in my humble opinion depends upon whether Canada remains ours in twelve months longer or not . . . . If a Governor General of all that remains of British possessions in North America can be appointed, Sir Guy Carleton is in my opinion preferable to any other person.[4]

After a further delay, the cabinet decided that Carleton would be made governor general of all British possessions on the mainland of North America. Upon reflection, however, the cabinet changed its mind. It gave Carleton, instead, a series of commissions: one as governor-in-chief, an official who represented the Crown in matters common to the government of all the colonies; one as governor of Quebec; one as governor of Nova Scotia; one as governor of Prince Edward Island; one as governor of New Brunswick; and one as governor of Cape Breton Island. In each of these provinces, the former governor would be demoted to lieutenant-governor. As for the governor-in-chief's gubernatorial powers, these were limited to when he was actually in each province. No change was made in the long-established principle that, in the absence of the governor of a province, his powers were exercised by a lieutenant-governor. Above all, the British government was not prepared to establish one common legislature for all the provinces.

Carleton accepted the office of governor-in-chief with one stipulation. Remembering how Hey as chief justice of Quebec had helped him govern, and how Livius had obstructed him, Carleton insisted that his friend and adviser William Smith be appointed chief justice of Quebec.[5] To this, there was some objection. Smith was known in London as a longtime opponent of Britain's taxation policies in the Thirteen Colonies, possessed no first-hand knowledge of Quebec, and had had little experience of the bench. However, Carleton was adamant, stressing that he would be responsible for Smith's conduct. And Carleton got his way.[6]

Before sailing for Quebec, Carleton received two honors. The British government was in the habit of giving pensions to honor or reward distinguished service. In connection with Carleton's appointment as governor-in-chief, Parliament bestowed upon him an annual pension of £1,000, a pension that would survive his death and be paid to his wife in her lifetime and, after her death, to his two eldest sons. This pension, first proposed by the Duke of Richmond, was sponsored in the House of Commons by Burgoyne, who reiterated how hard Carleton had struggled to make his ill-fated invasion of New York a success.[7] In addition, the King, on August 21st, 1786, made Carleton a baron. In a collateral branch of Carleton's family tree, there had been a Dudley Carleton who had been knighted by James I and had been created Lord Dorchester by Charles I. This peerage was now extinct. Carleton revived his distant relative's peerage by becoming the second Lord Dorchester. He adopted for his escutcheon two Canadian beavers on their hind legs supporting a shield, above which was a North American Indian holding an arrow. The motto was *Quondam His Vicimus Armis*—We used to conquer with these weapons.[8]

No money accompanied a peerage, but Lord Dorchester was now a rich man. He had, or shortly would have, an income of £5,000 a year: as governor of Quebec, £2,000; as a lieutenant-general £1,000; as governor of Charlemont £1,000; and £1,000 as a pensioner of the British government. If we consider the pound two hundred years ago as being at least twenty times as valuable as today, Dorchester's annual income was the equivalent of £100,000 or over $200,000. Furthermore, in the eighteenth century, personal incomes were tax-free. Dorchester may well have saved substantial amounts of money, especially in the years 1782-3. When serving as commander-in-chief in New York City, he received about £3 a day as a lieutenant-general and, as a commander-in-chief on overseas duty, an allowance of £10 a day.[9] Hence, his total income during the eighteen and a half months of his New York service was approximately £9,000. Since the British government paid all his living expenses while in New York City, including such extras as wine, he well may have saved several thousand pounds in this period alone. At any rate, in the summer of 1786, Dorchester bought an estate, Greywell Hill, a palatial residence with some seven hundred acres of land in Hampshire, about fifty miles from London. The price of this property must have been in the neighborhood of £10-15,000.[10]

Dorchester sailed from England on September 2nd, 1786, and arrived at Quebec on October 23rd. With him were his three eldest sons and William Smith, the new chief justice. Maria remained in England with the younger children. In 1785 she had given birth to a girl, Frances, and on August 1st, 1786 to a boy, Charles.[11]

For the next eight months Dorchester lived a bachelor's life in the Château St. Louis. On December 22nd, we catch a glimpse of him. Early in the morning he saw from the Château a fire burning on a wharf in the Lower Town. He dashed over to the Recollets, where a small contingent of soldiers was bivouacked, aroused them, and rushed them down into the Lower Town. The fire was on Grant's wharf, endangering forty hogsheads of rum. According to the Quebec *Gazette*, the military "animated by the presence of their Commander-in-Chief" put out the fire quickly. No rum was lost.[12]

During the winter of 1786-7 Carleton was taken ill, probably from the same ague that had attacked him in New York City. Hearing about this, his brother Thomas, the lieutenant-governor of New Brunswick, came to visit him. Using skis and camping out in the snow for eight consecutive nights, Thomas travelled from Saint John to Fredericton and then on through what is now the state of Maine to Quebec.[13]

In due course, Dorchester threw off whatever sickness had plagued him, and his sharp mind began to see an extra significance in Thomas' visit to the Château St. Louis. The port of Quebec was icebound each year from about December 1st to May 1st. During this long winter season, no direct mail service to or from Britain was possible. If Thomas, fifty-one years old, could travel overland in the depth of winter, so could younger, more vigorous men. If Dorchester could get mail to New Brunswick by ski or snowshoe, a packet could sail each month to England from the ice-free ports of either Saint John or Halifax. It took two years for the brothers to persuade London's bureaucracy to implement this mail system, but by the winter of 1788-9 the scheme was in operation. The closing date for mail leaving Quebec was announced in the *Gazette* and was usually four p.m. on the first Thursday of each month. The mail, always slow and somewhat uncertain, was even slower in winter, but the system worked.[14]

Dorchester soon discovered that his title of governor-in-chief was impressive but lacked substance. The lieutenant-governors of each province corresponded directly with London, continued to act as chief executives, and pretty much ignored Dorchester. One reason was geography. It was much quicker to write London direct than to do so via Quebec. Another was politics. Whether the British cabinet intended to give Dorchester a title that lacked real power is not clear. Yet London must have had some doubts as to the office of governor-in-chief, because Dorchester could only effectively be governor of Quebec. Nor do we know whether, at the start, Dorchester realized that he was getting a title and little else. He may have thought that his prestige and his London connections would, in practice, guarantee him the necessary influence as governor-in-chief. This did not happen. In May 1787, Dorchester was asked to entertain George III's son, Prince William (years later he became King William IV), who planned to visit Quebec during the summer. As the date of the prince's arrival and the length of his stay were unknown, Dorchester felt obliged to postpone his planned summer visit to the Maritime provinces. He did go a year later, but by that time Sydney and the lieutenant-governors were exchanging communications that totally excluded the governor-in-chief. Dorchester's (and Smith's) dream of administering Canada under a central government had little chance to work.

In the fall of 1787, Dorchester visited areas west and southwest of Montreal. Here lived some three thousand English-speaking families. Most of them farmers, scattered over a wide area, who wanted neighbors closer to them and would welcome American farm families willing to immigrate. However, there were delays, fees, and other burdens placed upon applicants for a land grant in the western part of Quebec. Dorchester had earlier divided these areas into four districts, and he now appointed for each district a local board. He then had the council state by proclamation: "All persons desiring settlements on lands of the Crown should go before the Boards appointed by the Governor. If such persons are deemed suitable, they shall be given two hundred acres."[15]

Dorchester's next problem was to establish courts for these newcomers. Here, he encountered difficulties. He had no authority to offer salaries, and few lawyers in Montreal or Quebec were interested in moving west and becoming judges where their incomes would be limited to fees both small and uncertain. The governor did appoint three English-speaking laymen—two of them Montreal merchants—as part-time judges, and decreed that their payment would be in the form of fees. These appointments, however, produced much dissatisfaction. The merchant-judges had a personal interest in some of the cases. None of the three was assiduous in carrying out his judicial duties. And when they did sit, their decisions were sometimes unorthodox, due to their ignorance of the law. The next year, Dorchester, realizing that he had made a mistake, removed the three part-time judges, appointed a lawyer, William Dummer Powell, to serve as judge, and assumed the responsibility of giving him a salary of £500 a year. Dorchester admitted to London that he had overreached his instructions, but said that a salaried judge was essential in this new settlement area. The British government sanctioned the arrangement, but told Dorchester never to take such action again without prior approval.[16]

Just as he had in the past, Dorchester tried to temper the severity of English criminal law. In December 1789, a John Miller of Beauport, a community close to Quebec City, was convicted of stealing ducks and turkeys, and sentenced to be whipped in the marketplace of the Upper Town.[17] Early in July the next year, a neighbor of Miller's, Antoine Guigue, was convicted of sheep stealing and sentenced to death. This time, Dorchester felt he had to intervene. He pardoned Guigue on condition that he left the province and never returned.[18]

In other ways, the governor tried to help the Québécois.

Farmers living along the St. Lawrence east of Quebec City had long wanted a bridge across the St. Charles River. This waterway had a strong current when the tide was going out, which made it difficult to get livestock and other produce to market in the city. It was also dangerous in the early part of the winter to walk across the river. Air holes formed in the ice, creating dangerous traps. Dorchester became a firm advocate of a bridge. The money needed for the construction was borrowed, with an understanding that tolls would be used to pay off the loan. On September 24th, 1789, the bridge was completed and opened, its name being, of course, the Dorchester Bridge. It was of a width sufficient for two carriages to pass, plus a footpath. Tolls were levied for crossing the bridge: a foot passenger, a sheep, and a pig, each one halfpenny; a man on horseback, an ox, and a cow, each twopence; a one-horse vehicle, fourpence; a two-horse vehicle, sixpence.[19] A couple of weeks after the opening of the bridge, an enterprising boatman started transporting people across the river at prices lower than the tolls. Dorchester promptly rushed through council an edict forbidding a ferry or canoe to transport men or animals across the St. Charles River for a fee. The fine for so doing was twenty shillings.

The year 1789 was known as the "Hungry Year,"[20] a twelve-month scarcity of nearly all farm products, especially corn and wheat. For the three previous years, Loyalist newcomers had been given free food, which reduced the carry-over of grain from one year to the next. In 1788, crops of wheat, corn and peas seem to have been much smaller than usual, yet there was a considerable export of agricultural produce. In 1789, the harvest, meagre everywhere, was almost nil in the Montreal area. Possibly due to the excessive rain,[21] a smut had formed on wheat and oats, reducing yields by fifty per cent in some fields and entirely ruining others. There was a great deal of suffering—and even starvation—due to the soaring prices of all foods, especially bread. The poor could not afford to buy it. In the files of the Quebec *Gazette*, there are accounts of the Merchant's Club of Quebec providing an ox and one hundred loaves of bread for the destitute. In Montreal, there was a public subscription, and six hundred people received, free, one half-pound of bread and one half-pound of beef per day for some weeks.

What did Dorchester do? Early in 1789 he started badgering Britain for help, but this would take time. So he put an embargo on the export of grain. On March 2nd, he ordered the senior naval officer on the Richelieu River, who was acting as a customs agent, to admit "free of duty by way of Lake Champlain and the river Sorel all bread, biscuit, wheaten flour or meal of rye, Indian corn, oats, barley, and other grains and all kinds of meat."[22] In June, with the approval of the council, Dorchester authorized the import of foodstuffs from the United States at the port of Quebec—a direct violation of a British statute. Writing to London, Dorchester admitted that his action was illegal, but said that what he had done he thought was necessary. He was not reproved.[23] Due to the shortage, many farmers failed to store seed for planting the next year. To make it easy to borrow money to purchase seed, Dorchester issued an ordinance that gave a seed loan precedence over any other loan a farmer might have contracted.

One of the most interesting results of the Hungry Year was the formation by Dorchester of the Agricultural Society. He persuaded—or quite possibly bulldozed—many important people to join. Every person on the council was a member of the society, as were the bishops, the superiors of the seminaries, and prominent French-speaking and English-speaking citizens. Dorchester refused to be president of the society, but agreed to be its "patron." Meetings were held at the Château St. Louis. The first formal meeting passed the following resolution: "That the Society make the means of preventing smut from affecting the crops of wheat and oats one of the first objects of their inquiry and that the best method of preparing the seed be recommended for trial the ensuing season throughout the Province."[24]

In August 1790, the society purchased the best seed for oats, barley, and other grain from England. Dorchester personally put up half the money for this purchase.[25] By 1791, the society had enlarged its range of interests to include hemp, which is valuable in making rope, sails, etc. By proclamation, Dorchester announced that two thousand bushels of hemp seed were to be given, gratis, to farmers who would promise to plant before May 1st, 1791, in accordance with the society's instructions. Dorchester gave the upper garden of the Château to the society for the purpose of planting fruit trees on an experimental basis. (The Quebec *Gazette* regretfully reported on May 19th, 1791, that Dorchester's fruit trees were doing badly.)

By December 1st, 1789, Britain had sent one thousand tons of flour, three thousand bushels of wheat, and twenty-four thousand bushels of peas. As a result, there was sufficient grain to carry the Province through the winter and spring, up to harvest time. The crisis was over. By August 1790, when it was clear that there was going to be a good harvest, the council was able to lift the embargo on the export of grain.[26]

CHAPTER 16

Dorchester's Later Years

As governor of the Province of Quebec, Dorchester continued his practice of personally chairing the first session of the council in the Château. Subsequent meetings were held in the Bishop's Palace, with Dorchester absent and Smith presiding. Smith, who became the most influential man in the Province, was really Dorchester's prime minister. The two worked so closely together that it is almost impossible to ascertain whether a particular policy originated with Dorchester and was adopted by Smith or vice-versa. Council meetings were often fiery affairs because of the bitterness between English-speaking and French-speaking members. However, no legislation was ever proposed without the prior approval of Smith. Everyone knew that he spoke for Dorchester. The governor, with power of absolute veto over any legislation, was the boss. It was unwise to try and thwart him. Everyone remembered that Dorchester had dismissed the former chief justice when he had introduced resolutions contrary to his wishes.

Dorchester still favored a central government for all of Canada. As late as February 4th, 1790, he wrote Grenville, who had replaced Sydney as colonial secretary, enclosing clauses drawn up by Smith for a bill to be passed by Parliament. The legislation proposed that Canada would have not only a governor general, but a legislative council and a general assembly with authority to levy taxes. Grenville's unenthusiastic response is expressed in the last sentence of his reply: "The formation of a general legislative government for all the King's provinces in America is a point which is under consideration but I think is liable to considerable objection."[1] The idea was rejected. Seventy-seven years would pass before the dream of a confederated Canada became a reality.

The prime concern of the British cabinet was not colonial union but amity between Quebec's English-speaking and French-speaking inhabitants. And there was little of that in the years immediately following 1783. English-speaking immigrants to Quebec tended to be more ambitious, thus more industrious, and hence wealthier, than the French-speaking inhabitants. The newcomers were quick to regard the Québécois as inferior. At the same time, the newcomers were scared; they knew they were in a minority. For their part, the French thought the English imperious and materialistic, always securing the best jobs for themselves. There was truth in this. From 1760 onward, the import-export trade with Britain had been in English hands and enriched English people. As a result, many of the French were bitter toward the English. Harmony between the two races might have been possible if there had been intermarriage, but there was almost none. The main reason for this was the language barrier, but religious and educational differences played their part.

Another cabinet concern was the international situation. The Thirteen Colonies had been lost, and no one in London wanted to lose Quebec. The twin fear was that the "new subjects" would revolt especially if, as expected, Britain should again be at war with France, and that the "old subjects," most of whom had come from the American colonies, would rebel and join the United States. The cabinet was also becoming alarmed over what Quebec was costing the British treasury. In 1786, the civil administration of the Province had cost £26,533.[2] Added to this, was an expenditure of £20,000 annually in gifts to Indians.[3] Yet, in 1786, the income collected in import duties was only £7,664.[4] The cabinet did not feel it could meet the deficit through higher taxes. A promise had been given not to increase import duties, and London well knew that a colony could be lost if the mother country increased taxes. The only solution was for Quebec to be given the right to levy its own taxes and pay part of its own way.

In the end, the British government, spurred by Grenville,

passed an act called the Constitutional Act, as a result of which Quebec was divided into two provinces.[5] The predominantly English-speaking region west of Montreal became Upper Canada. The predominantly French-speaking region became Lower Canada. This division, it was hoped, would eliminate the many frictions between the two groups.

Dorchester was asked to determine the boundary between the two provinces, and he suggested the line of the Ottawa River. The southern boundary between Upper Canada and the United States was already fixed by the Treaty of Paris (1783): a line running up the middle of the St. Lawrence River, the middle of Lake Ontario, the Niagara River, and Lake Erie. The western boundary between Upper Canada and the United States was another matter. In the peace treaty that recognized the independence of the Thirteen Colonies, Britain had surrendered to the Americans an enormous area west of lakes Michigan and Superior. In 1774, the Quebec Act had arbitrarily made this part of the Province. The British now knew that, in drawing up the Treaty of Paris in 1783, the leading American negotiator, Benjamin Franklin, had duped them into handing over lands that were fertile and also rich in furred animals. Within this vast area were several British army posts, which the Treaty of Paris stipulated that the British had to abandon and which, eight years later, were still occupied by redcoat garrisons. However, since London was not prepared to face up to this problem, the western boundary between Upper Canada and the United States remained in limbo.

Upper Canada and Lower Canada were each given their own legislature and the power to levy taxes. Each legislature was to consist of two houses, a legislative assembly, the elective counterpart of the House of Commons, and a legislative council whose members were to be appointed for life, as in the House of Lords. Dorchester was pleased by all this, with one exception. He strongly objected to having a legislative house that was hereditary.[6] However, London insisted upon leaving in the Constitutional Act the provision that the monarch could make some or all of the members of the appointive house provincial baronets so that their eldest sons would automatically enter the house. However, this hereditary feature was never put into practice.

Dorchester forwarded a list of individuals he thought should be members of the appointive chambers in both Upper and Lower Canada, and his recommendations were accepted *in toto*. Dorchester then suggested as lieutenant-governor of Upper Canada Sir John Johnson, a Loyalist and a man active in the affairs of the region. This time, Dorchester was ignored and Colonel John Graves Simcoe, a recently elected member of Parliament, was appointed lieutenant-governor.

The Constitutional Act stipulated that Crown land in Upper Canada was to be granted to newcomers for farming in "Free and Common Soccage," that is, free of rent, which was just what Dorchester and Smith had recommended. The system in Lower Canada whereby land was rented in perpetuity from a *seigneur* was not disturbed, again a safeguard that Dorchester had advised. Dorchester had suggested that for every thirty thousand acres given to farmers in a new township in Upper Canada, five thousand acres be retained by the Crown for the future support of a Protestant Church, schools, etc.[7] London agreed; one seventh of the land was to be so reserved. The Constitutional Act, of course, repealed the Quebec Act as far as Upper Canada was concerned. In Lower Canada, however, the Quebec Act, with its guarantees of the Catholic religion, French civil law, etc., was left in force.

Carleton had almost single-handedly persuaded Parliament to produce the Quebec Act, but his influence over the formation of the Constitutional Act was nowhere near as great. One reason was his distance from the London scene. However, there was another reason for Dorchester's limited influence. The population of Quebec in 1790 was about one hundred and fifty thousand.[8] After making numerous inquiries, Dorchester estimated that this population consisted of one English-speaking person for every five French-speaking persons. Of course, this one-to-five ratio was not an even distribution. In the farming districts between Quebec and Montreal, he estimated the ratio as one to forty. In Quebec and Montreal, it was one to two.[9] Along the Ottawa River, there was scarcely a single French Canadian. On the whole, the province had some twenty-five thousand people speaking English, sixteen per cent of the population. The remainder spoke French, but the immigration of English-speaking settlers to the region west of the Ottawa River was continuing. It would be a good many years, but still only a matter of time, before the English-speaking inhabitants outnumbered the French-speaking ones. When Carleton first arrived in 1766, less than one per cent of the population was English-speaking. In November of that year, he had written London:

> The Europeans who emigrate will never prefer the long inhospitable winter of Canada to the more cheerful climate and more fruitful soil of his Majesty's southern provinces . . . . But while this severe climate and the poverty of the country discourages all but the natives, its healthfulness is such that these multiply daily, so that barring a catastrophe shocking to think of, this country to the end of time must be peopled by the Canadian race.[10]

On the supposition that there would be no English-speaking immigration, Carleton had created the Quebec Act, had done everything he could on behalf of the Québécois. Now this supposition was demonstrated to be false. Quebec's population was to consist of a steadily increasing number of English-speaking inhabitants. How were the two groups to be united? For the newcomers to adopt the French language and culture was an impossibility. Should the French then be anglicized?

On November 7th, 1788, Smith had sent Dorchester a memorandum suggesting that the English-speaking people would assimilate the French Canadians. He wrote that New York, New Jersey and Pennsylvania had possessed non-English-speaking settlements, yet these elements had been gradually and quietly absorbed. Shouldn't this be the long-range plan for Canada? Dorchester had rejected the suggestion. He simply could not envision assimilation of the Québécois into the Anglo-Saxon culture. On the other hand, he was certainly not anti-English. In New York City, he encouraged Loyalists to immigrate to Quebec. As governor, he had tried to make it easy for Americans to settle in Quebec. All this left Dorchester with no clear view as to how to integrate the English with the French. On this subject he had written Sydney in June 1787: "For my own part I confess myself as yet at a loss for any plan likely to give satisfaction to a people so circumscribed as we are at present."[11] When a man does not have definite opinions to act on, his influence on events is limited.

In February 1790, Dorchester had written Grenville requesting permission "to return to take care of some private business and to confer over the Constitutional Act."[12] What the private business was we do not know, but his reference to conferring about the Constitutional Act is interesting. He seems to have realized, somewhat belatedly, that to be of influence he had to go to London.

While this letter of Dorchester's was in transit, London received alarming news. In May 1789, on the other side of the continent, two Spanish warships had sailed into Nootka Sound (located on the western shore of what is now Vancouver Island, British Columbia), pulled down the British flag, seized a British vessel, and arrested British fur traders. The captains of these warships claimed for Spain all the territory lying between what are now the states of Oregon and Alaska. Because of the distance involved, it was months before the British government heard about the Nootka incident. When it did, the official reaction was so violent that war with Spain seemed certain. Among other things, Grenville was afraid that the American government might use the opportunity of this international quarrel to seize the army posts in the Great Lakes region that the British had refused to abandon in 1783. Grenville hoped Dorchester could prevent any such move by the United States. Grenville also wanted tacit permission for British troops, possibly from Canada, to cross American territory in order to be able to attack Spanish-held Louisiana. So Grenville wrote Dorchester that he must stay in Quebec and negotiate with the Americans.[13] Dorchester had no option; he could not go to London.

While in New York City, Dorchester had been impressed by the work of Major George Beckwith, an intelligence officer, and had persuaded him to come to Quebec as his aide-de-camp. Beckwith was a friend of Angelica Church, the beautiful and beloved sister-in-law of the American secretary of the treasury, Alexander Hamilton.[14] Through her, and through other contacts in the United States, Beckwith and Dorchester knew that Hamilton was pro-British, that the American secretary of state,

Thomas Jefferson, was anti-British, and that Hamilton had enormous influence over President George Washington. Dorchester therefore sent Beckwith to New York to talk with Hamilton. The two men, almost the same age, got along famously. The United States wanted Spain to grant American vessels free access up and down the Mississippi River. Beckwith agreed. He had authority to promise that Britain would try to force Spain to grant this concession. On behalf of the American government, Hamilton assured Beckwith that there would be no attempt to seize the Great Lakes army posts.[15] And Hamilton also seemed to think that he could arrange for British troops to cross American territory. It looked as if Dorchester had achieved a minor diplomatic triumph, yet, in the end, it amounted to nothing. Contrary to everyone's expectations, Spain and Britain resolved their differences, and there was no outbreak of hostility between the two nations.

Late in July 1791, Dorchester received word that Parliament had passed the Constitutional Act. He was then granted permission to return to England for a visit. The lieutenant-governor of Lower Canada, Sir Alured Clarke, had arrived the year before, and the lieutenant-governor of Upper Canada, John Simcoe, would arrive shortly. Between them, these two men would implement the Constitutional Act. It was the end of an era for Dorchester.

On August 18th, 1791, Dorchester sailed for England[16] with Maria and their eight children, including his latest son, Dudley Carleton, born on June 22nd of the previous year.[17] (This child had been named for Dorchester's distant relative, the man who had become the first Lord Dorchester.) Shortly after reaching the capital, Dorchester purchased a lieutenantcy in the 3rd Guards for his oldest son Guy. In succeeding months, he purchased commissions for his next two sons, Thomas and Christopher. On February 7th, 1792, Dorchester went through the ceremony of taking his seat in the House of Lords, his sponsors being Lord Cathcart, a lieutenant-colonel in the army, and Lord Fife, an Irishman with large estates in Scotland.[18] On February 10th, 1792, his eleventh and last child, Richard, was born in a house in Queen Anne Street, London.[19] This is all we know of Dorchester's twenty-two-month stay in England.

On August 18th, 1793, Dorchester set sail again for Quebec. Now almost sixty-nine years of age, why did he go back? Why didn't he just resign? Lieutenant-Governor Alured Clarke had returned to Europe in June 1793 for some undisclosed reason, and Dorchester must have felt that it was his duty to go back immediately. Times were bad. In February, France had declared war on England. Edmond Charles Genet, a French agent, had landed in Charleston, South Carolina, in April 1793, with instructions to fit out American privateers to raid British ships and urge the United States to join France in the war against England. But Genet posed a special threat to Lower Canada. His instructions included a directive "to unite the American states with the beautiful star of Canada."[20] Knowing all this, Dorchester must have feared the reaction in Quebec and felt that his presence might deflect any efforts to subvert the Québécois. And there may have been another, more personal, motive. Perhaps he did not want to retire. Perhaps he could not give up public service, even at his age.

Dorchester returned to Quebec with peace very much in mind. On October 25th, he wrote Dundas, who had replaced Grenville:

> I must acknowledge that the interests of the King's American dominions require peace, and I think the interests of the states [the United States] require it still more though their conduct both to us and to the Indians has created many difficulties. What revolutions may take place there in the progress of time I think impossible to foresee, but am clearly of opinion that not war, but a pure and impartial administration of justice under a mild, firm, and wise government will establish the most powerful and wealthy people.[21]

But as fall stretched into winter, things began to look ominous. General Anthony Wayne was in command of an army raised to drive Indians out of parts of the Ohio territory. But rumor had it that "Mad Anthony" Wayne was going to attack the British posts in American-held territory and then start invading Canada. There were still other rumors. It was alleged that the state of

Vermont had offered to undertake the reduction of Canada, providing that the Vermont militia was permitted to plunder the inhabitants. In addition, agents of "Citizen" Genet were said to be circulating pamphlets in Quebec and Montreal urging the Québécois to "cast off the yoke of British bondage."[22]

This was the background to a large meeting of Indians of Lower Canada held in February 1794. Dorchester, in his address, used the occasion to warn them of the dangers that threatened the peace of the country. He had hoped that a new definite boundary line between Americans, Canadians and Indians would have been agreed upon but this had not happened. Dorchester therefore announced to his audience: "Since my return I find no appearance of a line remains; and from the manner in which the people from the states push on . . . . I shall not be surprised if we are not at war with them in the course of the present year; and if so a line must be drawn by the Warriors' children."[23] Dorchester not only delivered a provocative speech; he proceeded to take measures that were a mixture of defence and offence. Allegedly to protect the British fort at Detroit from an attack by General Wayne, he sent troops to occupy posts on the Miami River, posts that had been abandoned ten years earlier.

Dorchester's speech had been picked up by American newspapers and reached the attention of John Randolph, the new American secretary of state. Randolph protested to London in no uncertain terms. He considered the conduct of Dorchester as "hostility itself." On July 5th, Dundas wrote Dorchester, expressing apprehension that his speech to the Indians and the garrisoning of the Miami posts would provoke hostilities. Dorchester considered the letter a censure of his conduct. He replied stiffly on September 4th, saying that it was impossible for him to have given the Indians any hope for peace, and that he saw no reason for concealing his opinion on a subject that was of great interest to them. He continued:

> Private inclination and public duty apart, it would be folly in the extreme for any Commander-in-Chief circumscribed as I find myself here, without troops, without authority, amidst a people barely not in arms against the King, on his own to provoke hostility or to begin, as Mr. Secretary Randolph is pleased to call it,

"Hostility itself." You will perceive, sir, with me, that various reasons concur to make it necessary for the King's service that I retire from this command; I am therefore to request that you will have the goodness to obtain for me His Majesty's permission to resign the command of his Province in North America, and that I may return home by the first opportunity.[24]

The year before, it looked as if Dorchester had not wanted to retire after being idle in England for two years. What had changed his mind? Resuming his duties as governor may have been more onerous than he had expected. And, in December 1793, William Smith, not only his friend but his alter ego, had died. This must have depressed Dorchester and also increased the burdens of office. Dorchester was also convinced that war clouds were gathering. His professional soldiers, a little over two thousand, seemed hopelessly inadequate to check any serious American attack. He knew the futility of trying to use militia. Indians had, in 1790 and again in 1791, defeated American forces—hence his stirring speech to them—but, on August 20th, 1794, Wayne and his frontiersmen decisively defeated their Indian opponents near what is now Toledo, Ohio. Now, months later, he must have realized that his speech had been a mistake, that his judgement was slipping, that at seventy years old he should retire.

Dorchester, awaiting replacement, remained governor-in-chief for another two years. His activities can be covered briefly. His fears of war proved unfounded. In the fall of 1794, John Jay negotiated a new treaty in which the British agreed to withdraw, by June 1st, 1796, all troops at posts within the boundary lines established by the Treaty of Paris of 1783. Genet's mission in the United States failed. He was disowned, and his propaganda urging the inhabitants of Quebec to revolt stopped as quickly as it had started. The excesses of the French Revolution horrified the Catholic priests, the *seigneurs*, and other leaders in Lower Canada. They had no desire to be allies of an anti-clerical, god-forsaken France. As for purely domestic affairs, when Dorchester recommended the appointment of William Osgoode to succeed Smith, he delivered his old maxim of "no fees." Osgoode, agreeing to relinquish the fees of his office, became the new chief justice of Quebec.[25]

In May 1796, his replacement, General Robert Prescott, arrived. On July 9th, Dorchester and his family sailed for England on the *Active*. Six days later, it ran aground on Anticosti, a large island in the Gulf of St. Lawrence some three hundred and sixty miles below Quebec. No lives were lost, but the ship, which had run up on a rocky shore, could not be freed. A coastal schooner, standing by, carried the Dorchesters to a fishing village, Percé, sixty miles to the south on the Gaspé shore. Word was sent to Halifax, and the *Dover* was dispatched to pick up the Dorchesters. After a voyage without further incident, they reached Portsmouth on September 19th, 1796. It was Dorchester's fourteenth and last Atlantic voyage.

For the next twelve years, the Dorchesters lived in England, dividing their time among the three homes they owned. The largest and most beautiful was Greywell Hill in Hampshire. The size of the Greywell mansion can be appreciated by considering the living room. Today, with seven enormous couches and many chairs and tables in different groups, this room does not seem overly furnished. The Dorchesters' second residence was Kempshot House, not far from Greywell and reputedly much smaller. (The author was unable to find Kempshot House—if it is still standing.) The third residence was a mansion called Stubbings near Maidenhead, Berkshire. One of the attractions of Stubbings was that the trip from there to London was not arduous; it was only some thirty miles, whereas Greywell and Kempshot were some fifty miles from the capital.

On November 10th, 1808, Dorchester died suddenly at Stubbings in his eighty-fourth year. He was buried in the vault of Nately Scures, a tiny, twelfth-century chapel adjoining the Greywell Hill estate.

EPILOGUE

Guy Carleton is one of the decisive figures in eithteenth-century history because he kept Quebec (and, ultimately, Canada) within the British Empire, not on Britain's terms but on those of the Québécois. Distrusting the undercurrents of revolt flowing in the Thirteen Colonies and preferring the stable, orderly, semi-feudal society he found in Quebec, Carleton preserved that society by, in fact, disobeying his sovereign's Proclamation of 1763. That document decreed the use of English law, abolished the established Roman Catholic Church, promised freehold tenure of land after the English model, and also promised an elected legislative assembly after the British colonial model. Carleton perceived the long-term wisdom of retaining the loyalty of the Québécois by letting them live in their own way. This meant allowing the courts to follow the "Custom of Paris" in civil suits, continuing to grant land *en fief et seigneurie*, supporting the Roman Catholic Church (and occasionally using it as an implement of government), and refusing to call an elective assembly, which he knew a minority of provincial English-speaking immigrants would use to dominate and anglicize the French-speaking majority.

It was Carleton's genius that he was able to maintain *l'ancien regime* on the St. Lawrence and peruade King and Parliament to sanction this arrangement in the Quebec Act of 1774, a unique piece of British legislation for its time. The Quebec Act was the first tentative, almost unconscious, step in the construction of the second British Empire. Unknown to Carleton, George III and Parliament, it was also a step toward the creation of what came to be called the Commonwealth of Nations.

APPENDIX

THE QUEBEC ACT[1]
ANNO DECIMO QUARTO
GEORGE III, REGIS.
CAP. LXXXIII.

An Act for making more effectual Provision for the Government of the Province of *Quebec* in *North America*.

Whereas His Majesty, by His Royal Proclamation, bearing Date the Seventh Day of *October*, in the Third Year of His Reign, thought fit to declare the Provisions which had been made in respect to certain Countries, Territories, and Islands in *America*, ceded to His Majesty by the definitive Treaty of Peace, concluded at *Paris* on the Tenth Day of *February*, One thousand seven hundred and sixty-three: And whereas, by the Arrangements made by the said Royal Proclamation, a very large Extent of Country, within which there were several Colonies and Settlements of the Subjects of *France*, who claimed to remain therein under the Faith of the said Treaty, was left, without any Provision being made for the Administration of Civil Government therein; and certain Parts of the Territory of *Canada*, where sedentary Fisheries had been established and carried on by the Subjects of *France*, Inhabitants of the said Province of *Canada*, under Grants and Concessions from the Government thereof, were annexed to the Government of *Newfoundland*, and thereby

---

[1]The text of the Act is taken from the original folio black letter form in which it was first issued by the King's Printers. "London: Printed by Charles Eyre and William Strachan, Printers to the King's most Excellent Majesty. MDCCLXXIV."

Appendix

subjected to Regulations inconsistent with the Nature of such
Fisheries: May it therefore please Your most Excellent Majesty
that it may be enacted; and be it enacted by the King's most
Excellent Majesty, by and with the Advice and Consent of the
Lords Spiritual and Temporal, and Commons, in this present
Parliament assembled, and by the Authority of the same, That
all the Territories, Islands, and Countries in *North America*,
belonging to the Crown of *Great Britain*, bounded on the South
by a Line from the Bay of *Chaleurs*, along the High Lands which
divide the Rivers that empty themselves into the River *Saint
Lawrence* from those which fall into the Sea, to a Point in Forty-
five Degrees of Northern Latitude, on the Eastern Bank of the
River *Connecticut*, keeping the same Latitude directly West,
through the Lake *Champlain*, until, in the same Latitude, it meets
the River *Saint Lawrence*; from thence up the Eastern Bank of the
said River to the Lake *Ontario*; thence through the Lake *Ontario*,
and the River commonly called *Niagara*; and thence along by the
Eastern and South-eastern Bank of Lake *Erie*, following the said
Bank, until the same shall be intersected by the Northern Boundary, by the Charter of the Province of Pennsylvania, in case the
same shall be so intersected; and from thence along the said
Northern and Western Boundaries of the said Province, until
the said Western Boundary strike the *Ohio*: But in case the said
Bank of the said Lake shall not be found to be so intersected,
then following the said Bank until it shall arrive at that Point of
the said Bank which shall be nearest to the North-western Angle
of the said Province of *Pennsylvania*, and thence, by a right Line,
to the said North-western Angle of the said Province; and
thence along the Western Boundary of the said Province, until it
strike the River *Ohio*; and along the Bank of the said River, Westward, to the Banks of the *Mississippi*, and Northward to the
Southern Boundary of the Territory granted to the Merchants
Adventurers of *England*, trading to *Hudson's Bay*; and also all
such Territories, Islands and Countries, which have, since the
Tenth of *February*, One thousand seven hundred and sixty-
three, been made Part of the Government of *Newfoundland*, be,
and they are hereby, during His Majesty's Pleasure, annexed to,
and made Part and Parcel of, the Province of *Quebec*, as created

and established by the said Royal Proclamation of the Seventh of *October*, One thousand seven hundred and sixty-three.

Provided always, That nothing herein contained, relative to the Boundary of the Province of *Quebec*, shall in anywise affect the Boundaries of any other Colony.

Provided always, and be it enacted, That nothing in this Act contained shall extend, or be construed to extend, to make void, or to vary or alter any Right, Title, or Possession, derived under any Grant, Conveyance, or otherwise howsoever, of or to any Lands within the said Province, or the Provinces thereto adjoining; but that the same shall remain and be in Force, and have Effect, as if this Act had never been made.

And whereas the Provisions, made by the said Proclamation, in respect to the Civil Government of the said Province of *Quebec*, and the Powers and Authorities given to the Governor and other Civil Officers of the said Province, by the Grants and Commissions issued in consequence thereof, have been found, upon Experience, to be inapplicable to the State and Circumstances of the said Province, the Inhabitants whereof amounted, at the Conquest, to above Sixty-five thousands Persons professing the Religion of the Church of *Rome*, and enjoying an established Form of Constitution and System of Laws, by which their Persons and Property had been protected, governed, and ordered, for a long Series of Years, from the First Establishment of the said Province of *Canada*; be it therefore further enacted by the Authority aforesaid, That the said Proclamation, so far as the same relates to the said Province of *Quebec*, and the Commission under the Authority whereof the Government of the said Province is at present administered, and all and every the Ordinance and Ordinances made by the Governor and Council of *Quebec* for the Time being, relative to the Civil Government and Administration of Justice in the said Province, and all Commissions to Judges and other Officers thereof, be, and the same are hereby revoked, annulled, and made void from and after the First Day of *May*, One thousand seven hundred and seventy-five.

And, for the more perfect Security and Ease of the Minds of the Inhabitants of the said Province, it is hereby declared, That His Majesty's Subjects, professing the Religion of the Church of *Rome* of and in the said Province of *Quebec*, may have, hold, and enjoy, the free Exercise of the Religion of the Church of *Rome,* subject to the King's Supremacy, declared and established by an Act, made in the First Year of the Reign of Queen *Elizabeth,* over all the Dominions and Countries which then did, or thereafter should belong, to the Imperial Crown of this Realm; and that the Clergy of the said Church may hold, receive, and enjoy, their accustomed Dues and Rights, with respect to such Persons only as shall profess the said Religion.

Provided nevertheless, That it shall be lawful for His Majesty, His Heirs or Successors, to make such Provision out of the rest of the said accustomed Dues and Rights, for the Encouragement of the Protestant Religion, and for the Maintenance and Support of a Protestant Clergy within the said Province, as he or they shall, from Time to Time, think necessary and expedient.

Provided always, and be it enacted, That no Person, professing the Religion of the Church of *Rome,* and residing in the said Province, shall be obliged to take the Oath required by the said Statute passed in the First Year of the Reign of Queen *Elizabeth,* or any other Oaths substituted by any other Act in the Place thereof; but that every such Person who, by the said Statute is required to take the Oath therein mentioned, shall be obliged, and is hereby required, to take and subscribe the following Oath before the Governor, or such other Person in such Court of Record as His Majesty shall appoint, who are hereby authorized to administer the same; *videlicet,*

I A. B. *do sincerely promise and swear, That I will be faithful, and bear true Allegiance to His Majesty King* GEORGE, *and him will defend to the utmost of my Power, against all traiterous Conspiracies, and Attempts whatsoever, which shall be made against His Person, Crown, and Dignity; and I will do my utmost Endeavour to disclose and make known to His Majesty, His Heirs and Successors, all Treasons, and traiterous Conspiracies, and Attempts, which I shall know to be against Him, or any of Them; and all this I do swear without any Equivocation, mental Evasion, or secret Reservation, and renouncing all Pardons and Dispensations from any Power or Person whomsoever to the Contrary.*
SO HELP ME GOD.

And every such Person, who shall neglect or refuse to take the said Oath before mentioned, shall incur and be liable to the same Penalties, Forfeitures, Disabilities, and Incapacities, as he would have incurred and been liable to for neglecting or refusing to take the Oath required by the said Statute passed in the First Year of the Reign of Queen *Elizabeth*.

And be it further enacted by the Authority aforesaid, That all His Majesty's *Canadian* Subjects, within the Province of *Quebec*, the religious Orders and Communities only excepted, may also hold and enjoy their Property and Possessions, together with all Customs and Usages relative thereto, and all other their Civil Rights, in as large, ample, and beneficial Manner, as if the said Proclamation, Commissions, Ordinances, and other Acts and Instruments, had not been made, and as may consist with their Allegiance to His Majesty, and Subjection to the Crown and Parliament of *Great Britain*; and that in all Matters of Controversy, relative to Property and Civil Rights, Resort shall be had to the Laws of *Canada*, as the Rule for the Decision of the same; and all Causes that shall hereafter be instituted in any of the Courts of Justice, to be appointed within and for the said Province, by His Majesty, His Heirs and Successors, shall, with respect to such Property and Rights, be determined agreeably to the said Laws and Customs of *Canada*, until they shall be varied or altered by any Ordinances that shall, from Time to Time, be passed in the said Province by the Governor, Lieutenant Governor, or Commander in Chief, for the Time being, by and with the Advice and Consent of the Legislative Council of the same, to be appointed in Manner herein-after mentioned.

Provided always, That nothing in this Act contained shall extend, or be construed to extend, to any Lands that have been granted by His Majesty, or shall hereafter be granted by His Majesty His Heirs and Successors, to be holden in free and common Soccage.

Provided also, That it shall and may be alwful to and for every Person that is Owner of any Lands, Goods, or Credits, in the said Province, and that has a Right to alienate the said Lands, Goods, or Credits, in his or her Life-time, by Deed of Sale, Gift, or otherwise, to devise or bequeath the same at his or her Death, by his or her last Will and Testament; any Law, Usage, or Custom, heretofore or now prevailing in the Province, to the Contrary hereof in any-wise notwithstanding; such Will being executed, either according to the Laws of Canada, or according to the Forms prescribed by the Laws of *England*.

And whereas the Certainty and Lenity of the Criminal Law of *England*, and the Benefits and Advantages resulting from the Use of it, have been sensibly felt by the Inhabitants, from an Experience of more than Nine Years, during which it has been uniformly administered; be it therefore further enacted by the Authority aforesaid, That the same shall continue to be administered, and shall be observed as Law in the Province of *Quebec*, as well in the Description and Quality of the Offence as in the Method of Prosecution and Trial; and the Punishments and Forfeitures thereby inflicted to the Exclusion of every other Rule of Criminal Law, or Mode of Proceeding thereon, which did or might prevail in the said Province before the Year of our Lord One thousand seven hundred and sixty-four; any Thing in this Act to the Contrary thereof in any Respect notwithstanding; subject nevertheless to such Alterations and Amendments as the Governor, Lieutenant-governor, or Commander in Chief for the Time being, by and with the Advice and Consent of the legislative Council of the said Province, hereafter to be appointed, shall, from Time to Time, cause to be made therein, in Manner herein-after directed.

And whereas it may be necessary to ordain many Regulations for the future Welfare and good Government of the Province of *Quebec*, the Occasions of which cannot now be foreseen, nor, without much Delay and Inconvenience, be provided for, without intrusting that Authority, for a certain Time, and under proper Restrictions, to Persons resident there: And whereas it is at present inexpedient to call an Assembly; be it therefore enacted by the Authority aforesaid, That it shall and may be lawful for His Majesty, His Heirs and Successors, by Warrant under His or Their Signet or Sign Manual, and with the Advice of the Privy Council, to constitute and appoint a Council for the Affairs of the Province of *Quebec*, to consist of such Persons resident there, not exceeding Twenty-three, nor less than Seventeen, as His Majesty, His Heirs and Successors, shall be pleased to appoint; and, upon the Death, Removal, or Absence of any of the Members of the Council, in like Manner to constitute and appoint such and so many other Person or Persons as shall be necessary to supply the Vacancy or Vacancies; which Council, so appointed and nominated, or the major Part thereof, shall have Power and Authority to make Ordinances for the Peace, Welfare, and good Government, of the said Province, with the Consent of His Majesty's Governor, or, in his Absence, of the Lieutenant-governor, or Commander in Chief for the Time being.

Provided always, That nothing in this Act contained shall extend to authorise or impower the said legislative Council to lay any Taxes or Duties within the said Province, such Rates and Taxes only excepted as the Inhabitants of any Town or District within the said Province may be authorised by the said Council to assess, levy, and apply, within the said Town or District, for the Purpose of making Roads, erecting and repairing publick Buildings, or for any other Purpose respecting the local Convenience and Oeconomy of such Town or District.

Provided also, and be it enacted by the Authority aforesaid, That every Ordinance so to be made, shall, within Six Months, be transmitted by the Governor, or, in his Absence, by the Lieutenant-governor, or Commander in Chief for the Time being, and laid before His Majesty for His Royal Approbation; and if His Majesty shall think fit to disallow thereof, the same shall cease and be void from the Time that His Majesty's Order in Council thereupon shall be promulgated at *Quebec*.

Provided also, That no Ordinance touching Religion, or by which any Punishment may be inflicted greater than Fine or Imprisonment for Three Months, shall be of any Force or Effect, until the same shall have received His Majesty's Approbation.

Provided also, That no Ordinance shall be passed at any Meeting of the Council where less than a Majority of the whole Council is present, or at any Time except between the First Day of *January* and the First Day of *May*, unless upon some urgent Occasion, in which Case every Member thereof resident at *Quebec*, or within Fifty Miles thereof, shall be personally summoned by the Governor, or, in his Absence, by the Lieutenant-governor, or Commander in Chief for the Time being, to attend the same.

And be it further enacted by the Authority aforesaid, That

nothing herein contained shall extend, or be construed to extend, to prevent or hinder His Majesty, His Heirs and Successors, by His or Their Letters Patent under the Great Seal of *Great Britain*, from erecting, constituting, and appointing, such Courts of Criminal, Civil, and Ecclesiastical Jurisdiction within and for the said Province of *Quebec*, and appointing, from Time to Time, the Judges and Officers thereof, as His Majesty, His Heirs and Successors, shall think necessary and proper for the circumstances of the said Province.

Provided always, and it is hereby enacted, That nothing in this Act contained shall extend, or be construed to extend, to repeal or make void, within the said Province of *Quebec*, any Act or Acts of the Parliament of *Great Britain* heretofore made, for prohibiting, restraining, or regulating, the Trade or Commerce of His Majesty's Colonies and Plantations in *America*; but that all and every the said Acts, and also all Acts of Parliament heretofore made concerning or respecting the said Colonies and Plantations, shall be, and are hereby declared to be, in Force, within the said Province of *Quebec*, and every part thereof.

Finis.

NOTES

Chapter 1

1. The Carleton memorial in the Nately Scures chapel gives his birth as 1722. His previous three biographers, other historians and all reference books I have consulted place his birth in 1724. They give no source but probably follow Burdy. Circumstantial evidence, such as Carleton's entering the army at eighteen in 1742, supports 1724 as his birthdate.

2. Berkshire County Archivist.

3. Samuel Burdy, *Complete Works of Philip Shelton with His Life*, Chapter 1.

4. Berkles Wilson, *The Life and Letters of James Wolfe*, p. 228. Wolfe wrote his mother: "I hear that Mr. Conolly is relapsed, probably gone by this time. Carleton will feel the loss . . . . He [Conolly] was his patron and protector."

5. Ibid., p. 72. The first letter of Wolfe's to mention Carleton is in 1747.

6. Ibid., p. 196

7. Ibid., p. 358.

8. Ibid., p. 392.

9. Ibid., p. 354.

10. Ibid., p. 356.

11. Ibid., p. 411.

12. Francis Parkman, *Montcalm and Wolfe*, vol. 2, p. 204, and

Jean-Claude Hébert, *Le Siège de Québec en 1759 par trois témoins*, p. 130.

13. New York Historical Society, *Journal of Captain John Montresor*, p. 219.

14. Parkman, *Montcalm and Wolfe*, vol. 2, p. 225; Hébert, *Le Siège de Québec*, p. 130, says Carleton had three hundred soldiers.

15. Parkman, *Montcalm and Wolfe*, pp. 285-6. Parkman has made this legend celebrated, although its historical evidence is tenuous. See C.P. Stacey, *Quebec 1759*, pp. 122-3.

16. Wilson, *Wolfe*, p. 511. A Captain Leslie wrote to his father, September 13th, 1759: "Guy Carleton was wounded in the head, but no danger is apprehended." George M. Wrong, *Canada and the American Revolution*, p. 222, says Carleton was badly wounded.

17. Alan Valentine, *Lord George Germain*, p. 499.

18. Christopher Hibbert, *Wolfe at Quebec*, p. 130. A friend of Wolfe's, Katherine Lauther, gave Wolfe the volume with the poem. Alongside the poem are comments in Wolfe's handwriting.

Chapter 2

1. The author personally visited Belle-Ile-en-Mer. In the museum of the citadel at Le Palais is a pamphlet describing the capture of the island.

2. The author's sources for the capture of Havana are Willis Fletcher Johnson, *The History of Cuba*, and W. Adolph Roberts, *Havana, the Portait of a City*.

3. William Wood, *The Father of British Canada*, p. 153.

4. Berkles Wilson, *The Life and Letters of James Wolfe*, p. 153.

5. Smithsonian Institution, *The Road to American Independence*, p. 15.

6. Jean McIlwraith, *The Life of Sir Frederick Haldimand*, p. 119.

7. New York Historical Society, *Journal of Captain John Montresor*, p. 384.

8. Quebec *Gazette*, September 26, 1766.

9. The description of the Château St. Louis is based upon a sketch made in 1698 and reproduced in J. Camile Pouliot, *Quebec and the Isle of Orleans*, p. 146. The Château, with its massive stone wall facing Lévis and its copper roof, seems not to have been seriously damaged by Wolfe's cannon balls. However, according to Jean-Claude Hébert, *Le Siège de Québec en 1759 par trois témoins*, p. 125, the Château did suffer significant damage. See also Francis Parkman, *The Old Regime of Canada*, pp. 419-21.

10. Gustave Lanctot, *A History of Canada*, vol. 3, p. 249. The census of 1765 showed a population of 69,810, but some localities are missing.

11. Reginald Coupland, *The Quebec Act*, p. 109.

12. Adam Shortt and A. G. Doughty, eds., *Canada and Its Provinces*, vol. 4, p. 527.

13. Lanctot, *A History of Canada*, vol. 3, p. 126. There were one hundred and sixty-three priests in 1759, but the number must have dropped in the next six years, because there was no bishop and hence no new priests could be ordained.

Chapter 3

1. A. G. Bradley, *Sir Guy Carleton*, p. 33.

2. A. L. Burt, "Sir Guy Carleton and His First Council," *Canadian Historical Review*, December 1923, p. 322.

3. Ibid., p. 323.

4. *Report on American Manuscripts in the Royal Institution of Great Britain*, vol. 3, p. 421. Carleton ordered three cases of claret for his personal use, and bought wine often.

5. A. L. Burt, "Carleton First Council," p. 324.

6. Adam Shortt and A. G. Doughty, eds., *Documents Relating to the Constitutional History of Canada, 1759-1791*, p. 303.

7. Peter Force, *American Archives*, vol. 5, part 2, p. 246.

8. Shortt and Doughty, *Documents*, p. 277.

9. Edgar W. McInnis, *Canada, A Political and Social History*, p. 139.

10. Shortt and Doughty, *Documents*, p. 281.

Chapter 4

1. Quebec *Gazette*, June 4th, 1765.

2. Adam Shortt and A. G. Doughty, eds., *Canada and Its Provinces*, vol. 2, p. 405.

3. A. G. Bradley, *Sir Guy Carleton*, p. 36.

4. Adam Shortt and A. G. Doughty, eds., *Documents Relating to the Constitutional History of Canada, 1759-1791*, p. 290.

5. R. H. Mahon, *General James Murray*, pp. 366-8. Four days before his departure for London, Murray collected fees totalling £599 6s. His son signed the receipt, but it is not clear what time period the fees were for.

6. This was the lieutenant-governor's salary in 1774 and there is no evidence that salaries had changed in the previous ten years.

7. Mahon, *Murray*, pp. 366-8.

8. Quebec *Gazette*, May 21st, 1767.

9. K. G. Davies, *Documents of the American Revolution*, vol. 1, pp. 131-2.

10. Mandements des Evêques de Québec, p. 189.

11. Quebec *Gazette*, October 29th, 1767.

12. Alfred Leroy Burt, *The Old Province of Quebec*, pp. 260-1.

13. Quebec *Gazette*, April 10th, 1768.

14. Ibid., May 30th, 1769.

15. Ibid., June 2nd, 1768.

16. Ibid., July 7th, 1766.

17. Shortt and Doughty, *Documents*, p. 272.

18. Ibid., p. 273.

19. Mahon, *Murray*, p. 377.

20. Quebec *Gazette*, November 3rd, 1768.

Chapter 5

1. Adam Shortt and A. G. Doughty, eds., *Documents Relating to the Constitutional History of Canada, 1759-1791*, p. 568n.

2. K. G. Davies, *Documents of the American Revolution*, p. 182.

3. Shortt and Doughty, *Documents*, pp. 401-16.

4. Samuel Johnson, *The Rambler*, number 82.

5. Shortt and Doughty, *Documents*, p. 294.

6. Reginald Coupland, *The Quebec Act*, p. 132.

7. Ibid., p. 134.

8. Shortt and Doughty, *Documents*, p. 294.

9. Ibid., p. 392.

10. Ibid., p. 369n.

Chapter 6

1. K. G. Davies, *Documents of the American Revolution*, vol. 4, p. 13.

2. Ibid., p. 247.

3. Ibid., p. 384.

4. Ibid., p. 97.

5. Ibid., p. 118.

6. Bradley mistakes Maria's brother for her father. The then Lady Dorchester told Bradley this story seventy-five years or so

ago. This lady's daughter and granddaughter, Lady Dorchester and the Duchess of Malmesbury, recounted this version of the story to me in 1977.

7. Baroness Von Riedesel, *Riedesel and the American Revolution,* p. 122; and Lieutenant James M. Hadden, *A Journal Kept in Canada and upon Burgoyne's Campaign,* p. 20. Christopher Carleton was the son of Carleton's oldest brother, William Carleton.

8. William Wood, *The Father of British Canada,* p. 52.

9. *Collins Peerage of England.*

10. *Gentleman's Magazine,* May 1772.

11. Alfred Leroy Burt, *The Old Province of Quebec,* p. 513, n3. In the spring of 1767, Carleton had said that the only perquisite he had ever accepted was the prize money at Havana.

12. Berkles Wilson, *The Life and Letters of James Wolfe,* p. 111.

13. *Report on American Manuscripts in the Royal Institution of Great Britain,* vol. 1, p. 65.

14. R. Cole Harris and John Warkentin, *Canada before Confederation,* p. 177.

15. Tablet in Nately Scures chapel, Hampshire, England.

16. George Otto Trevelyan, *The American Revolution,* vol. 1, part 2, p. 248.

17. Adam Shortt and A. G. Doughty, eds., *Documents Relating to the Constitutional History of Canada, 1759-1791,* pp. 504-8; Sir Henry Cavendish, *Debates in the House of Commons in the Year 1774,* p. 153. One hundred and fifty thousand is too high. It is likely that Cavendish, a member of the House of Commons who took notes and later wrote up the debates, made a mistake in recording what Carleton had said. The French-speaking population was around ninety thousand.

18. Cavendish, *Debates 1774,* pp. 153-6.

19. Ibid.

20. Ibid.

21. Reginald Coupland, *The Quebec Act*, p. 96.

22. Shortt and Doughty, *Documents*, pp. 294-6.

23. Edmund Burke, *The Works and Correspondence*, vol. 2, p. 463.

24. Ibid. Burke wrote the Committee of Correspondence for the General Assembly of New York: " . . . particularly the post of Niagara, which Mr. Carleton, I am told, was earnest to have within his government, but by the [Quebec] act is excluded."

25. Coupland, *The Quebec Act*, p. 193.

Chapter 7

1. Quebec *Gazette*, September 22nd, 1774.

2. George M. Wrong, *Canada and the American Revolution*, p. 346. Murray's wife had refused to accompany him to Canada.

3. Peter Force, ed., *American Archives*, vol. 5, part 2, p. 794.

4. Adam Shortt and A. G. Doughty, eds., *Canada and Its Provinces*, vol. 6, p. 283.

5. A corrected and authenticated version of the Quebec Act was published in the *Gazette* on December 8th, 1774.

6. Adam Shortt and A. G. Doughty, eds., *Documents Relating to the Constitutional History of Canada, 1759-1791*, p. 591.

7. Ibid., p. 588.

8. Gustave Lanctot, *Canada and the American Revolution, 1774-1783*, p. 245. Lanctot gives the complete text of the letter in an appendix.

9. Quebec *Gazette*, May 18th, 1775.

10. Force, *American Archives*, vol. 5, part 2, p. 246.

11. Shortt and Doughty, *Documents*, p. 594.

12. Alfred Leroy Burt, *The United States, Great Britain and British North America*, pp. 33-4. Lieutenant Digby said of Carleton: "In

time of danger he possesses a coolness and steadiness which few can attain."

13. John André, artist, poet and rejected suitor, had purchased a lieutenantcy in the 7th Foot in 1771. In the late fall of 1774, he joined the regiment in Quebec.

14. William Bennet Munroe, *The Seigneurs of Old Canada*, pp. 143-4.

15. H. A. Verreau, ed., *Invasion du Canada: Collection des mémoires recuellis et annotés*, pp. 143-4.

16. Quebec *Gazette*, August 3rd, 1775, states that there were sixteen hundred Indians—a gross exaggeration. Verreau gives a total of six hundred.

17. General Riedesel, *Memoirs, Letters and Journals*, pp. 46-7. Riedesel was present at the meeting of Carleton and the Indians in this same church a year later. He states that there were several meetings in this church, all similar in ceremony, and I have used his description.

18. George Otto Trevelyan, *The American Revolution*, vol. 1, part 3, p. 83n.

19. Henry Steele Commager and Richard B. Morris, *The Spirit of Seventy-six*, pp. 186-7.

20. Trevelyan, *The American Revolution*, vol. 1, part 3, 83n.

21. Shortt and Doughty, *Documents*, p. 596.

22. Robert McConnell Hatch, *Thrust for Canada*.

23. Quebec *Gazette*, August 3rd, 1775.

Chapter 8

1. Quebec *Gazette*, July 27th, 1775.

2. The records of the English Cathedral at Quebec City show that Carleton and his wife signed the baptismal registry on this date.

3. Quebec *Gazette,* September 26th, 1775.

4. Ibid., August 9th, 1775; Adam Shortt and A. G. Doughty, eds., *Canada and Its Provinces,* vol. 3, p. 400.

5. A. G. Bradley, *Sir Guy Carleton,* p. 100.

6. Gustave Lanctot, *Canada and the American Revolution,* p. 78.

7. H. A. Verreau, ed., *Invasion du Canada: Collection des mémoires recuellis et annotés,* p. 49.

8. Christopher Ward, *The War of Revolution,* p. 160; Verreau, *Invasion du Canada,* pp. 89-93.

9. Lanctot, *Canada and the American Revolution,* p. 90.

10. Allen French, *The First Year of the American Revolution,* p. 429.

11. Verreau, *Invasion du Canada,* p. 234. Senau(t) is French for trysail. A brig is a two-masted boat, which in this case had its rear mast fitted with a trysail.

12. Alfred Leroy Burt, *The Old Province of Quebec,* p. 219.

13. Verreau, *Invasion du Canada,* p. 39.

14. Adam Shortt and A. G. Doughty, eds., *Documents Relating to the Constitutional History of Canada, 1759-1791,* p. 660.

15. Ibid., pp. 637-8.

16. Ibid., p. 671.

17. Quebec *Gazette,* November 16th, 1775.

18. Alan Valentine, *Lord George Germain,* p. 305.

19. George Otto Trevelyan, *The American Revolution,* vol. 1, part 2.

20. Verreau, *Invasion du Canada,* p. 338. These letters were sent to New York via the governor of New York. A Brooke Watson wrote from New York City on June 19th, 1775, that he had a letter from Chatham to Carleton and letters to Maria from her mother and sisters. These letters do not seem to have reached the Carletons until September.

Chapter 9

1. Quebec *Gazette*, November 23rd, 1775.

2. Thomas Ainslie, *Canada Preserved, a Journal*, p. 24.

3. New York Historical Society, *Journal of the Most Remarkable Occurrences in Quebec by an Officer of the Garrison*, entry for November 14th. This count was made five days before Carleton arrived in Quebec.

4. Henry Steele Commager and Richard B. Morris, *The Spirit of Seventy-six*, p. 202.

5. Maria Tremaine, *A Bibliography of Canadian Imprints*, p. 101.

6. Quebec *Gazette*, October 26th, 1775.

7. Thomas Fleming, *1776: Year of Illusions*, p. 10. The officer in note 3 above estimated the number of seamen at four hundred.

8. Lieutenant James M. Hadden, *A Journal Kept in Canada and upon Burgoyne's Campaign*, pp. 549-50.

9. Harrison Bird, *Attack on Quebec*, p. 140.

10. Commager and Morris, *Spirit of Seventy-six*, p. 202.

11. Bird, *Attack on Quebec*, p. 175.

12. Adam Shortt and A. G. Doughty, eds., *Canada and Its Provinces*, vol. 3, pp. 88-9.

13. Peter Force, ed. *American Archives*, vol. 4, pp. 289-90.

14. New York Historical Society, *Journal by an Officer*, p. 212.

15. John Codman, *Arnold's Expedition to Quebec*, p. 262.

16. Hadden, *Journal*, p. 43.

17. Some journals by American soldiers, including John Henry and Abner Stocking, give December 31st-January 1st as the night of the battle. Carleton and Arnold, however, both record it as December 30th-31st.

18. Canadian and American accounts differ diametrically over

Près-de-Ville. I have followed American accounts dealing with American troops and Canadian accounts dealing with Canadian troops.

19. Some American accounts refer to Carleton's seamen and militia being drunk. Codman disagrees. Davies, *Documents of the American Revolution*, VIII, p. 103, has a letter from Maclean complimenting Barnsfair and Coffin. I doubt he would have written this letter if the men had been drunk.

20. H. A. Verreau, ed., *Invasion du Canada: Collection des mémoires recuellis et annotés*, p. 120. Ainslie, *Canada Preserved*, gives the figure as sixty, followed by another sixty, which seems much too low.

21. However, there were still airholes in the ice and some of the escapees may have drowned.

22. Ainslie, *Canada Preserved*, p. 19.

23. Force, *American Archives*, vol. 4, p. 656.

24. Codman, *Arnold's Expedition*, p. 254.

25. New York Historical Society, *Journal by an Officer*, p. 190.

26. Commager and Morris, *The Spirit of Seventy-six*, p. 210.

Chapter 10

1. John Codman, *Arnold's Expedition to Quebec*, pp. 266-7.

2. H. A. Verreau, ed., *Invasion du Canada: Collection des mémoires recuellis et annotés*, p. 69; Fred C. Wurtele, *Blockade of Quebec 1775-1776 by the American Revolutionists*, 8 series, II, p. 37.

3. Codman, *Arnold's Expedition*, p. 275.

4. New York Historical Society, *Journal of the Most Remarkable Occurrences in Quebec by an Officer of the Garrison*, p. 234.

5. Verreau, *Invasion du Canada*, p. 127.

6. Kenneth Roberts, *Journals of the Members of Arnold's Expeditions*, p. 448.

7. Thomas Fleming, *1776: The Year of Illusions*, p. 221; Thomas Ainslie, *Canada Preserved*, p. 88.

8. Verreau, *Invasion du Canada*, p. 240.

9. Peter Force, ed., *American Archives*, vol. 1, pp. 1168-70.

10. Fleming, *1776*, p. 385.

11. George Otto Trevelyan, *The American Revolution*, vol. 1, part 2, p. 83.

12. Roberts, *Journals*, p. 293.

13. Ibid.

14. Ibid., p. 539.

15. Force, *American Archives*, vol. 3, p. 988.

16. A. L. Burt, *The Old Province of Quebec*, p. 240.

17. A. G. Bradley, *Sir Guy Carleton*, p. 139n.

Chapter 11

1. Baby, Taschereau and William, *Journaux*, consists of the reports of these three commissioners.

2. Thomas Anburey, *With Burgoyne from Quebec*, p. 46.

3. Adam Shortt and A. G. Doughty, eds., *Documents Relating to the Constitutional History of Canada, 1759-1791*, p. 675.

4. F. J. Hudleston, *Gentleman Johnny Burgoyne*, p. 107.

5. Allen French, *The First Year of the American Revolution*, p. 401.

6. Anburey, *With Burgoyne from Quebec*, p. 86.

7. Shortt and Doughty, *Documents*, pp. 674-6.

8. Ibid., p. 817; pages 816-40 contain the instructions in full.

9. Quebec *Gazette*, September 12th, 1776.

10. Lieutenant James M. Hadden, *A Journal Kept in Canada and upon Burgoyne's Campaign*, p. 541.

11. Christopher Hibbert, *Wolfe at Quebec*, p. 88.

12. General Riedesel, *Memoirs, Letters and Journals*, vol. 1, p. 71.

13. Ibid., p. 174.

14. Ibid.

15. Ibid., p. 172.

16. Anburey, *With Burgoyne from Quebec*, p. 71. It must be pointed out that Anburey did not reach Quebec until a year later, and this report is hearsay. However, Riedesel supports these facts.

17. Hadden, *Journal*, p. 452.

18. Christopher Ward, *The War of the Revolution*, p. 397.

19. Peter Force, ed., *American Archives*, 5th series, vol. 2, p. 1040.

20. Ibid., p. 1028, states: "Post consisted of ten thousand men, well supplied and in high spirits."

21. Henry Steele Commager and Richard B. Morris, *The Spirit of Seventy-six*, p. 222.

22. Hadden, *Journal*, p. 34.

23. Baroness Von Riedesel, *Riedesel and the American Revolution*, p. 123.

24. Quebec *Gazette*, October 31st, 1776.

25. General Riedesel, *Memoirs*, vol. 1, p. 83.

26. A carryall must be differentiated from a cariole. A carryall had four wheels and sat four in two seats. A cariole had only two wheels and one seat for two people. Both vehicles were drawn by a single horse.

27. Baroness Von Riedesel, *Riedesel*, p. 123.

28. Quebec *Gazette*, January 4th, 1776.

Chapter 12

1. Lord George Germain was not a peer. Because he was the younger son of a duke, he carried the courtesy title of lord. When Wolfe wrote to him, his courtesy title was Lord George Sackville. As secretary of state for the colonies, his title was Lord George Germain. In 1782 he was made a peer in his own right.

2. Alan Valentine, *Lord George Germain*, p. 156.

3. A. L. Burt, "The Quarrel between Germain and Carleton: an Inverted Story," *Canadian Historical Review*, September 1930, p. 203.

4. Valentine, *Lord George Germain*, p. 152.

5. Burt, "The Quarrel between Germain and Carleton," p. 208.

6. Ibid., p. 206.

7. Ibid., p. 208.

8. Ibid., p. 210.

9. Ibid.

10. Peter Force, ed., *American Archives*, vol. 5, pp. 1103-5.

11. Jane Clark, "The Command of the Army for the Campaign of 1777," *Canadian Historical Review*, June 1929, p. 130.

12. Valentine, *Lord George Germain*, p. 146.

13. Ibid., p. 156.

14. A. L. Burt, *The Old Province of Quebec*, p. 244.

15. A. G. Bradley, *Sir Guy Carleton*, p. 165.

16. F. J. Hudleston, *Gentleman Johnny Burgoyne*, p. 114.

17. James Flexner, *George Washington in the American Revolution 1775-1783*, p. 178.

18. Hudleston, *Gentleman Johnny Burgoyne*, p. 115.

19. Burt, "The Quarrel between Germain and Carleton," p. 218.

20. George Otto Trevelyan, *The American Revolution*, vol. 1, part 3, p. 74.

21. Lieutenant James M. Hadden, *A Journal Kept in Canada and upon Burgoyne's Campaign*, p. 346.

22. Hudleston, *Gentleman Johnny Burgoyne*, p. 127.

23. Thomas Anburey, *With Burgoyne from Quebec*, p. 132.

24. Burt, "The Quarrel between Germain and Carleton," p. 215.

25. General Riedesel, *Memoirs, Letters and Journals*, p. 137.

26. Anburey, *With Burgoyne from Quebec*, pp. 4-5.

27. Hadden, *Journal*, pp. 433-4.

28. Ibid., p. 433.

29. Valentine, *Lord George Germain*, p. 193.

30. Ibid., p. 260.

31. Records of the English Cathedral at Quebec.

32. Valentine, *Lord George Germain*, p. 193.

33. Quebec *Gazette*, January 8th, 1778.

Chapter 13

1. Adam Shortt and A. G. Doughty, eds., *Documents Relating to the Constitutional History of Canada, 1759-1791*, p. 678.

2. Edwin C. Guillet, *The Pioneer Farmer and Backwoodsman*, vol. 2, p. 95.

3. A. L. Burt, "The Tragedy of Chief Justice Livius," *Canadian Historical Review*, September 1924, p. 201.

4. Ibid., p. 202.

5. William Smith, "The Struggle over the Laws of Canada," *Canadian Historical Review*, June 1924, pp. 178-9.

6. Burt, "The Tragedy of Chief Justice Livius," p. 203.

7. Ibid., p. 206.

8. H. A. Verreau, ed., *Invasion du Canada: Collection des mémoires recuellis et annotés*, pp. 151-3.

9. Jane Clark, "The Command of the Canadian Army for the Campaign of 1777," *Canadian Historical Review*, June 1929, p. 130n; Alan Valentine, *Lord George Germain*, p. 385.

10. Smith, "The Struggle over the Laws of Canada," p. 181.

11. Burt, "The Tragedy of Chief Justice Livius," p. 205.

12. Quebec *Gazette*, July 5th, 1778.

13. A. Aspinall, *The Later Correspondence of George III*, p. 146.

14. Valentine, *Lord George Germain*, p. 500n.

15. Ibid., p. 185.

16. Ibid., p. 149.

17. Burt, "The Tragedy of Chief Justice Livius," p. 206.

18. Ibid., p. 207.

19. Malmesbury, *Letters of the First Earl of Malmesbury, His Family and Friends*, May 2nd, 1780.

20. *Gentleman's Magazine*, July 1779.

21. Adam Shortt and A. G. Doughty, eds., *Canada and Its Provinces*, vol. 11, p. 18.

22. Archevêché du Québec, *Lettres*, May 1780.

23. George Otto Trevelyan, *George III and Charles Fox*, p. 306.

24. Valentine, *Lord George Germain*, p. 444.

25. Ibid., p. 446.

Chapter 14

1. *Report on American Manuscripts in the Royal Institution of Great Britain*, vol. 3, p. 1; George Otto Trevelyan, *The American Revolution*, vol. 1, part 3, p. 354, gives a figure of 33,300.

2. *Report on American Manuscripts,* vol. 3, p. 421; Piers Mackesy, *The War for America, 1775-1783,* p. 474.

3. George Athan Billias, ed., *George Washington's Opponents,* p. 129.

4. Henry Steele Commager and Richard B. Morris, *The Spirit of Seventy-six,* p. 885.

5. James Flexner, *George Washington in the American Revolution 1775-1783,* p. 479.

6. Donald Barr Chidsey, *The Loyalists,* p. 150.

7. Thomas Jefferson Wertenbaker, *The History of New York during the Revolution,* pp. 231-2.

8. Mackesy, *The War for America,* p. 491.

9. Commager and Morris, *The Spirit of Seventy-six,* pp. 889-91.

10. Flexner, *George Washington in the American Revolution 1775-1783,* p. 482.

11. Ibid., p. 480.

12. Ibid., p. 482.

13. Lieutenant James M. Hadden, *A Journal Kept in Canada and upon Burgoyne's Campaign,* p. 424.

14. Ibid., p. 422.

15. Lord Edmund Fitzmaurice, *The Life of William Earl of Shelburne,* vol. 3, p. 199.

16. Ibid.

17. A. G. Bradley, *Sir Guy Carleton,* p. 212.

18. Page Smith, *A New Age Begins,* p. 1756.

19. George M. Wrong, *Canada and the American Revolution,* p. 383.

20. Ibid., p. 381.

21. Wertenbaker, *The History of New York,* p. 262.

22. Adam Shortt and A. G. Doughty, eds., *Canada and Its Provinces*, vol. 13, p. 142.

23. Ibid., p. 148.

24. Ibid., pp. 28-9.

25. Wertenbaker, *A History of New York*, p. 163.

26. Ibid., p. 162.

27. *Report on American Manuscripts*, vol. 3, p. 353; Wertenbaker, *A History of New York*, p. 162.

28. Adam Valentine, *Lord George Germain*, p. 444.

29. Wertenbaker, *A History of New York*, p. 163.

30. Ibid., p. 169.

31. *Report on American Manuscripts*, vol. 3, pp. 177-8. This is the quotation in the report.

32. Ibid., vol. 4, p. 106.

33. Ibid., p. 78. This is again the quotation in the report.

34. Ibid., vol. 3, p. 106.

35. Rockland County Society, *The Rockland Record*, p. 48.

36. Kenneth Roberts, *Journals of the Members of Arnold's Expedition*, vol. 2, p. 794, says: "Carleton had the same commanding presence, the same level glance, the same firm mouth and square jaw as Washington."

37. Thomas H. Radall, *The Path of Destiny: Canada from the British Conquest to Home Rule*, p. 10.

38. Isabelle K. Savell, *Wine and Bitters Historical Society of Rockland County*, p. 22.

39. T. Harry Williams, *History of the United States*, p. 164.

40. *Rockland Record*, p. 48; *Wine and Bitters*, pp. 26-30.

41. There are three accounts of this Tappan meeting. One prepared under Washington's direction, one by Colonel Richard

Varick, and one by Judge William Smith. They differ chiefly in emphasis.

42. Smith, *A New Age Begins*, p. 1758.

43. Shortt and Doughty, *Canada and Its Provinces*, vol. 13, p. 143.

44. Flexner, *George Washington in the American Revolution 1775-1783*, p. 523.

45. Smith, *A New Age Begins*, p. 1754.

Chapter 15

1. Adam Shortt and A. G. Doughty, eds., *Documents Relating to the Constitutional History of Canada, 1759-1791*, gives a memo of Smith's sent by Dorchester to London which shows how the two men were thinking. It is impossible to determine whether this proposal contains Smith's ideas as they were absorbed by Dorchester or vice-versa, or a little of each.

2. *Collins Peerage of England*.

3. Shortt and Doughty, *Documents*, p. 810.

4. Alfred Leroy Burt, *The Old Province of Quebec*, p. 427.

5. Adam Shortt and A. G. Doughty, eds., *Canada and Its Provinces*, vol. 3, p. 119.

6. Jean McIlwraith, *The Life of Sir Frederick Haldimand*, p. 315n.

7. A. Aspinall, *The Later Correspondence of George III*, p. 146 and p. 232n.

8. *Burke's Peerage and Baronetage*.

9. Alan Valentine, *Lord George Germain*, p. 124. This was Gage's bonus when he was commander-in-chief and Carleton presumably received the same.

10. Early in 1788 Warren Hastings purchased a mansion and six hundred and fifty acres in the English countryside for £12,425 and the two estates appear comparable.

11. *Collins Peerage*; Nately Scures chapel memorial.

12. Quebec *Gazette*, December 28th, 1786.

13. Shortt and Doughty, *Canada and Its Provinces*, vol. 7, pp. 152-7.

14. A. G. Bradley, *Sir Guy Carleton*, p. 243.

15. Quebec *Gazette*, April 2nd, 1778.

16. William Renwick Riddell, *The Life of William Dummer Powell*, p. 12.

17. Quebec *Gazette*, December 17th, 1789.

18. Quebec *Gazette*, July 30th, 1790.

19. Ibid., September 27th, 1789.

20. Guillet calls 1788 the Hungry Year. The famine started in 1788 and ended in 1790.

21. Ruth Kirk, *Snow*, p. 32. Possibly the blight might have been caused by snow mould.

22. Quebec *Gazette*, March 2nd, 1789.

23. Edwin C. Guillet, *Early Life in Upper Canada*, pp. 208-9.

24. Ibid., p. 220.

25. Quebec *Gazette*, August 30th, 1790.

26. Ibid.

Chapter 16

1. Adam Shortt and A. G. Doughty, eds., *Documents Relating to the Constitutional History of Canada, 1759-1791*, p. 1027.

2. Adam Shortt and A. G. Doughty, eds., *Canada and Its Provinces*, vol. 4, p. 13.

3. John Ehrman, *The Younger Pitt*, p. 362.

4. Ibid., p. 356.

5. Shortt and Doughty, *Documents*, pp. 1031-51, reproduces the Constitutional Act in full.

6. Alfred Leroy Burt, *The Old Province of Quebec*, p. 493.

7. Shortt and Doughty, *Documents*, p. 947.

8. Burt, *The Old Province of Quebec*, p. 531n, estimates the population in 1788 at one hundred thirty thousand; Shortt and Doughty, *Canada and Its Provinces*, vol. 3, p. 146, estimates it in 1790 as one hundred sixty thousand.

9. Shortt and Doughty, *Documents*, pp. 958-60.

10. Ibid., p. 281.

11. Ibid., p. 947.

12. Ibid., p. 1005.

13. Ibid., p. 1027.

14. Robert Hendrickson, *Hamilton*, vol. 2, pp. 56-7.

15. S. E. Morison, *Oxford History of the United States, 1783-1917*, vol. 1, p. 145.

16. Quebec *Gazette*, August 21st, 1791.

17. Ibid., June 24th, 1790.

18. Records of the House of Lords.

19. *Collins Peerage of England*.

20. Morison, *Oxford History of the United States*, vol. 1, p. 151.

21. Shortt and Doughty, *Canada and Its Provinces*, vol. 3, pp. 148-9.

22. Ibid., p. 148.

23. Ibid., p. 149.

24. Ibid., p. 150.

25. William Wood, *The Father of British Canada*, p. 212.

BIBLIOGRAPHY

"A pied dans le vieux Québec" (pamphlet). Author and date unknown.

Ainslie, Thomas. *Canada Preserved, a Journal*. Quebec: 1905.

Anburey, Thomas. *With Burgoyne from Quebec*. Toronto: 1963.

Archevêché du Québec. *Lettres*, Quebec: 1888.

Aspinall, A. *The Later Correspondence of George III*. Cambridge: 1962.

Baby, Taschereau, et Williams, *Journeaux*. Quebec: 1927-28.

Bancroft, George. *History of the United States*. Vol. 3. New York: 1834.

Benoit, Pierre. *Lord Dorchester*. Quebec: 1961.

Billias, George Allan, ed. *George Washington's Opponents*. New York: 1969.

Bird, Harrison. *Attack on Quebec*. New York: 1968.

Bradley, A. G. *Sir Guy Carleton (Lord Dorchester)*. Toronto: 1966.

Burdy, Samuel. *Complete Works of Philip Shelton with His Life*. Vol. 1. London: 1792.

Burke, Edmund, *The Works and Correspondence*. Vol. 1. London: 1852.

Burke's Peerage & Baronetage. New York: 1975.

Burt, A. L. "Sir Guy Carleton and His First Council." *Canadian Historical Review*, December 1923.

Burt, A. L. "Guy Carleton, Lord Dorchester, 1724-1808." Canadian Historical Association booklet. Ottawa: 1968.

Burt, A. L. "The Quarrel between Germain and Carleton, an Inverted Story." *Canadian Historical Review*, September 1930.

Burt, A. L. "The Tragedy of Chief Justice Livius." *Canadian Historical Review*, September 1924.

Burt, Alfred Leroy. *The Old Province of Quebec*. New York: 1970.

Burt, Alfred Leroy. *The United States, Great Britain, and British North America*. New York: 1961.

Cavendish, Sir Henry. *Debates of the House of Commons in the Year 1774*. London: 1792.

Chidsey, Donald Barr. *The Loyalists*. New York: 1969.

Clark, Jane. "The Command of the Canadian Army for the Campaign of 1777." *Canadian Historical Review*, June 1929.

Clinton, Sir Henry. *The American Rebellion, a Narrative of His Campaigns 1775-1782*. New York: 1944.

Codman, John. *Arnold's Expedition to Quebec*. New York: 1901.

Collins, Arthur. *Collins Peerage of England*, 9 vols. New York: 1812.

Commager, Henry Steele, and Morris, Richard B. *The Spirit of Seventy-six*. New York: 1958.

Connecticut Historical Society. *Journal of the Expedition against Canada*, by Benjamin Trumbull. Hartford: 1899.

Coupland, Sir Reginald. *The Quebec Act*. Oxford: 1925.

Davies, K. G., ed. *Documents of the American Revolution*. 8 vols. Shannon: 1972.

Derry, John W. *William Pitt*. New York: 1963.

Doughty, A. G. *The Siege of Quebec and Battle of the Plains of Abraham*. Quebec: 1901.

Ehrman, John. *The Younger Pitt*. New York: 1969.

Evans, Elizabeth. *Weathering the Storm, Women of the American Revolution*. New York: 1975.

Fitzmaurice, Lord Edmund. *The Life of William Earl of Shelburne*. 3 vols. London: 1876.

Fleming, Thomas. *1776: Year of Illusions*. New York: 1975.

Flexner, James *George Washington in the American Revolution 1775-1783*. New York: 1967.

Flexner, James *The Traitor and the Spy*. New York: 1962.

French, Allen. *The First Year of the American Revolution*. Boston: 1934.

Force, Peter, ed. *American Archives*. Fourth series, six volumes; Fifth series, three volumes. Washington: 1848-1853.

Garraty, John, and James, Edward. *Dictionary of American Biography*, 10 vols. Totowa: 1974.

Gentleman's Magazine. London: 1778 to 1808.

Guillet, Edwin C. *Early Life in Upper Canada*. Toronto: 1933.

Guillet, Edwin C. *The Pioneer Farmer and Backwoodsman*. 2 vols. Toronto: 1963.

Hadden, Lieutenant James M. *A Journal Kept in Canada and upon Burgoyne's Campaign in 1776 and 1777*. Albany: 1884.

Halpenny, Frances, ed. *Dictionary of Canadian Biography*. Toronto: 1974.

Harris, R. Cole, and Warkentin, John. *Canada before Confederation*. Toronto: 1974.

Hatch, Robert McConnell. *Thrust for Canada*. Boston: 1979.

Hendrickson, Robert. *Hamilton. Vol. 2 (1789-1804)*. New York: 1976.

Hébert, Jean-Claude, ed. *Le Siège de Québec en 1759 par trois témoins*. Quebec: 1972.

Hibbert, Christopher. *Wolfe at Quebec*. Cleveland: 1959.

Hubbard, Timothy William. "Battle at Valcour Island, Benedict Arnold as Hero." *American Heritage*, October 1966.

Hudleston, F. J. *Gentleman Johnny Burgoyne*. Indianapolis: 1927.

Jenkins, Kathleen. *Montreal, Island City of the St. Lawrence*. New York: 1966.

Johnson, Samuel. *The Works*. London: 1806.

Johnson, Willis Fletcher. *The History of Cuba*. New York: 1920.

Kirk, Ruth. *Snow*. New York: 1977.

Kingsford, William. *The History of Canada*. Vols. 5, 6 and 7. Toronto: 1892.

Knox, Captain John. *Account of the Battle of Quebec*. Old South Leaflets, Vol. 3. Boston: 1896.

Lanctot, Gustave. *Canada and the American Revolution, 1774-1783*. Toronto: 1967.

Lanctot, Gustave. *A History of Canada*. Cambridge: 1965.

Leroy, Perry Eugene. *Sir Guy Carleton as a military leader during the American invasion and repulse in Canada, 1775-1776*. Ph.D. thesis in Quebec Archives: 1960.

Lewis, Paul. *The Man Who Lost America*. New York: 1973.

Lower, Arthur M. *Colony to Nation*. New York: 1946.

Mackesy, Piers. *The War for America, 1775-1783*. Boston: 1965.

Mahon, R. H. *General James Murray*. London: 1921.

Malmesbury, 3rd Earl, ed. *Letters of the First Earl of Malmesbury, His Family and Friends*. London: 1870.

Mandements des Évêques du Québec. Quebec: 1888.

Marshall, Douglas, and Peckham, Howard H. *Campaigns of the American Revolution*. Maplewood: 1976.

Marshall, John. *History of the American Colonies*. Philadelphia: 1824.

McCarthy, Justin. *History of Our Times*. New York: 1880.

McIlwraith, Jean. *Life of Sir Frederick Haldimand*. London: 1926.

McInnis, Edgar, W. *Canada, a Political and Social History*. New York: 1959.

Mitchell, Broadus. *Alexander Hamilton, Youth to Maturity, 1755-1788*. New York: 1957.

Morgan, H. J. *Sketches of Celebrated Canadians*. Quebec: 1908.

Morison, S. E. *The Oxford History of the United States, 1783-1917*. Vol. 1. London: 1927.

Munroe, William Bennet. *The Seigneurs of Old Canada*. Toronto: 1922.

New York Historical Society. *Silas Deane Papers*. 5 vols. New York: 1887-1891.

New York Historical Society. *The Golden Letter Books*. Vol. 2. New York: 1880.

New York Historical Society. *Journal of Captain John Montresor*. Vol. 14. New York: 1881.

New York Historical Society. *Journal of the Most Remarkable Occurrences in Quebec by an Officer of the Garrison*. Vol. 14. New York: 1881.

New York Historical Society. *Journals of Lieutenant John Charles Philip Von Craft*. Vol. 15. New York: 1887.

Parkman, Francis. *Montcalm and Wolfe*. 2 vols. Boston: 1890.

Parkman, Francis. *The Old Régime of Canada*. Boston: 1890.

Pearson, Michael. *Those Damned Rebels*. New York: 1972.

Pell, John. *Ethan Allen*. Lake George: 1929.

Pell, S. H. P. "Fort Ticonderoga" (Pamphlet). Ticonderoga: 1975.

Pennypacker, Morton. *General Washington's Spies*. Long Island Historical Society. Brooklyn: 1939.

Pouliot, J. Camile. *Quebec and the Isle of Orleans*. Privately published. Quebec: 1927.

Quebec *Gazette*, 1766 to 1789.

Quebec Archives. *Documents relatifs à la revolution américaine de 1775*. Quebec: 1946.

Raddall, Thomas H. *The Path of Destiny: Canada from the British Conquest to Home Rule*. New York: 1957.

Reid, Marjorie G. "The Quebec Fur Traders and Western Policy, 1763-1774." *Canadian Historical Review*, March 1925.

Report on American Manuscripts in the Royal Institution of Great Britain. 4 vols. London: 1904.

Riddell, William Renwick. *The Life of William Dummer Powell*. Lansing: 1924.

Riedesel, Baroness Von. *Baroness Von Riedesel and the American Revolution*. London: 1827.

Riedesel, Major General. *Memoirs, Letters and Journals*. Albany: 1904.

Roberts, Kenneth, ed. *Journals of the Members of Arnold's Expedition*. New York: 1938.

Roberts, Kenneth. *Oliver Wiswell*. New York: 1940.

Roberts, W. Adolph. *Havana, the Portrait of a City*. New York: 1953.

Rockland County Society. *The Rockland Record*. Nyack: 1925.

Savell, Isabelle K. *Wine and Bitters*. Rockland County, New York: 1975.

Saywell, John. *Canada Past and Present*. Toronto: 1969.

Schachner, Nathan. *Aaron Burr*. New York: 1937.

Scott, Duncan Campbell. *John Graves Simcoe*. Quebec: 1926.

Sen, S. P., ed. *Dictionary of National Biography*. 4 vols. Columbia: 1972.

Shellabarger, Samuel. *Lord Vanity*. Boston: 1953.

Shortt, Adam, and Doughty, A. G., eds. *Documents Relating to the Constitutional History of Canada, 1759-1791*. 2 vols. Ottawa: 1907.

Shortt, Adam, and Doughty, A. G., eds. *Canada and Its Provinces*. 24 vols. Toronto: 1914.

Smith, Page. *A New Age Begins*. New York: 1976.

Smith, William. "The Struggle over the Laws of Canada, 1763-1783." *Canadian Historical Review*, June 1924.

Smithsonian Institution. *The Road to American Independence*. New York: 1976.

Sparks, Jared, ed. *Correspondence with George Washington*. Boston: 1832.

Spaulding, E. Wilder. *His Excellency, George Clinton*. New York: 1938.

Stacey, C. P. *Quebec, 1759*. Toronto: 1959.

Tremaine, Maria. *A Bibliography of Canadian Imprints*. Ottawa: 1952.

Trevelyan, George Otto. *The American Revolution*. Vol. 1, Parts 2 and 3. New York: 1907.

Trevelyan, George Otto. *George III and Charles Fox*, New York: 1915.

Valentine, Alan. *Lord George Germain*. London: 1962.

Verreau, H. A., ed. *Invasion du Canada: Collection des mémoires recueillis et annotés*. Montreal: 1873.

Vidal, Gore. *Burr*. New York: 1973.

Wade, Mason. *The French Canadian Outlook*. Toronto: 1964.

Walpole, Horace. *Letters*. (8 vols., edited by Peter Cunningham.) London: 1963.

Ward, Christopher. *The War of the Revolution*. New York: 1952.

Wertenbaker, Thomas Jefferson. *History of New York during the Revolution*. New York: 1887.

Williams, T. Harry; Current, Richard N.; and Freidel, Frank. *A History of the United States*. New York: 1964.

Wilson, Berkles. *The Life and Letters of James Wolfe*. London: 1909.

Wood, William. *The Father of British Canada, a Chronicle of Carleton*. Toronto: 1916.

Wrong, George M. *Canada and the American Revolution*. Toronto: 1935.

INDEX OF PERSONS